S0-BHZ-906

13 - 16

PRAYING FOR UNITY

PRAYING FOR UNITY

A Handbook of Studies, Meditations and Prayers

Edited by

MICHAEL HURLEY, S.J.

BX
8.2
.H96.

BTQ
403
H96

73661

BTQ 403 .H96

ST. JOSEPH'S UNIVERSITY   STX

Praying for unity;

3 9353 00008 4879

With a Foreword by

THE BISHOP OF DOWN AND CONNOR

and Introductory Messages from

THE CHURCH OF IRELAND ARCHBISHOP OF DUBLIN

THE MODERATOR OF THE GENERAL ASSEMBLY OF THE PRESBYTERIAN CHURCH IN IRELAND

THE PRESIDENT OF THE METHODIST CHURCH IN IRELAND

THE FURROW TRUST

GILL & SON, DUBLIN

First published in 1963 by
M. H. Gill and Son Limited
50 Upper O'Connell Street
Dublin 1
in association with
The Furrow Trust
Maynooth

© *The Furrow Trust 1963*

Cover designed by Stan Davison

Printed in the Republic of Ireland by LEINSTER LEADER
LTD., NAAS. *Nihil Obstat*: PATRICIUS HARRIS, Censor
Deputatus. *Imprimatur*: ✠ THOMAS, Ep. Darensis et
Leighlinensis. 21:1:'63.

To the descendants of

THE CHILDREN OF FOCHLAD

CONTENTS

CONTRIBUTORS

MOST REVEREND WILLIAM J. PHILBIN is Bishop of Down and Connor.

MOST REVEREND GEORGE OTTO SIMMS is Church of Ireland Archbishop of Dublin.

RIGHT REVEREND W. A. MONTGOMERY is Moderator of the General Assembly of the Presbyterian Church in Ireland.

REVEREND FREDERICK E. HILL is President of the Methodist Church in Ireland.

REVEREND AUSTIN FLANNERY O.P. is Editor of *Doctrine and Life*.

DR DAPHNE POCHIN MOULD is author of many books on Celtic spirituality and other subjects.

RIGHT REVEREND JOSEPH DOWDALL O.S.B. is Lord Abbot of St Columba's Abbey, Glenstal, County Limerick.

DR DAVID THORNLEY is lecturer in Political Science at Trinity College, Dublin.

REVEREND DERMOT RYAN is Professor of Oriental Languages at University College, Dublin.

REVEREND MICHAEL HURLEY S.J. is Professor of Dogmatic Theology at Milltown Park, Dublin.

REVEREND ENDA MCDONAGH is Professor of Moral Theology at St Patrick's College, Maynooth. Author of *Roman Catholics and Unity*; contributor to *Christian Unity*.

REVEREND PATRICK O'CONNELL S.J. is Professor of Church History at Milltown Park, Dublin.

REVEREND PÓL Ó SÚILLEABHÁIN O.F.M. is attached to St Isidore's, Rome.

THE EARL OF WICKLOW is a director of the publishing house of Clonmore and Reynolds.

REVEREND KEVIN MCNAMARA is Professor of Dogmatic Theology at St Patrick's College, Maynooth. Editor of and contributor to *Christian Unity*.

REVEREND DENIS FAUL is on the teaching staff of St Patrick's Academy, Dungannon.

REVEREND WILFRID HARRINGTON O.P. is Professor of Sacred Scripture at St Mary's, Tallaght and at St Patrick's College, Maynooth.

LEON Ó BROIN, ESQ. is a well-known author and Secretary of the Department of Posts and Telegraphs, Dublin.

MOTHER JOAN SWEETMAN R.S.C.J. is on the teaching staff of Sacred Heart Convent, Monkstown, County Dublin.

DR GEOFFREY HAND is lecturer in History at the University of Southampton.

REVEREND DESMOND WILSON is on the teaching staff of St Malachy's College, Belfast.

REVEREND SEÁN O'RIORDAN, C.SS.R. is Professor of Moral Theology at St Alphonsus' Institute, Rome.

SEAMUS GRACE, ESQ. is on the teaching staff of Blackrock College, County Dublin.

FOREWORD

William J. Philbin

Bishop of Down and Connor

CHRISTIANITY is a many-sided inheritance and in the course of centuries one aspect after another comes into prominence. Oversights are constantly being corrected and emphases adjusted. In our own times the conscience of believers has been uniquely moved by the claims of the underprivileged on the rest of the community, and on humanity in general, and in another field the Church's character as the Mystical Body of Christ has exerted a widely fruitful influence. In general, our age has seen the social side of religion assume a new value. One feature of this development is the growth of concern about relations with other Christians 'who are not of this fold' and the stirrings of an uneasy feeling that we have been lacking in charity towards them, or at least allowed ourselves all too often so to appear. A drastic re-thinking of the attitude of Christians towards one another is the most extraordinary religious phenomenon of recent years. It is almost as if it remained for our age to realize acutely how anti-Christian is ill-feeling towards anyone who is endeavouring to follow Christ.

It can scarcely be doubted that this is one of the fruits of the Holy Spirit, forever abiding with Christ's followers and leading them to all truth. We are re-discovering an aspect of Our Lord's own attitude to those who did not entirely reject him.

We are familiar with his treating his followers as one group, one family, never authorizing them to set up separate communities on their own, praying not merely for their union but for a unity among them such as existed between the Father and himself. The apostles so understood him: they established a tightly-organized body which made a great point of maintaining close relations and the same strict discipline among communities that necessarily were geographically separated. St Paul indignantly repudiated the idea of a Christianity naming itself after him or Apollo or Peter or other great missionary figures. We are all members one of another, according to his favourite way of thinking, and this mystical communion is to be evidenced in a mutual help and brotherhood that transcend national bounds and overlook the most rooted separateness the ancient world knew, the apartness of Jew from Gentile.

It would be elaborating the obvious to refer to all the indications of Christian oneness in the Bible and in post-Biblical times. The intention of Christ, the dispositions made by him, the understanding of those nearest to him and those he appointed to implement his wishes are as clear as could be. One of the most striking features of infant Christianity was the way dissent was universally repudiated. It is equally evident, however, that from the outset there was not universal and absolute acceptance of Christ's wishes in this matter among all who sought to follow him. Many who believed in him and loved him have failed him in this respect, just as some closer to him in organized unity failed him in other of his demands. Sin extends over the whole spectrum. With the passing of time dissenting Christian groups became more numerous, more organized and more fully and rootedly at variance with the parent body and with one another. Long before our age positions had become entrenched and had been sanctified by tradition and by the memory of high-minded leaders who have not been lacking in any religious persuasion.

The important factor that has intervened in our age is the incalculable element of prayer. Our consciences have suddenly been troubled and as in any other trouble we have had recourse to God. There has been prayer all round. The Church Unity Octave has found the whole divided Christian world united in supplication. There have been many other dramatic evidences of a humble common seeking to know God's will, to be led by him to the unity we know to be his desire. A share in the blame for division is willingly accepted on many sides. United prayer has been accompanied by many other evidences of charity and brotherliness. A climate has been established in which it is no longer a kind of sacred duty to hold that all the attitudes and habits that have grown up around the frontiers of doctrine have been well-judged or even permissible. It is no longer held to be treachery to recognize elements of value and truth among those differing from us and with whom we still find it necessary to disagree. There is a general re-thinking of policies, a questioning of the need and even of the justification of so much differing, a realization that seems to be increasingly general that we have obscured the things we are at one about in insisting on our divergences.

Re-reading the New Testament we are finding that side by side with the organizational unity of the community that Christ established, with its stress on uniformity and cohesiveness, there is plenty of evidence of an immense tolerance and love on the part of Our Lord for those whose faith in him did not extend to a full perception of the allegiance he demanded towards his merely human delegates. We find the Master saying indeed: 'He that is not with me is against me' (*Matt.* 12:30). But how wide the content of that 'with me' may be appears from the sharply-contrasting words in which he rebuked the apostles when he was told they had forbidden a man to cast out devils in his name 'because he was not following us'. 'Forbid him not', Jesus said, 'for there is no one that shall work a miracle in my name and shall be able soon to speak ill of me, for he that is not against us is for us. Yes, whosoever shall give you a cup of water to drink because ye are Christ's, amen I say to you, he shall not lose his reward' (*Mark* 9:38-40).

In spite of the strict, uncompromising demands Our Lord made on the group who stood consistently with him, he recognised that to come some way towards him was better than not to come at all. He did not exclude from his loving-kindness those on the fringes of his Society. He who knew what was in man knew all about the vagaries of conscience,

the blind spots of the understanding, the way in which
feelings and irrational elements, habits of thought and un-
recognized prejudices impede the functioning of intellect.
We may wonder how far the Centurion whose servant was
healed (*Matt*. 8:5) and the Samaritan woman (*John* 4:7)
and the woman of Canaan (*Matt*. 15:22) and the Centurion
at the foot of the Cross (*Luke* 23:47) and others who figure
so enviably in the Gospels conformed with the full pattern
of what Our Lord prescribed. What happened the followers
of Our Lord who withdrew because they would not accept
his Eucharistic teaching? (*John* 6). There is room for much
fruitful enquiry in this field and much supplementary
thinking about the hard lines we have allowed to grow
around a charity that should be like the charity of Christ.

Without suggesting that we can always find exact
analogies to modern circumstances in such instances, we
must recognize that they are an example to us of for-
bearance and slowness to judge or condemn. The argument
often is not *a pari* but *a fortiori*. In the Gospels we find
no justification for a self-satisfied faith or for any cold-
shouldering of those who are not fully of our community.
'Where two or three are gathered together in my name there
am I in the midst of them' (*Matt*. 18:20) is a large saying
that seems to exceed the bounds of a context concerning
his presence with the apostles and disciples.

We must not forget Our Lord's refusal to repudiate those
in marginal positions, while at the same time we must not
fail to give full value to his will for complete unity. His will
for unity is, of course, his dominant thought for all: 'And
other sheep I have that are not from this fold; these also
I must bring and they shall hear my voice and they shall
be one flock, one shepherd' (*John* 10:16). No leniency is
allowed to blunt his peremptory demand of obedience to
Church authority (e.g. *Matt*. 18:17).

In the same connexion we must come back to the classical
exposition of what he meant by unity in the very last words
he spoke to his apostles on the eve of the Passion (*John*
17:20 *seqq*.). However clearly he recognized the limitations
that misunderstanding imposed on the faith of many who
believed in him and loved him, his passionate wish and

prayer for all his followers was that they should be one after the model of the perfect unity subsisting between the Father and him. He makes that point that it is only by such an incorporation of all of them in him and in one another that the world can be truly led to believe in him. The world would be able with something like a good conscience to hold aloof from Christians as long as Christians held aloof from one another. The scandal of disagreement would be an excuse for the weak in faith. The miracle of perfect agreement and of mutual love of Christians was to be the miracle that would clinch the case for Christ, their Founder. This would be a miracle that could not be resisted, that would not be wasted.

Full agreement still remains a goal that can only be reached by a miracle. Yet considering its fruits and potential consequences, surely it is a miracle we all must pray for, even pray for with confidence. Who can say it is not a miracle we are stumbling towards? What a prospect may be opening before our generation in the task we seem to be committing ourselves to and becoming more and more involved in, almost, one might think, without realizing what we are about! It is nothing less than releasing again the dynamism of the apostolic age when, for a brief space, there existed generally the unity we—and Christ—have dreamt of. For such an end surely even the most cherished prejudices are well sacrificed. 'All things are possible to him that believes' (*Mark* 9:23). Many may feel that the climate already established is little short of miraculous.

The essays in this volume form a series of exploratory surveys in the direction of Christian union. They may be regarded as marking an Irish initiative in a field in which we have been thought behindhand. One may hope that in regard to them a proverb may bear adjustment: *Má's mithid, is maith*—Worthwhile, if tardy.

INTRODUCTORY MESSAGE

George Otto Simms

Church of Ireland Archbishop of Dublin

WHEN the subject of Christian Unity is discussed year by
year by the General Synod of the Church of Ireland, a
motion is regularly carried with the unanimous support of
the members, phrased in some such terms as these: 'That the
Synod respectfully requests the House of Bishops to appoint
a Week of Intercession for Christian Unity to be observed
in all the churches of the Church of Ireland'.

Thus it has been the practice of the House of Bishops to
appoint the days in January specially associated with the
Feast of the Conversion of St Paul, 25 January, for intercession on behalf of a divided Christendom. In this way,
the teaching of St Paul concerning the Church, as the Body
of Christ, is brought to mind in a vivid way; the familiar
words of the epistle to the Ephesians are recalled for
meditation and for guiding thoughts: 'one Lord, one faith,
one baptism, one God and Father of us all'. Furthermore,
the direction to pray for unity is made at a time when other
traditions are also engaged upon the same theme, when one
Church confession has the experience of praying in spirit
and in concord with other, differing confessions.

Such prayer for unity has been made, at the official
instigation of the Church of Ireland, for a number of years.
Each year fresh suggestions about subjects for special
mention in prayer encourage more of our number to participate in this simultaneous action. Often the prayer, printed

elsewhere in this volume, from the Book of Common Prayer, with its familiar reference to 'our unhappy divisions' is used during this week; it incorporates in its petitions much New Testament teaching about the Church and wears well. Furthermore, the great intercessory prayer in the order of Holy Communion makes petition for unity each time the sacrament is celebrated in the timeless phrases, familiar to every communicant: 'We humbly beseech thee, most mercifully to receive these our prayers, which we offer unto thy Divine Majesty; beseeching thee to inspire continually the universal Church with the spirit of truth, unity and concord: And grant, that all they that do confess thy holy Name may agree in the truth of thy holy Word, and live in unity and godly love'.

If a profound aim of prayer is 'to become' rather than 'to receive', then prayer for unity that is made through Jesus Christ our Lord is offered in order that we may become more like him, more closely united to him in truth. We try to make our own his prayers for unity; this is indeed an ambitious endeavour and there is always in practice a sense of sorry imperfection and failure after our devotions are over. However, the words of the great seventeenth chapter of St John's Gospel serve as a constant inspiration and guide, not least in this week of concentrated prayer for unity. That high-priestly prayer of our Lord, made on behalf of those whom he loved, links together requests for unity, for holiness and for truth: 'for their sakes, I sanctify myself that they also may be sanctified through the truth; neither pray I for these alone, but for them also which shall believe on me through their word; that they all may be one'.

The meaning of intercession is made clear during this week of prayer; for the word denotes a going in among the concerns of those with whom we would pray in a spirit of charity and goodwill, beside whom we would offer our petitions. Intercession encourages us to extend our interests through the whole world, in company with many fellow-Christians with whom we are friendly, yet not in organic communion on account of differences. The week is well spent also in study, in a deeper appreciation of doctrinal differences, in a clearer understanding of our own beliefs and convictions, with a readiness to declare them to others without complacency. There are treasures in our own tradition which we hold very dear; treasures in the ethos and basis of our membership in the Body of Christ, and it may be that some of the most valuable work for unity will be done by showing these treasures at their best and in all their fullness.

It is possible also that the most effective work for unity may be performed not by praying directly for unity, but for other things which help towards a better understanding. Prayer should be made for peace, for a new vision of truth, and a renewal of our Christian life. The peace that has come upon the Christian scene in many places throughout the world gives us hope to persevere, to exercise patience, and to be long-suffering in many matters difficult of solution. If differing traditions present a divided Christendom and the outsider is baffled by the confusion of confessions, we can at least claim that there is today a greater longing to co-operate and to share experiences where possible, and a keener desire for us all to join in upholding Christ in a world that sorely needs his reconciling love.

INTRODUCTORY MESSAGE

W. A. Montgomery

Moderator of the General Assembly of the Presbyterian Church in Ireland

I WELCOME the opportunity to provide an introductory message to the volume entitled *Praying for Unity*, to be issued under the Furrow Trust of Maynooth College. I pray that the Holy Spirit may lead us all into deeper truth. We all have convictions which are dear to us and we are growing increasingly tolerant towards others who differ from us, giving them credit for a sincerity at least equal to our own. I understand that Cromwell once sent a message to Scottish Presbyterians saying: 'Pray consider it possible that you may be mistaken'. It is very difficult sometimes for us to consider even the *possibility* that we may be mistaken. If, as at present, we cannot all be one in faith and doctrine, surely we can be one in charity. What we need in all matters affecting Church Unity is not ignoble compromise but real reconciliation. This we must seek under the guidance of the Holy Spirit.

The state of the world calls for the fullest measure of Christian co-operation. We continue to proclaim that in Christ is the secret of peace and unity. But how can we say so and saying so hope to be taken seriously, when the Church is itself divided as it is today? How can we expect men to believe our claim that the Church can bridge divisions in human society when it is itself in competing fragments? A Church at strife is not likely to be heeded when it essays to disarm the animosities of a warring world. We need to confront the world with a united witness and a compact influence in the name of Christ.

The mission-field calls for united witness. Our missionaries testify that the divisions of Christians are holding up progress and weakening our witness. The Hindu, the Moslem etc., just cannot understand why Christians should be in competing camps.

No one can doubt that it is the will of God that we should seek Christian unity. The evangelists do not often admit us to the privacy of our Lord's prayer-life. We do have the words he used in Gethsemane and we have a very precious fragment in the fourth gospel. Here (17:11 ff.), three separate times the great desire of his soul is voiced—even when his thoughts might well have been pre-occupied with pressing, personal concerns—he prayed earnestly, repeatedly that 'they might be one'. These words should be in the forefront of our thoughts and talks and writings about Christian Unity.

Christ prayed that his disciples may be one 'that the world may believe that Thou hast sent Me'. Church Unity is like Justice. Justice must not only be done but must also be *seen* to be done. But so long as we retain our denominational walls, as at present, the world will not see much of the Christian Unity for which our Lord prayed.

'Grace be with all those who love the Lord Jesus Christ in sincerity and in truth'.

INTRODUCTORY MESSAGE

Frederick E. Hill

President of the Methodist Church in Ireland

IT has always been the desire of Methodism to be 'the friends of all and the enemies of none'. Recalling the words of our founder, who having obtained the assurance of sins forgiven 'felt his heart strangely warmed', we have been called 'the people of the warmed heart'. We have always laid a particular emphasis on Christian fellowship, which in early Methodism found its expression in the Class Meeting where little groups met together to share their experiences, pray with and for one another, and help each other to attain to the ideal of Scriptural Holiness on which John Wesley laid such great emphasis. In these days of ecumenicity, these emphases, which in the beginning were held within the confines of the Methodist societies, assume a new importance and are now challenging us to find a wider fellowship and to share what we know to be a rich inheritance with others.

John Wesley in a letter to a Roman Catholic wrote: 'Then if we cannot as yet think alike in all things, at least we may love alike. Herein we cannot possibly do amiss. For of one point none can doubt a moment. "God is Love; and he that dwelleth in Love dwelleth in God and God in him".' He continues in the same letter: 'Let us resolve to speak nothing harsh or unkind of each other . . . to harbour no unkind thought, no unfriendly temper towards each other . . . and endeavour to help each other on in whatever leads to his kingdom'. One cannot help but reflect on how much strife and bitterness and misunderstanding could have been avoided in the years gone by, if all branches of Christ's Church had followed the advice of this good man.

But the publication of this little volume does at least indicate that we are agreed to help each other on in one thing, which we are sure leads to his kingdom, for surely there can be no better way of helping each other on than by praying for one another. It was a challenging word spoken by a wise man when he said: 'If we are friends then it is natural to pray for one another. If we are enemies then we are *commanded* to do so'.

The purpose of this little volume is to help us to pray intelligently for one another, to help us to understand one another better, and perhaps to enable us to realize how much we have in common, and how much each has that is good, bestowed upon us through no merit of our own but by the infinite grace of our Lord and Master who is the Head of the Church. It must be a source of satisfaction to all Christian men of goodwill to know that at last some of the barriers that have divided us are going down and that we can look into the future with greater hope that past bitterness and rivalries will be forgotten. We cannot doubt that the universal urge towards unity in Christendom today is the work of the Holy Spirit. At whatever cost we must follow his leading, realizing that unity can only be achieved through repentance, rebirth and renewal. The way of reconciliation is always costly, for it is the way of the cross, and in reconciling the world to himself God has set us the pattern. Churches as well as individuals are called to follow the way of sacrifice and self-giving and 'in dying behold we live'.

It is my earnest hope that during the week of prayer for Unity, as we pray for one another, that every branch of the Christian Church will be willing to submit in humble obedience to God all that is good and all that it treasures, all that may be defective, and all that may be in error, praying for itself and the Church throughout the world, in which Methodism holds and cherishes a true place, in the words of the ancient prayer

> Fill it with Truth; in all Truth with Peace.
> Where it is corrupt purge it;
> Where it is in error direct it;
> Where anything is amiss reform it,
> Where it is right confirm and strengthen it;
> Where it is in want furnish it;
> Where it is divided and rent asunder, do Thou make up the breaches in it, O Thou Holy One of Israel.

INTRODUCTION

The Editor

THIS is a book in which Irish parents, teachers and priests try to give a practical answer to the question: 'How can I help my children, my pupils, my parishioners and myself to enter into the spirit of the Week of Prayer for Christian Unity (18-25 January) and to celebrate it fittingly as recommended by so many Popes and by our own bishops as early as 1936?' It does not for a moment suggest that Christians can be reunited by prayer alone without good works, or that ecumenism (and this book) is just something for one short week in the whole year. It does suggest however (what experience itself seems to show only too clearly) that without the prayer there can be no good works, that without the special week there can be no sustained movement. The book is born of the simple conviction that the ecumenical movement is impossible without the public, organized observance of the January Unity Week.

The reasons for this are not far to seek. In the first place ecumenism in all its various manifestations is still for many Catholics a new and strange and disturbing and even scandalous thing. Yet it seems quite clear that the achievement of Christian unity does demand contact and co-operation at all levels with our separated brethren in order to remove the antipathy and ignorance and misunderstanding caused by isolation and inbreeding and to enable us slowly but surely to grow together in love and truth. One answer to this pastoral problem is undoubtedly the public observance of the Unity Week. Ecumenism, like all the other new things which the Church in the course of

time brings forth from its treasure house, needs a liturgical
context in order to take root and to grow. It is not through
cold theological instruction but through active participation
in the Church's Sunday liturgy that the mysterious insights
and energies of Christianity become ours for every day
and lose their strangeness but not their mystery. The same
paedagogy, it would seem, must be applied in the case of
ecumenism. And the parish which regularly observes the
Unity Week does invariably find that gradually and without
any crisis its attitudes and outlook have all changed and
so changed that the various good works associated with
ecumenism are seen no longer as scandalous but rather as
plain Christian duty.

In the second place, Christian unity is too obviously a
humanly impossible goal for anyone to doubt that it calls
for prayer, for that prayer of faith which moves Churches
as it moves mountains. We pray for Christian unity not for
lack of something else or of something better to do but
because in this cause prayer is simply the one thing necessary.
It is not however to acquire or deepen this particular conviction that we need a Unity Week. We all readily acknowledge that it is in answer to persevering prayer that God in
his mysterious providence bestows his gifts and when once
we sense our need of some divine gift we easily turn to
prayer. What we do lack and very generally lack and what
only a Unity Week can begin to provide is rather the conviction that Christian unity is a gift of God which our world
very sorely and urgently needs, that Christian disunity in
itself and in its effects is an immense evil which can no
longer be tolerated, that without Christian unity the world
will not, perhaps cannot, believe in Christ and in the Gospel.
We need a Unity Week to be roused out of our indifference
and apathy, and we look forward to the day when our own
foreign missionaries, like those of our separated brethren,
will provide us with this inspiration. It is still unfortunately
true that, with regard to ecumenism, Catholics owe almost
nothing and other Christians almost everything to their
respective foreign missionaries.

Once roused however to a vivid appreciation of the need
for Christian unity, how do we pray for this great gift of

God? We still need to be initiated into the spirit and forms of ecumenical prayer, and this is another need which, like a retreat, only a Unity Week can begin to satisfy. To pray for Christian unity is to pray for people and not only for others but for ourselves also. To pray for Christian unity is with Pope Paul humbly to ask pardon of God and of our separated brethren for our share of the faults which caused the division of Christendom in the past and maintain it in the present. To pray for Christian unity is to beg of God that he would fill our hearts with the Spirit of love and charity and empty them of all that pride and prejudice, all that arrogance and antipathy by which we hinder the fulfilment of his will for the unity of his people. To pray for Christian unity is to ask grace to know Christ in his brethren and his brethren in him, to know him and them according to the spirit and not according to the flesh. To pray for Christian unity is to recall the wonderful gifts of faith and order we still possess in common, and to realize that these already bind us together in Christ more intimately than we ordinarily care or dare to admit. To pray for Christian unity is to pray for ourselves and for our separated brethren that the graces of baptism work themselves out to the full in their lives as in our own and that soon we all be renewned and consummated in one by the power and operation of the Holy Ghost overcoming our foolishness and our slowness of heart to believe. Finally to pray for Christian unity is to pray *with* our separated brethren. Prayer is a mediation of love and unity, an effect and cause of love and unity. Prayer therefore *for* one another leads naturally to that greater act of love and unity which is prayer *with* one another. And eventually, when we have at length achieved unity of faith in charity, this prayer *with* one another will find its consummation in communion with one another in the celebration of the Eucharist. 'The family that prays together, stays together'. Such prayer with one another, as a public service in church, requires of course not only authoritative sanction from the bishop but also ecumenical education in the whole community; it represents a fairly advanced stage of ecumenism. In homes however and in private these precise conditions are not required[1] and such common prayer (with approved texts) is a practice that can with due prudence be adopted.

With its precise aim of promoting the public observance of the Unity Week here in Ireland and thus making the ecumenical spirit a permanent characteristic of each parish as well as of each individual, this is not just another general book on Christian unity but consists rather of essays, meditations and prayers of immediate practical value. It provides a vision of the meaning and scope of the Unity Week which is perhaps richer and more satisfying than many may have imagined. To promote the Unity Week is by no means to allow the unity movement to 'get bogged down in prayer'; ecumenical prayer flows over gradually and naturally into ecumenical action, into good works of conversation, co-operation and common witness. It caters in a modest way for the 'thoroughgoing revision of received ideas and attitudes' which the Editor of the Maynooth Union Summer School lectures on Christian Unity wrote of as desirable but which is already to a large extent a reality in this country under the influence of recent Popes and the 'intense educative effort' being made, notably by our national seminary at Maynooth. It provides a certain outlet for all the resultant pent-up ecumenical feeling and zeal which is now so urgently calling for direction and expression if it is not to go sour and peter out in frustration and bitterness. It envisages the busy priest and teacher and parent who at home, in class room, at meetings of various organizations as well as in church want so much 'to do something about it' and are quite at a loss as to how to proceed. It provides them with material for talks and

---

1. Cf. e.g., Vermeersch-Creusen, *Epitome Juris Canonici*, 7th ed. (Paris-Bruxelles 1954) II, n. 578, p. 411: 'Orationes privatas cum acatholicis fundere, remoto omni scandalo, non vetamur.'; A. Vermeersch, *Theologiae Moralis*, 3rd ed. (Rome 1937), II, p. 43: 'Privatas orationes, in se bonas, secluso scandalo et propriae perversionis periculo, cum acatholicis fundere, nec iure naturali neque hodierno iure positivo prohibemur.'; H. Jone-U. Adelman, *Moral Theology* (Cork 1948) n. 125, p. 74: 'But it is not forbidden to pray or sing privately with heretics if the prayers or songs are not heretical and no scandal is given.'

sermons or private reading and in particular with a factual
appreciative account of the main Christian bodies who are
not in communion with us and whom, in this way to begin
with, we must get to know and to love. It also provides
meditations (suitable for groups or individuals) on the true
authentic Christian values particularly emphasized by these
bodies so that we may come to know them interiorly and
to appreciate our common ground and existing unity with
them and thus obtain the necessary courage and hope to
pray and work for the consummation of this unity according
to God's will. It also provides a collection of prayers which,
among other things, will show clearly that not all Protestant
prayers are 'Protestant' (i.e. heretical and unusable by
Catholics), that to speak as Pope Paul did of the 'riches of
their religious inheritance' is no mere polite empty phrase
and that the hymns, e.g., of our Methodist brethren are
such as to put us to shame and fill us with envy and make
us long for a permanent share in such treasures.

It is not necessary that family prayers and evening
devotions in school chapels or parish churches should
invariably consist of the rosary. The fact that they do is
due, at least partially, to the impoverishment of our religious
and liturgical education. Last Lent however the Sunday
afternoon religious programmes on Telefís Éireann introduced us to a form of service which with its bible-readings,
prayers, psalms, hymns and homily is not only more
ancient but also more varied and interesting and for this
reason alone perhaps worthy of consideration by all those
concerned to revive attendance at Sunday evening church
devotions. The material in this book is suitable for some
such form of service and will contribute, it is hoped, to its
development up and down the country, with, in time, the
happy consequence that all in each place who believe in
Christ may join together in repentant humble supplication
for the ending of our divisions, in obedience to God's will,
and in order that the world may believe. Meantime the
material can be used whenever, during the Unity Week or
any other time, it may seem desirable and prudent to invite
friends or neighbours not in communion with us to join in
family prayers at home in private.[2]

2. Cf. footnote p. 27

John Raleigh Mott, the great American Methodist and architect in so many ways of the modern ecumenical movement, devoted his life to work for university students in particular but when asked shortly before his death, 'If you had your time over again what would you do?' he replied at once: 'The same, God willing, but I would start with schoolchildren and not wait until they reached student-age'. This book believes with John Mott that ecumenism must begin in our homes and in our schools: six at least of the contributors are parents or schoolteachers and it is to the children of Ireland that the book itself is respectfully dedicated. It was our children who in the past brought St Patrick and Christianity to Ireland, it is our present children who will enjoy the fruits of the Second Vatican Council and be in a position as a result more effectively to promote the cause of Christian unity, it is our future children who will see the consummation of this unity. Nothing can be too good for children. No effort surely can be spared to save them in their Christlike innocence and simplicity from our traditional unecumenical attitudes and to ensure that the image they acquire of their Protestant brethren and fellow-Irishmen is no longer influenced by old unhappy far-off things and battles long ago. Those who teach religion and history in Irish schools, and all who are in any way entrusted with the formation of our children, might do well to remember the words of Christ: 'But he that shall scandalize one of these little ones that believe in me, it were better for him that a mill-stone should be hanged about his neck, and that he be drowned in the depth of the sea' (*Matt.* 18:6). If Christianity be true, there is surely nothing so scandalous as uncharity or indifference towards any of our brethren in Christ.

This book is honoured and enhanced by a Foreword from the Most Reverend Dr Philbin, Bishop of Down and Connor. It is here, around Belfast, that our Irish separated brethren are most heavily concentrated and it is here too that our most notable Irish ecumenical achievement, the Churches' Industrial Council (to which the Catholic Church officially belongs), operates so successfully. Dr Philbin's Foreword is not however an honour which for these reasons

we by any means take for granted. We are very conscious
of the distinction his name and office confer on this book.
We are even more conscious of the encouragement and
recommendation his contribution provides for the difficult
task of promoting Christian unity here in Ireland. 'For
such an end surely even the most cherished prejudices are
well sacrificed'. On behalf of the publishers, contributors
and readers as well as on my own behalf I wish to offer His
Lordship our sincere appreciation and thanks.

It gives me great pleasure gratefully to record here that
our Irish Anglican, Presbyterian and Methodist brethren
have taken a sympathetic and helpful interest in this book.
The chapters on Anglicanism, Presbyterianism and Methodism were kindly examined by individual members of these
Churches and in their private, unofficial judgment, readers
will be glad to know, these parts of the book contain at least
no error in fact or unfairness in comment. In addition, the
Anglican Archbishop of Dublin, the Moderator of the
Presbyterian General Assembly and the President of the
Methodist Church in Ireland have graciously consented to
contribute introductory messages. These contributions are
not only admirable in themselves, both in spirit and content,
they are also in this context acts of Christian courtesy and
charity which put us all in debt to their authors and co-
religionists. We are deeply grateful to the Most Reverend
Dr Simms, the Right Reverend Dr Montgomery and the
Reverend Mr Hill. Their messages are edifying in the best
sense of that word and they provide us with welcome
encouragement in our stumbling ecumenical efforts.

It remains for me to thank all those without whose help
this book would quite certainly never have appeared. There
is first and foremost the Reverend Dr J. G. McGarry of
Maynooth College who knows as few others how to encourage and to whom through *The Furrow* the cause of
renewal and unity here in Ireland owes so much. It was Fr
McGarry who welcomed and approved my idea of this
book, who undertook to publish it, who invited me to edit
it and whose interest and advice have enabled me to accomplish the task. Secondly, there are the nineteen contributors
who, despite other commitments, have given so generously

of their time and talents to this book and who have been so painstaking—and so patient—in their collaboration. It will be noted and, I feel sure, with considerable satisfaction and hope for the future of the Church in Ireland, that six of the contributors are distinguished members of our laity and another a nun. Lastly, there is Michael Gill of Gill & Son, who has taken a personal interest in the publication of this book and the staff of the *Leinster Leader* who have so kindly and efficiently expedited its production. To all these, and to Dom Bede Lynch of Glenstal for help in choosing hymns, I offer my very sincere thanks. Grateful acknowledgment is also made to The Epworth Press, The Faith Press and Sheed & Ward for permission to print copyright material. Acknowledgment is made for permission to quote from the New English Bible, New Testament; copyright 1961 Oxford and Cambridge University Presses.

RECENT POPES AND CHRISTIAN UNITY

Austin Flannery

AN essay on the recent popes and ecumenism cannot avoid what must seem a disproportionate emphasis on the achievement of the late Pope John XXIII. The plain fact is that he does overshadow his predecessors and that the present Holy Father, Pope Paul VI, has not yet had time to challenge his pre-eminence. Besides, until the lines of his pontificate have been given a chance to reveal a characteristic pattern, Pope Paul's policy can hardly be dissociated from that of Pope John. He himself has been at considerable pains to declare his adherence to Pope John's programme and methods.

However, such comparisons between Pope John and his predecessors can be misleading, unless one is prepared to view their respective situations in an historian's perspective. An historian would remind us that there are many factors which vary from one age to another and which should be taken into account when comparing their achievements. Each age will have its own set of more urgent problems which, inevitably, will acquire priority at that time. Each age, it is likely, will have problems which seem well-nigh insoluble at the time but which will become amenable to solution later, as fresh opportunities and possibilities emerge. It is true, too, that when the time is ripe, God does give the Church leaders whose qualities seem fully to match the needs and opportunities of their times. Such men were, for example, Leo XIII, Pius XII and John XXIII.

One is ignoring a great deal of history if one thinks it

remiss of Pius IX, let us say, not to have done for Christian unity in the eighteen-sixties what John XXIII did in the nineteen-sixties. If Pius IX worked from a different scale of priorities than did John XXIII, the times too were different and the problems and opportunities. Of course, one must not so exaggerate the role of external factors as to suggest that a pope's policy will be entirely determined by them. But the fact remains that the programme of even the most talented and forceful pope will to a considerable extent be dependent on the opportunities that his predecessors have fashioned for him. And it is undoubtedly true that all the popes of the past century or so have helped to make the opportunities that now open before us in the nineteen-sixties.

Leo XIII (1878-1903)

The first of the modern popes to make a sustained effort to end the disunity of Christendom was Leo XIII. In 1897 he wrote that one of the two great aims of his pontificate had been 'to promote the reunion of those who have fallen away from the Catholic Church by heresy or schism, since it is undoubtedly the will of Christ that all should be united under one Shepherd'.[1] He made the Eastern Churches his special concern. He was conscious of the need to dissipate the fears of many Orientals that the Latin Church wanted to do away with their ancient privileges and traditions. Thus, the encyclical, *Grande Munus*, which he published in 1880, speaks with tenderness and respect of the ancient Slavonic liturgies and in *Orientalium Dignitas*, published in 1894, he expressly ordered the preservation of the Eastern liturgies. In 1893 he had given permission for what was an object-lesson in respect for the Eastern liturgies, at the Eucharistic Congress in Jerusalem. Mass was celebrated there every day in a different Eastern rite and the Orthodox

---

[1] This and the following three quotations will be found in C. Boyer, *Christian Unity and the Ecumenical Movement*, London, 1962, p. 59.

were invited to join with the Catholics in common homage
to Christ in the Eucharist.[2]

It was during the next few years, however, that Pope Leo
published his major statements on the problems of unity.
One of them, *Praeclara Gratulationis* (1894), is the sort of
document that we nowadays would refer to as being in the
spirit of Pope John XXIII. It is a stirring invitation to unity.
The language is conciliatory; the words 'heresy' or 'schism'
are studiously avoided. Addressing himself to the Easterns,
Pope Leo said: 'It is not for any human motive, but impelled
by divine charity and a desire for the salvation of all, that
we advise reconciliation and union with the Church of
Rome'. What he said to the Protestants is startingly like
something that Pope John was to say to the observers at
the Vatican Council almost seventy years later. Pope Leo
wrote: 'Our heart appeals to you even more than our words,
to you, our brethren, who for three centuries and more
differ from us on Christian faith; and to you all likewise
who in later times for any reason whatsoever have turned
away from us. Let us all meet in the unity of faith and of the
knowledge of God'. He quoted a remark addressed by
Bessarion to the Greek Orthodox Church: 'What are we
going to say to the Lord when he asks us to render an
account of this separation from our brothers, he who came
down from heaven to unite us in one fold, who was made
flesh and crucified?'

Pope Leo's name, however, has been rather more readily
associated with two other documents which, though no less
charitable in tone, had a less agreeable function to discharge.
They are the encyclical, *Satis Cognitum* (1896) and the
apostolic letter, *Apostolicae Curae* (1896). The first of these
outlined the doctrine and attitudes to which the Church
is committed on the question of Christian unity, the second
one pronounced against the validity of Anglican orders.

Students of ecumenism assign a particular importance
to Pope Leo's *Praeclara Gratulationis*. It is said to have
inaugurated a new period in the history of the Church's
relationship to other Christian confessions. One biographer

[2] G. Goyau, 'Léon XIII', *Dictionnaire de théologie catholique*, IX (I),
col. 351, Paris, 1926

refers to it as the high point of the Pope's pontificate.[3] It is certain that, on the threshold of the twentieth century, *Praeclara Gratulationis* and *Satis Cognitum* between them expressed the combination of doctrinal firmness and deeply-felt charity which should be the mark of Catholic ecumenism.

Saint Pius X (1903-1914)

The pontificate of Saint Pius X coincided with a period of great beginnings in Protestant ecumenism. It was in 1910 that the twentieth-century ecumenical movement was launched by the World Missionary Conference at Edinburgh. The same period, however, also saw the high-water mark of Modernism, a factor which considerably inhibited Catholic ecumenism at this time. But Saint Pius X, it has been said, did see the Church through the crisis of Modernism without a schism. And in 1909 he approved the Unity Octave for January. In 1897 Pope Leo XIII had decreed that a novena for Christian unity be celebrated before Pentecost each year.

Benedict XV (1914-1922)

Pope Benedict XV found himself in the unhappy position of having to discourage Catholics from taking part in a movement towards Christian unity which had won the support of many of the most generous souls outside the Church. In 1919 a set of letters of the Holy Office were published in the *Acta Apostolicae Sedis* forbidding Catholics to join the 'Association for the Promotion of the Unity of Christendom'. Father Gregory Baum, O.S.A., thus resumes the reasons given for this decision: 'The Association is based on an ecclesiology which is incompatible with the Catholic faith. According to the Roman letters, the underlying theory of the Association recognizes the Church of Christ as existing in three Catholic bodies, Anglican,

[3] Ibid., col. 252; G. Baum, *That They May Be One*, London, 1958, p. vii

Roman and Greek, which are united in charity, the essentials of faith and an ecclesiastical tradition, while they remain structurally distinct'.[4]

The Pope himself, that same year, felt he had no choice but to refuse a very courteous invitation to him to attend a 'Faith and Order' conference. As the official response which was handed to the deputation who waited on the Pope put it: 'The teaching and practice of the Roman Catholic Church regarding the unity of the visible Church of Christ is well known to everybody, and therefore it would not be possible for the Catholic Church to take part in a congress such as the one proposed. His Holiness, however, by no means wishes to disapprove of the congress in question for those who are not in union with the chair of Peter'.[5]

The rather bleak impression left by these words is offset by the remembrance of Pope Benedict's support for the Church Unity Octave, which he enriched with indulgences and by the reflection that it was he who created the Congregation for the Oriental Churches and the Pontifical Institute of Oriental Studies. Admittedly, the short-term purpose of these institutions was to assist the Eastern Churches in communion with Rome; but they also had a long-term aim, the promotion of contacts with Eastern Orthodoxy and the study of the problems of Christian unity.

Pius XI (1922-1939)

The pontificate of Pope Pius XI is best remembered in the West for the approval he gave to the Malines conversations and for his encyclical *Mortalium Animos*. At first sight, they seem contrasting enterprises, the conversations seeming to open a door and the encyclical seeming to shut it. In fact, however, both are expressions of a single coherent policy. Pius XI desired Christian unity, but he knew that a movement towards unity would founder unless guided by a sound theology and, in particular, a sound ecclesiology.

[4] G. Baum, op. cit., p. 103
[5] G. H. Tavard, *Two Centuries of Ecumenism*, London, 1960, p. 117

The Malines conversations between Anglican and Catholic theologians represented the sort of patient and painstaking enterprise that seemed best calculated to further the slow work of fostering Christian unity. Their long-term effects were, undoubtedly, beneficial. Father Y. Congar, O.P. remarks that they were a concrete demonstration of the possibility of dialogue and friendship with the Catholic Church and with Catholics.[6]

The immediate fruits of the Malines conversations, however, were disappointing for those who had hoped for too much from them. Such hopes were to some extent based on a misunderstanding of the Catholic position on Christian unity. It was in order to remove misunderstandings and to dissuade people from entertaining unrealizable hopes that Pope Pius XI felt it necessary to state the Church's position in the encyclical, *Mortalium Animos*. It is one of the classic statements of the Catholic conception of Church unity.

Pope Pius XI, however, was himself more interested in the problem of reunion with the Orthodox Christians and it is in this domain that he made his main contribution to ecumenism. And it was a very important contribution indeed. Father Baum points out that his efforts were 'continuous and systematic, and their aim is perpetuated by the schools and institutes which he created'.[7] He reorganized the Oriental Institute in 1922 and he was instrumental in having the study of Oriental theology introduced into Catholic faculties of theology and into major seminaries. It was at his prompting that the Benedictines set up a monastery devoted to unity at Amay in Belgium, which was later transferred to Chevetogne. The work done at Chevetogne epitomizes what Pope Pius XI had in mind: prayer, deep study, 'benevolence'. Pope Pius's writings, too, contributed not a little towards the progress of ecumenism. Father Baum says of him that his language 'is indicative of a new age in the history of Christian disunity'.[8] One famous passage summarises Pope Pius's thought and programme:

[6] *Divided Christendom*, London, 1939, p. 168
[7] G. Baum, op. cit., p. 163, note 19
[8] Ibid., p. 110

For a reunion it is above all necessary to know and to
love one another. To know one another: because if the
efforts of reunion have failed so many times, this is in
large measure due to mutual ignorance. If there are
prejudices on both sides, these prejudices must vanish.
Incredible are the errors and equivocations which
persist and which are handed down among the separated
brethren against the Catholic Church; on the other
hand, Catholics also have sometimes failed in justly
evaluating the truth or, on account of insufficient
knowledge, in showing a fraternal spirit. Do we know
all that is valuable, good and Christian in the fragments
of ancient Catholic truth? Detached fragments of
gold-bearing rock also contain the precious ore. The
ancient Churches of the East have retained so true a
holiness that they deserve not only our respect but
also our sympathy.[9]

Pius XII (1939-1958)

The impact of the personality of Pope Pius XII in this
age of expanding mass-media and increasing travel was
truly enormous. Not only Catholics but thousands of other
Christians attended his numerous public audiences each
year and many of these undoubtedly were persuaded by his
obvious holiness and his magnetism to think better of the
Church which he headed. The same was true of the millions
who heard him on the radio or saw him on television or
cinema screens. The importance of all this cannot be lightly
dismissed, especially since much of anti-Catholic prejudice
was in fact focused on the papacy.

Pope Pius XII did not have the wholehearted personal
enthusiasm for ecumenism which Pope John was to show,
but many appeals for a return to unity with Rome do occur
in his writings and addresses. His principal direct contribution to ecumenism was the Instruction, *Ecclesia
Catholica*, which was issued by the Holy Office on 20
December 1949. In this document the attitude towards the

[9] Quoted ibid.

ecumenical movement is much more positive than the attitudes which previous popes had felt justified in adopting. The desire for unity among Christians not in communion with Rome is attributed to 'the grace of the Holy Spirit'. The bishops are invited to engage in ecumenical activities and are told that they 'must not be content to observe this movement'. They are to assist those who seek the truth and to protect 'the faithful from the dangers that easily result from the activity of this movement'. The Instruction gives practical directives for ecumenical meetings between Catholics and other Christians.

Looking back at Pope Pius's reign in the aftermath of Pope John's reign, one can see that many of Pope Pius's activities prepared the way indirectly for the ecumenism of Pope John and Pope Paul. This is true, in the first place, of the influence of Pope Pius within the Church itself. The programme of renewal which is so essential a part of Pope John's ecumenism would scarcely have been possible were it not for the encouragement and guidance given by Pope Pius XII to biblical studies and to the liturgical movement. Further, the progress made by Catholic scholars in both these fields has facilitated much fruitful contact between themselves and other Christian scholars over the past thirty years.

In a number of other instances Pope Pius XII, though addressing himself to Catholics, contributed to the formation of a climate favourable to ecumenism. This is true of his statement of the Catholic doctrine on subjects which have often been points of particular difficulty for Protestants. They are, principally, his teaching on tolerance and on Church-State relations as well as his teaching on the nature of the Church in the encyclical *Mystici Corporis*.

Pope John XXIII (1958-1963)

It is not easy to write adequately about Pope John XXIII and unity. One does, indeed, approach the task with enthusiasm, but one is also conscious of a gnawing conviction that one will not do his achievement justice. One

senses the near-impossibility of gauging the scope and
depth of his influence and the difficulty of diagnosing its
nature and origins.

The truth is that Pope John's influence has been both
profound and widespread and that its scope is still being
widened. It is in the Catholic Church, of course, that it has
been most emphatically and deeply felt. There it has been,
to use an overworked phrase, epoch-making. In the four
and a half years of his pontificate Pope John gently nudged
the Catholic Church into a new epoch in inter-confessional
relations. This is how Father Hans Küng puts it:

> Almost overnight the reunion of our separated brethren
> has ceased to be the concern only of a brave little van-
> guard, themselves objects of admiration, ridicule, pity
> or hostility; it has become the concern of the universal
> Church, even in purely Catholic countries, and of the
> Church's leaders; something to be not only proposed
> in theory but worked out in practice. Theological and
> pastoral work with an ecumenical slant are no longer
> regarded as hobbies for individuals but as a necessity
> for the entire Church. Within the Church today there
> is a longing and striving and praying for reunion of a
> totally new power and intensity.[10]

It is universally realized that Pope John's concern for
reunion can be traced back to his days in Bulgaria, where
he was in day-to-day contact with disunity. It is not perhaps
sufficiently realized to what extent his Bulgarian experiences
moulded his outlook. This is not a question for an historian but for a theologian. Pope John was deeply imbued
with a sense of Divine Providence guiding events and he
had a profound awareness of God influencing him through
people and events.

How deeply his Bulgarian experiences affected Pope John
is suggested by a story told by Father Leone Algisi, in his
John XXIII, a book which was read and approved in proof
by Pope John himself:

[10] H. Küng, *The Council and Reunion*, London, 1961, p. 1

Roncalli liked to recall the grief of an elderly Armenian bishop who had spent himself in apostleship in various European countries. During one of the early years of his apostolic visitation the venerable prelate had knelt before him in tears and as he kissed his hands had said: 'Your Excellency, we read in the Gospel that Our Lord forgives all sinners but that one sin will never be forgiven, neither on earth nor in heaven. Which is that, Excellency? Would it not be the sin of the division of the Church?'[11]

The sense of the evil of disunity and of the evil consequences it has brought in its train was deeply engraved on Pope John's mind. He referred to it, for example, in the letter he wrote in 1957 as Patriarch of Venice to encourage his diocesans to observe the Church Unity Week in January. He referred to the social, political and national evils that follow from disunity and said that disunity can poison relations between peoples and nations. He went on to say that he could attest from his own experience to the existence of 'profound and fervent aspirations' towards unity all over the world.

When speaking of the role of Pope Pius XII in ecumenism I said that, from his time onwards, especially, tourism and the mass media had been focusing attention to a hitherto undreamt-of extent on the pope's personality. If the personality of Pius XII accomplished an enormous amount with the help of tourism and the mass media, Pope John's personality was able to accomplish much more. Under the close scrutiny of television cameras, especially, he came into his own. The world quickly came to see with certainty that here was a man of great and universal charity whom one could trust absolutely. The popular magazines are a good indication of what the world thinks, and the description most commonly applied to him by them after his death was 'a good man'.

This universal affection for Pope John meant that when he wrote or spoke his words were commended to his public by his personality. Not that his words, as words, lacked

[11] L. Algisi, *John XXIII*, London, 1963, pp. 88-9

persuasiveness, they did not. But, ultimately one felt that he himself accomplished more than his words did.

When therefore Pope John spoke of himself in his first discourses as the pastor, and when he spoke of the Eastern Churches, to whom he extended a 'most loving heart' and 'open arms', inviting them to return—'They will not find a strange house, but their own; a house which in times past was enriched by the teaching and virtues of their forbears' —his words won a hearing because of what he was himself.[12]

On several occasions in the first few months of his pontificate Pope John manifested his concern about Christ-ian disunity. Then in January 1959 he decided, 'in obedience to a sudden inspiration', to link his longing for unity with an ecumenical council. Quickly enough his plans were explained more clearly in addresses and particularly in the encyclical *Ad Petri Cathedram*. The Council would not be a summit-meeting at which plans for reunion could be hammered out, though eventually it was decided to invite observers from other Christian denominations. The Council would concern itself with the renewal of the Church's life and the deepening of the faith of Catholics and, when the work of renewal had been accomplished, all Christians would see in the spectacle 'of truth, unity and charity' a 'gentle invitation to seek that unity for which Jesus Christ prayed so ardently to the heavenly Father'.

This was Pope John's programme. Death took him before he had completed it. Already, however, more of his pro-gramme than many of us realized had been accomplished. The dissident Christians have seen in the Council the proof that the Church is not a monolith in which difference or debate is impossible. The rights of bishops, which were not described in the acts of the First Council of the Vatican, were seen there in exercise. The observers themselves were treated with charity and consideration by the conciliar fathers. One observer, an American Methodist, wrote: 'And we could not fail to observe how our silent presence was taken into account when speaker after speaker insisted that a given schema or chapter be more pastoral and

[12] Cf. 'Digest of Papal Documents', *Doctrine and Life* 9 (1959), p. 26

ecumenical, following the Pope's direction in his opening address'.[13]

Pope John's opening address, it now seems clear, profoundly affected the deliberations at the first session of the Council.[14] Two passages, in particular, have important ecumenical significance. The first is:

> Our duty is not limited to the mere custodianship of this precious treasure [the deposit of faith], as though antiquity were our sole concern. Rather should we set about meeting the needs of our own age, energetically and courageously. This is what the Church has been doing for twenty centuries.
>
> The aim of the council, therefore, is not the discussion of this or that fundamental point of the Church's teaching, with wide-ranging appeals to the teaching of the Fathers and of ancient and modern theologians. One can presuppose that all this is already sufficiently well known.
>
> One did not need a council for that. What is expected, by the Christian, Catholic and Apostolic spirit of the entire world, is a step forward towards a doctrinal penetration and a formation of conscience which is in more perfect accord with authentic teaching, itself studied and expounded with the help of modern methods of research and in modern literary forms. And this must take place in a renewed, serene and tranquil adherence to the Church's teaching, in its entirety and its precision, as it still exists resplendent in the Acts of the Councils of Trent and Vatican I. The substance of the ancient doctrine, the *depositum fidei*, is one thing, its presentation is another. And it is this which must be taken very much into account— patiently, where there is need for patience—measuring everywhere by the forms and proportions of a *magisterium* which is pre-eminently pastoral.

The second passage, one which is of even more direct relevance in the ecumenical dialogue, is as follows:

[13] F. Hildebrandt, *Doctrine and Life* 13 (1963), p. 200
[14] Cf. X. Rynne, *Letters from Vatican City*, London, 1963, pp. 72-3

The Church has always been opposed to these errors,
she has often condemned them with the greatest
severity. Nowadays, however, the Spouse of Christ
prefers to use mercy rather than severity. She aims to
meet the needs of the day rather by showing the
validity of her teaching than by issuing condemnations.

The Pope went on to say that this did not imply that there
is now an end to errors nor of the need to dispel them;
rather is it that 'they are so obviously contrary to decency
and so ruinous in their fruits that men are apt of themselves
to condemn them'. He went on:

In this state of affairs the Catholic Church raises the
torch of religious truth, by means of this Ecumenical
Council. She wants to show herself the loving mother
of all men, kind, patient, full of mercy and goodness,
even towards the sons who are separated from her.[15]

On 13 October 1962 Pope John received the observers
attending the Vatican Council. What he said to them might
easily escape the notice of a reader on the look-out for
major statements of policy or theology; it was nonetheless
profoundly significant. He received the delegates in the
Hall of the Consistory and then sat down with them in
much the same formation as with cardinals in a consistory.
He himself sat, not on a throne, but on a chair of the same
kind as the delegates sat on. Addressing the delegates he
told them, in effect, that the problem of Christian unity was
in the hands of God. He quoted Psalm 67: 'Blessed be God
every day; he carries our burdens, God our salvation'. As
for the Pope's own attitude, he told them: 'you can read it
in my heart, you will find it more revealing, perhaps, than
my words'. He went on to speak of his days in Sofia, Athens
and Istanbul—'twenty happy and eventful years'—and of
his years in Paris. He spoke of the many Christians of other
denominations he had known. He went on:

Never, to my knowledge, did we experience a confusion

---

[15] *Doctrine and Life* 13 (1963), pp. 253, 254

of principles nor did we have a dispute when we dispensed charity together to those who were suffering. We did not organize conferences, we simply talked (*nous n'avons pas 'parlementé', mais parlé*); we did not hold discussions, we loved one another.

One day, many years ago, I sent a medal of Pius XI to a venerable old prelate of the Orthodox Church. The gift was no more than a simple courtesy. Shortly afterwards the old man, on his death-bed, directed that the medal be placed on his breast after his death. I saw it myself and the memory has never left me.

It is of set purpose that I allude to this episode. In its touching simplicity it is like a wild flower that one plucks in the springtime to offer as a gift. May the grace of the Lord always thus accompany us on our ways.[16]

It is easy to miss the wisdom of these words—to read them, assent to them as to something always taken for granted, and then to pass on. The point is that many of us take the Gospel simplicities too much for granted, as a member of a family can be taken so much for granted that for all practical purposes he is ignored. Pope John has shown the power and the relevance of charity in the modern world and in particular its relevance in the ecumenical dialogue. He showed the power and the persuasiveness of simple charity, of charity informing the hum-drum routine of daily life—the visits to the sick, the small kindnesses, the ready smile, the total lack of pretentiousness. His charity was more than an example, it was an apostolate. It has been like the mighty wind of Pentecost, blowing away the fogs of prejudice which for too long have obscured the long path towards Christian unity. When he was Patriarch of Venice he once said at a Unity Week meeting: 'The road to unity between the different Christian creeds is love, so little practised on either side'.[17] At the end of his own pontificate the second part of that statement was no longer true.

[16] Ibid., pp. 257-8
[17] Quoted by Algisi, *op. cit.*, p. 267

Pope Paul VI

Pope Paul VI has already shown, on at least four occasions, that he will use all his powers to push forward the ecumenical programme initiated by Pope John. His public utterances on the subject have been full of warmth and full of promise. The day after his election he said:

> Lastly, it will be part of our task as Pope to continue the great work begun so successfully and with such high hopes by our predecessor, John XXIII, to the end that the earnest prayer of the divine Redeemer, *ut unum sint*, may at last be granted. All men long for this and John XXIII gave his life for it.
>
> For this reason, the restoration of the unity of Christians, which was shattered centuries ago, will be our aim and the object of our prayers. We are acutely conscious, as Christ's Vicar on earth, of the import of the words with which Jesus Christ admonishes us: 'Simon, Simon . . . I have prayed for thee, that thy faith fail not; and thou being converted, confirm thy brethren' (*Luke* 22:31-32). For this reason we open our arms to those who glory in the Name of Christ, we address them by the sweet name of brothers. We would have them realize that in us they will find unfailing understanding, that in the Roman Church they will find their Father's house, where the glorious pages of their past history, their culture and their religious heritage are held in high honour and are endowed with new splendour.[18]

In July 1963 the bishop of Lausanne, Geneva and Fribourg was sent by the Secretariat for Promoting Christian Unity to Moscow for the celebration of the Jubilee of the episcopal consecration of the Patriarch Alexius. On 18 August the Holy Father referred to this when he visited the Greek-rite monastery of Grottaferrata. He said:

This gesture reveals the Catholic hierarchy's intention

[18] *Doctrine and Life* 13 (1963), p. 427

of paying homage to ancient memories, of eschewing emulation, prestige, ambition and—all the more so—pride; of showing that the Catholic Church has no desire to perpetuate disharmony and differences which, though they may have been sharply in focus at times in the past, seem anachronistic today. . . .

Further, the Supreme Pontiff wants also to make his own the wish which, with unexpected and spontaneous generosity came from the hearts of our predecessors and, especially, John XXIII. It is that most intense desire and he wished he had a voice as powerful as the angel's trumpet to express it: come, let us break down the barriers which separate us, let us explain the points of doctrine which we do not have in common and which are still the subject of controversy; let us endeavour to profess our *Credo* unanimously and jointly, to achieve a hierarchic union which is both articulated and compact. We wish neither to absorb nor to destroy the great Oriental Churches, but—yes!—we wish them to be re-grafted on to the one tree, the one Church of Christ.

This is not one of those very carefully prepared papal addresses. It would appear to have been in large measure delivered spontaneously and it is published in the *Osservatore Romano* (19-20 August) in an unsatisfactory mixture of direct and indirect speech. However, it is the sentiment of the address that counts most, the arms-open approach, the humility. The Pope went on to acknowledge that Catholics sometimes lacked understanding of 'the great tradition and religious inheritance of the Oriental Churches'. In a reference to the Gospel of the day, the curing of the man born deaf and dumb, he said: 'We are all a little deaf and dumb. May the Lord open our eyes and our mouths'.

It is fitting that this short survey should end with Pope Paul's address in Grottoferrata. Catholics in the English-speaking world may be conscious of greater social and cultural affinity with Protestants, but the popes, the recent popes especially, have always been more forthcoming on the subject of the Eastern Churches.[19] This is especially true of Leo XIII and Pius XI. It is true, but in a different way, of John XXIII. Leo XIII and Pius XI were wholly warm and welcoming towards the Eastern Churches; they both enormously assisted the development of knowledge of the Eastern Churches among Catholics, the growth of understanding and a conciliatory attitude and of the acknowledgment of our own faults. Circumstances forced both of them to inject a note of caution and reserve into Catholic-Protestant relations, however.

Pope John, on the other hand, was able to extend towards Protestants all of the warmth and the longing for unity that his experiences in the East had bred in him. Pius XII had considerably improved Catholic-Protestant relations, but John XXIII's charity and humanity had given it a wholly new dimension. This is the dimension in which we now live and in which Pope Paul's appeal at Grottoferrata takes on a relevance it could not have had fifty years ago:

> Let us ask the Lord unceasingly to grant that, if our age does not see it—this would be too much to hope for—at least the very next ages may witness the remaking of the unity of all true Christians, especially unity with the venerable Oriental Churches.

[19] Cf. G. Baum, *The Quest for Christian Unity*, London, 1963, pp. 28-50

Suggestions for Further Reading

L. Algisi, *John XXIII,* London: Darton, Longman and Todd, 1963

G. Baum, O.S.A., *That They May Be One.* A study in papal doctrine from Leo XIII to Pius XII. London: Bloomsbury Publishing Co., 1958
The Quest for Christian Unity, London: Sheed and Ward, 1963

C. Boyer, S.J., *Christian Unity and the Ecumenical Movement,* Faith and Fact Book no. 138, London: Burns and Oates, 1962

Y. J. Congar, O.P., *Divided Christendom,* London: Geoffrey Bles, 1939

C. J. Dumont, O.P., *Approaches to Christian Unity,* London: Darton, Longman and Todd, 1959

M. Hurley, S.J., *Towards Christian Unity,* Dublin: CTSI, 1960.

E. McDonagh, *Roman Catholics and Reunion,* Starbooks, London: Mowbrays, 1962

K. McNamara (ed.), *Christian Unity.* Lectures of Maynooth Union Summer School 1961. Dublin: Furrow-Gill, 1962

G. Noel, *The Montini Story,* London: B. Herder, 1963

G. Tavard, *Two Centuries of Ecumenism,* London: Burns and Oates, 1961

J. M. Todd, *Catholicism and the Ecumenical Movement,* London: Longmans, 1956

THE UNITY WEEK FOUNDERS

Daphne Pochin Mould

THE ancient hope of every new subdivision of Christian belief was that its views would prevail over the others and so bring about unity. In fact, history records a continued splintering and hiving-off, so that the number of Churches and groups with the name of Christian has steadily risen. Scottish Presbyterianism provides a kind of text-book example first of the formation of new divisions for conscience sake, and then, over the last hundred years, of their reuniting in response to the modern longing for Christian unity. In 1843, at the famous Disruption, nearly a third of the ministers of the Scottish Church seceded, abandoning homes and incomes because they would not submit to what they called 'moderation ["Broad Church" liberal views] and the evils of patronage'. Their courage was supported by their congregations, and the Scottish Free Church came into being. In 1929 reunion with the Church of Scotland was to an extent achieved. The sceptic can, of course, say that these reunions and other moves towards unity are a result of a general weakening of theological belief, that men today wish rather to present a united front than to split dogmatic hairs. And there is this danger in ecumenical activity, in which all need to remind themselves constantly that true unity can only be based on the fullness of truth.

Awareness of the scandal of disunity and efforts to heal it have existed from around the time of the famous Scottish Disruption. On the Catholic side there has been an increasing awareness of the problem, as the reader may see

even by studying papal encyclicals from those of Leo XIII
on, and a cautious advance into dialogue with the other
Churches.[1] On the Protestant side, there has been the great
coming together of Churches which has culminated in the
formation of the World Council of Churches, representing
more than two hundred groups.[2] A wind of change in
relations between Christians of different Churches, a deep
and urgent longing for unity, this is the background to the
work of the men who originated organized united prayer
for unity. One has the impression that their work was a
realization of a need already felt, rather than any sudden
novelty thought up by a single individual.

The idea of a week of special prayer connected with unity
seems to have originated in 1836 with St Vincent Pallotti.
He, with the Eastern Churches particularly in mind, wished
to show the unity in diversity of the Catholic Church, the
splendour and variety of her liturgies, that the familiar
Latin rite was only one among many different rites, all
truly Catholic. So, in the week following the feast of the
Epiphany, the feast that celebrates the bringing of salvation
to all nations (represented in the persons of the magi), St
Vincent arranged to have a different liturgy celebrated on
each successive day in the Theatine church of St Andrew.
This impressive week of the celebration of the different
Catholic liturgies in a single church still continues to be
held in Rome.

Again, on the Catholic side, Leo XIII wrote several
encyclicals on the theme of unity, and in particular was at
pains to vindicate the status of the eastern rites, that they
were never to be regarded as inferior to the Latin one. In
1895 Blessed Helena Guerra, the foundress of the Congregation of Oblates of the Holy Spirit, petitioned the Pope
for a novena of prayer before Pentecost, for the return of all
men and nations separated from the Church. The idea was
to emulate the example of the apostles, Mary and the other
first followers of Christ praying for the coming of the Holy
Spirit. Leo XIII, in a brief, *Provida Matris*, dated 5 May

[1] Cf. 'Recent Popes and Christian Unity' in the present volume,
pp. 32-49
[2] Cf. Dr Thornley's essay on the World Council, below, pp. 83-99

1895, approved the idea; in an encyclical, *Divinum Illud* (9 May 1897) he ordered the novena to be held everywhere. Indulgences were attached to the novena before Pentecost, and also granted to those who prayed for the same intention for the eight days following Pentecost.

Meantime in England in the Anglican Church, the Oxford Movement originated by Newman and his associates had led to a rediscovery of the Fathers and their thought and of the sacramental doctrines of the Church. For Newman and many others the result was a personal reunion with Rome, but their conversions did not initiate a mass movement in that direction in the Church of England. What took place was a progressive, often hotly contested, Catholicizing of Anglican liturgy and thought. To the Oxford Movement we owe the modern restrained yet gracious liturgy of the English cathedrals, as well as the more flamboyant extremes of those Churches described as 'more Roman than the Pope'.

Born Catholics must be completely puzzled by the Anglican Church's ability to glory in her comprehensiveness in which the traditional Protestant lamb lies down beside the Papalist lion, and yet there is only an occasional snarl or bleat between them. Each may try to convince the other, but always in the context of their basic loyalty to the Church, which they have no idea of leaving.

Newman, during his days as an Anglican, and the Oxford Movement believed that though the Reformation had many regrettable sides to it, it had neither broken the essential continuity of the historic Catholic Church, nor interrupted the apostolic succession. Just as the Orthodox Church had valid Orders and sacraments, so had the Church of England. High Churchmen believed in a 'branch theory' in which the true Catholic Church was subdivided into three great bodies, Roman Catholic, Orthodox and Church of England. Bodies like the Church of Scotland which had rejected episcopacy were regarded as heretical and not as part of the true Catholic Church.

The branch theory had the result of highlighting the scandal of the schism between the branches, and it also suggested that corporate reunion between the branches was a workable possibility. In 1857 a group which included Catholics as well as Anglicans met in London and founded the Association for the Promotion of the Unity of Christendom. The English Catholic hierarchy were highly suspicious of this society and in the end, in 1864, the Holy Office forbade Catholics to belong to it, on the grounds that it held the branch theory, gave the impression one religion was as good as another and that the presence of Catholics in it would give scandal by suggesting that they approved the organization's basic assumptions. Catholics therefore ceased to belong to the Association, but it continued its work for unity.

A popular manual for the ordinary High Anglican laity first published in 1893 not only listed the seven sacraments and taught much of Catholic doctrine, but gave space and prominence to the scandal of disunity and urged the faithful to pray for unity. Divisions were contrary to the mind of Christ expressed in his prayer at the Last Supper; they hindered the world's conversion and were 'a ground of perpetual reproach'. 'It is our duty to possess a spirit desirous of reunion and to keep up such a spirit by earnest prayer, and in all ways of speech and feeling as ever ready for reunion when the path shall be opened to us'.[3]

This is the background to the work of Lewis Thomas Wattson (1863-1940), founder of the Chair of Unity Octave of Prayer. He was the son of an American Episcopalian clergyman, his father's whole clerical career had in fact been blighted as the result of suspicions of his Roman leanings in student days. But by the time his son was growing up and attending an American theological college, High Church views had become respectable.

Thomas Wattson was not a profound thinker, nor theologian nor philosopher. He was transparently good and sincere, a man of prayer, an eloquent preacher, with a huge faith in God that must have been maddening to ordinary 'practical' people. A controversialist with little idea of breaking a new idea gently to other people; a person

[3] *The Catholic Religion. A Manual of Instruction for Members of the Anglican Church*, by Rev. Vernon Staley, Mowbray: London and Oxford, p. 65

who believed that he received sudden divine inspirations, though one may suspect this was simply the way the man's mind worked, in sudden leaps. One of these sudden ideas, or inspirations, came to him as a teenager—that he would found an Order.

Ordained in 1886, by special dispensation as he was under age, he worked first in an ordinary parish; later, in 1895, was invited to become superior of a group of unmarried clergy living and working together in Omaha.

It was on 9 July 1893 that, becoming more and more convinced of his vocation to found an Order, young Thomas Wattson sought a sign by means of the *sortes biblicae*. After celebrating the Communion service he opened the bible at random three times. The texts he hit on were reasonably apt for his purpose, being *John* 7:37-39, *Romans* 5:11 and the account of the institution of the Eucharist in the eleventh chapter of 1 *Corinthians*. The second of the three texts gave him the name of his Order. In the English Authorised version it reads: 'And not only so, but we also joy in God, through Our Lord Jesus Christ, by whom we have now received the atonement'.

Atonement is an English word for which the Douai translation uses the Latinism *reconciliation*. It is typical of the way that Father Wattson's mind worked that *atonement* caught his eye, that he broke it down into its constituent syllables, at-one-ment, and saw in it both the name and the vocation of the Order he wished to found. It would be the Society of the Atonement.

Father Wattson also discovered his own abilities as a journalist. In 1894 he started a small parish magazine called *The Pulpit of the Cross* whose policy was to be 'aggressive rather than defensive'. He was deeply concerned over Christian unity; he set himself in the magazine to expound Catholic doctrine but at this stage he rejected the Pope. In July 1895 he wrote: 'The argument from history as well as from Scripture is fatal to the papal theories of the Church of Rome and we cannot regard the Roman Catholic hierarchy in America in any other light than being the representatives of a foreign bishop'. Outsiders perhaps saw the road he was following more clearly than he did. *The*

New York Sun commented that the editor of the *Pulpit of the Cross* might soon be expected to become a Catholic. The editor snapped back that the *Sun* was many years behind the times: 'we were baptized into the Holy Catholic Church over thirty years ago'.

Father Wattson had hoped that the Omaha community might be the nucleus of his Order; in fact, in later years, he used to joke about his efforts to make monks of men 'who did not want to become monks'. One cannot but be convinced that the Order never would have become concrete reality if he had not come into contact with a remarkable American woman called Lurana Mary White. She was the sheet anchor of the whole project. She it was who found the Graymoor property on which the infant Society settled, who fell first under the spell of St Francis, and brought about the Franciscan character of the group. She was consoler, inspirer, adviser, and her activity ranged from initiating ideas in the unity apostolate to designing the habit for the new friars.

She began to correspond with Father Wattson in 1896 when she was already an Anglican sister with private vows. In 1897 she went to England to make a formal novitiate with the Sisters of Bethany in London as preparation for founding the Sisters of the Atonement with Father Wattson. Meantime, Father Wattson began to think again about the Roman claims; passing the time after he had missed a train, he wandered into a Catholic church, and his mind made another of its sudden jumps. He looked at his history books with new insight and became convinced that the papal claims were just and true. At the same time, he did not renounce the Catholicity of the Episcopalian Church or the validity of its orders; he regarded it as in schism and that every effort must be made to bring it to corporate reunion with Rome.

Mother Lurana came back to America and she and Father Wattson made a Triduum of prayer at her sister's house at Warwick, New York. At its close, on 7 October 1898, they made a solemn gift of themselves to God for the founding of the new Society. Mother Lurana, with two other girls, moved at once to the Graymoor property to face a bitter winter in a shack; Father Wattson followed them there a year later after making his religious novitiate with the Episcopal Order of the Holy Cross in Westminster, Maryland.

In 1900 Father Wattson vowed poverty, chastity and obedience, and on 28 October of that year formally launched the tiny Society (which consisted essentially of Mother Lurana and himself) on its extraordinary apostolate of vindicating papal claims from outside the Church. In a sermon on this occasion, Father Wattson who had now taken the names of Paul James Francis in religion, declared that the Faith 'is the Faith of the Holy Roman Church, and the Chair of Peter at Rome is the divinely-constituted centre of a reunited Christendom'. All the members of the infant Society were asked to sign a declaration agreeing with the main points of this sermon; those who refused were asked to leave.

In season and out of season Father Wattson set himself to preach corporate reunion with Rome. Not unnaturally, the new Society soon ceased to be popular and its leader, once in great demand as a preacher, found that street corners were becoming his only pulpit! He turned to the written word to get his message across, launching *Rose Leaves from Our Lady's Garden at Graymoor* in 1901, and *The Lamp* in 1903. Mother Lurana sent her sisters on begging tours to raise money to publish *The Lamp*; she also suggested its subtitle *Ut omnes unum sint*—That all may be one.

The Lamp, which is still being published, was liked, hated, argued over; it roused controversy and it carried Father Wattson's ideas far and wide. In the first Editorial (2 February 1903), the founder wrote that he believed all that the Church of Rome teaches, including papal infalli- bility, but also in 'Anglican Orders and the perpetuity of the Anglican Church. The breach with Rome is going to be repaired in God's good time and the same relations re- established between the Vatican and the *Ecclesia Anglicana* which existed prior to the sixteenth century'.

The historian may smile at so naïve a view of the past and of the events of the Reformation, but it was sincerely held, and when in 1907 American Episcopalians drew closer to Presbyterian and other non-episcopal groups, opening their pulpits to them, the High Church were profoundly shocked. In the February 1908 issue of *The Lamp* Father Wattson wrote that: 'Something like a mania to decatholicize the Episcopal Church in the interests of Protestant Christianity seems to have gotten possession of the Anglican Episcopate the world over'. Thus at this stage Father Wattson thought of reunion only between the true 'Catholic episcopal' Churches, Roman, Anglican and Orthodox, but in terms of conversion from heresy in the case of other Christian Churches.

As early as 4 October 1901 he had planned a 'Church Unity Army', whose members would pray and work for this reunion of Catholics, Episcopalians and Orthodox. It never flourished, but the idea was there in Father Wattson's mind. In England, the Association for the Promotion of the Unity of Christendom was still going strong and in 1902 the Reverend Spencer Jones published a book based on a series of sermons he had preached for the Association. It was entitled *An Essay Toward Reunion* and called for the corporate reunion of Anglicans with Rome. Rev. Spencer Jones and Father Wattson began to correspond after the book was published and Spencer Jones to contribute to *The Lamp*. In 1907 the two men collaborated in a book called *The Prince of the Apostles*. Mother Lurana had, in fact, suggested the project, and wrote a large part of the first chapter, though her share remained anonymous.

That same year of 1907 Spencer Jones wrote to Father Wattson suggesting a special sermon on unity be preached on 29 June each year. Replying on 30 November 1907 Father Wattson wrote: 'The Peter Sermon suggestion is fine. By all means let us set it in motion at once. In addition to that, what do you think of inaugurating a Church Unity Week beginning with St Peter's Chair at Rome, January 18th, and ending with St Paul's day? During that week a series of addresses on reunion might be made every night, or someone outside the parish might be invited to give a conference; or a Church Unity mission might be conducted. We have to make this a popular movement and we will not do it until we preach these things repeatedly and constantly to our people'.

The Lamp accordingly launched the idea, and the first Unity Octave took place in 1908. Its intentions were the 'recognition by all Christians of the Chair of Peter as the divinely-constituted Centre of Unity', and for the reunion of Orthodox, Anglicans, Protestants, lapsed Catholics, the conversion of England and America to Catholicism and the conversion of pagans and Jews. The prayer to be said for unity during the Octave was that already used for the same intention by Anglicans: the prayer which immediately follows the *Agnus Dei* in the Catholic Mass.

Father Wattson's position was quite obviously becoming more and more illogical. It came to the point where he believed all the Pope and Rome taught, except about the validity of Anglican Orders. In the end he conceded this final point, and he claimed that the first fruits of the Octave were the corporate reunion of the Society with Rome on 30 October 1909. Corporate reunion was still his dream, and he succeeded in bringing the Society of the Atonement (which consisted of himself, Mother Lurana, a lay brother, two professed sisters and two novices, together with ten lay people associated with the foundation) into the Church as a group which would continue its apostolate and religious life as originally planned by its founder.

Only then did Father Wattson's position begin to make sense and the Octave to flourish. Asked why he chose an Octave and not a Novena he claimed that, in addition to fitting in with the two feast days, an 'Octave, as in music, is a scale of harmony, [so it] may very well typify harmony and unity among Christians'. The year following Graymoor's reception the Octave was observed, under Catholic auspices, in America and it spread rapidly. On 25 February 1916 Benedict XV issued a Brief which extended the observance to the whole Church and indulgenced it. Father Wattson tried to persuade the Holy See to make the observance compulsory, but this was prudently rejected. In 1927, to avoid any ambiguity of meaning, the title of 'Church Unity Octave' was changed to 'The Chair of Unity Octave'—the new name was suggested by Mother Lurana.

This is not the place to detail the early struggles of the
Society of the Atonement to establish itself, or the very
many good works and projects carried out by Father
Wattson and the Society. Meantime Graymoor's example
of joining the Church as a group, encouraged others who
were merely in schism to seek corporate reunion—in
particular Mar Ivanios and the Jacobites in India.

It will be noted however that Father Wattson, at least
in the first half of his career, was an uncompromising
controversialist. To the ordinary Christian, apart from the
High Anglican group, his Octave would appear aggressively
papal. How could a sincere Presbyterian, say, join other
followers of Christ in praying for something to come about
(submission to the Pope) which he believed to be contrary
to the mind of Christ? Yet this same Presbyterian might
passionately desire the unity of Christians. How could
means be found for him to pray with a Catholic for unity,
in such a way however that each respected the rights of the
other's conscience and belief?

To a Frenchman, the Abbé Paul Couturier (1881-1953),
we owe the deepening, the spiritualization, one might say,
of the idea behind the week of prayer for unity, so that it
has become something in which all followers of Christ can
join in complete sincerity. Unhappily, controversy has
arisen between the followers of the 'Wattson' way and the
'Couturier' way, the former claiming that Couturier had
'watered down' the Octave. But what we are really seeing
is not a 'watering down' but a development, the evolution
of a form of prayer for unity which corresponds to the
contemporary evolution of ecumenical work. Catholics,
who used to think only in terms of 'submission' and 'conversion', have now learned to talk of 'dialogue', to realize
that deeply-held beliefs are not changed overnight, and
that one must go out of one's way to understand them, to
appreciate all that is true in them and to love and understand the people, the individuals, who hold them. The
Church, in fact, has moved from an attitude in which she
condemns the errors held by the other Churches, to one

in which she appreciates, and even learns from, the truths which they hold and believe.

A detail of the new courtesy and understanding between Christians is the fact that Abbé Couturier spoke of a *week* of prayer, not an *octave*. Born Catholics may not realize that both octave and novena are highly irritant words to many Christians, suggesting as they do a superstitious juggling with magical numbers.

Paul Couturier was born in Lyons in 1881 and his career was ordinary to the point of dullness. He followed the normal, not then very inspiring or adventurous, studies for the priesthood and as he showed no very particular gifts for parish work or preaching, came to teach mathematics and natural science at the college of the Prêtres de Saint-Irénée, of which group he became a member. His pupils remembered him more for his obvious holiness than for his teaching ability. In 1920 Abbé Couturier came into contact with Père Albert Valensin, S.J., who gave a series of retreats at Saint Égrève. If there had been any possibility of Abbé Couturier sinking into a spiritual rut, Père Valensin pulled him out of it. He taught the primacy of charity and Couturier took up the idea wholeheartedly. At the same time, western Europe received many Russian refugees and Abbé Couturier began to work to help those in Lyons. This brought him into contact with Orthodox clergy and with the Eastern Church.

Meantime in 1925, at Amay in Belgium, another remarkable man, Dom Lambert Beauduin, O.S.B., had founded a Benedictine community dedicated to work for unity, especially for unity with the East. For that reason the community which is now at Chevetogne is of two rites with a daily simultaneous celebration of the Latin and the Byzantine rite. Dom Lambert was a friend of Cardinal Mercier who had taken part in the famous Malines Conversations with the Anglican Church.

The Amay community were already working to extend the observance of the January Octave of prayer, and also that of Pentecost. Posters, bearing pictures of Russian icons, and booklets were printed and distributed to Belgian parishes.

In 1932 Abbé Couturier visited the Amay community, saw what they were doing and learned about the Octave of prayer for unity. He discovered as well Cardinal Mercier's testament for unity that 'in order to be united it is necessary to love one another; in order to love one another it is necessary to know one another; in order to know one another it is necessary to meet one another'. Making these personal contacts and friendships was, and is, one of the fundamental activities of the Amay (Chevetogne) Benedictines. Abbé Couturier seems to have been profoundly impressed by their work and associated himself directly with them by becoming an oblate of the community, taking the name of Benedict Irenaeus.

Couturier immediately introduced the Unity Octave in Lyons, beginning in 1933 with a triduum preached by his friend, Père Valensin, and backed by a massed Slavonic choir.

But he meditated on the problem and on the form that prayer for unity should take. He realized that Christian reunion would be a miracle and one for which all Christians, who all share in the guilt of disunity, must ask God. How could they find a formula in which they could unite to ask for unity? There was such a formula and Abbé Couturier discovered it. Each one could unite himself with Christ and pray that the unity of all Christians may come as Christ wills and by the means he wills. 'Christian Unity will be attained when the Praying Christ has found enough Christian souls in all confessions in whom He Himself can freely pray to His Father for Unity'.

This new approach did not mean that Abbé Couturier hid his own Catholic Faith or convictions. Equally it did not mean that he appeared as a man spiritually superior, boastful of possessing the fullness of truth. It was, in fact, his complete Catholic convictions, his faith, his priesthood, combined with his love and understanding that made members of other Churches love him.

An Anglican monk, Dom Benedict Ney, wrote of him in these terms: 'Indeed, I am convinced that it was precisely because his faith in all the Roman Church teaches was so deep and strong that he saw so clearly that the more his separated brethren deepened their hold on and lived by the truths they believed in common with the Roman Church, the more eager they would be for reunion with her. That is why he always came back to the primacy of the spiritual life in all his work and thoughts about unity of Christians'.

As the present prior of Chevetogne, Dom Thomas Becquet, points out, there is always a danger in ecumenical work of becoming so immersed in human contacts as to forget God. Couturier (whom Dom Becquet knew well) was the corrective to this possibility. He was a man who gave an impression of calm, of patience, humility and above all of an intense preoccupation with God. He struck his Catholic friends as a man who could, and did, spend long hours in prayer. He was the very opposite of the fighting controversialist, yet beneath his quiet calm was an extraordinarily ardent spirit.

Accordingly, Abbé Couturier never set out to make debating points. What he tried to do was to deepen the love of God in all Christians. He was fond of saying, 'Ex igne lux ut de luce ignis', meaning that from the fire of charity would come light and out of this light would come more fire. But his idea of charity was far from being merely sentimental good will. His papers include a list of 'Lives sacrificed for Christian Unity', of people who had offered their lives and their sufferings for this cause. He regarded them as forming a new army of martyrs.

Abbé Couturier was also a moving spirit in organizing meetings for prayer and study between Protestants and Catholics, meetings which now form so important a part of modern ecumenical work. He also rejoiced in the formation of the World Council of Churches.

Thus the week of prayer for unity has evolved and deepened and widened its scope and its ideas, just as ecumenical work and thought in general has evolved over the same period of time. There are enormous difficulties in the way of reunion, especially with Protestant groups, but the change already so apparent in relations between the Churches gives great hope for the future. However we may be certain that unity will not, indeed cannot, come until all Christians desire it and pray for it. To Abbé

Couturier we owe a form of prayer for unity in which all can sincerely join without doing violence to conscience or present belief.

Suggestions for Further Reading

C. Boyer, S.J. (ed.), *Unitas*, Duckett, Summer 1963 (a commemorative issue for the centenary of Father Wattson's birth), Rome/London

*G. Curtis, C.R., *Life of Abbé Couturier*, S.C.M. Press, 1964 (?) (in preparation; exact title and date of publication not yet announced), London

D. Gannon, S. A., *Father Paul of Graymoor*, Macmillan, 1959, New York

M. Villain, *Abbé Paul Couturier*, Haywards Heath, Sussex: Holy Cross Convent, 1959

*Anglican author

THE MASS 'FOR THE UNITY OF THE CHURCH'

Joseph Dowdall

AT every Mass we celebrate the entire mystery of our Redemption through the death and resurrection of our Lord Jesus Christ. Yet in order to help us enter more fully into this mystery the Church presents in successive feasts throughout the year different facets of it. She concentrates our attention upon one or other of the basic elements contained within it. Thus the mystery of Redemption is presented under the aspect of the coming of God into the human race at Christmas, and of its bringing us a share of the glorified life of Christ at Easter, and of the indwelling in each of us of the Divine Spirit at Pentecost, and so forth. The existence of a visible society founded by Christ and in which his Spirit dwells is an essential part of God's plan for redeeming mankind, and this society—the Church—is One, Holy, Catholic and Apostolic. In the Mass *For the Unity of the Church* the origin and mystery of her own unity is presented to the faithful by the Church.

The prayers and readings of the Church's Liturgy are drawn up for her own believing members only. They do not treat directly of those outside of her fold, nor do they reflect all the refinements of theology, or the language of controversies. Rather does the Church present her own doctrine serenely in them for the enlightenment of her own faithful. Nevertheless, the principles of doctrine which inspire these texts are of universal application, and we can turn to them humbly and confidently for guidance in the present tragic division of Christendom to which we are the heirs. Having first then seen something of the historical background of this special Mass for the Unity of the Church we shall go on to examine its texts more closely and understand their message. Finally, before concluding, we shall see how the theme of unity is prominent elsewhere in the liturgy and indeed in every Mass.

Historical Background

This Mass was composed especially to heal the great schism in the Church during the fourteenth and fifteenth centuries.[1] For forty years the Western Church was divided into two and later into three parties, each supporting a rival claimant to the papacy. The schism opened in 1378 with the election of Clement VII and the repudiation by the cardinals of the election of the Italian Pope Urban VI. Fourteen years later Clement VII issued a papal Bull, *Pia Mater Ecclesia*, calling upon all to celebrate publicly each week this new Mass and to urge the faithful to pray for the ending of the schism:

> Holy Mother Church, deeply afflicted by the hateful schism in which the world is placed by the action of the Evil one, is plunged in an anguish and bitterness of unspeakable suffering; she weeps with constant compassion for the betrayal of her sons who, in their folly, seek to tear the seamless robe of our Lord, viz. the unity of the Church itself. . . .
> We earnestly seek all ways and means whereby those who are gone astray may, casting off the dark shadow of their blindness, return to the true path of salvation, and re-join the devoted sons of the Church. Considering therefore that the faithful wait and hope for a solution, coming rather from the appeal of humble and confident prayer than from any human methods and following the counsel of our brothers, we have composed a

[1] R. Amiet, 'La Messe "pro unitate Ecclesiae" ', *Ephemerides Liturgicae* 76 (1962), pp. 296-334. The original text of the Bull *Pia Mater Ecclesia* is given on pp. 308-9.

special Mass for the ending of this schism. . . . We command you to instruct with all your prudence both clergy and faithful in this matter, to admonish them by urgent exhortation, and to guide them by profitable reflection that they consider how harmful and deadly is this schism and how much danger it brings to souls. Exhort them, therefore, to celebrate this Mass with humble and contrite hearts, so that God may flood with the light of his truth the hearts of those who are blinded by the error of such schism as this, and that he may illuminate them by the ray of true vision, and finally may re-unite their hearts in the unity of the same Church.

Rival kings and states, opposing historians, canonists and theologians, even persons later officially recognized as saints—all these forces combined to prolong the division and to keep open the wound in the Church's unity. Yet the prayers of the common faithful and the repeated Masses offered for the reunion of the Christian people prevailed. Although the claims of Clement VII to be the true Head of the Church were not recognized by her, this Mass, so rich in doctrine, was taken over, with only slight and unimportant textual changes, into the Missal of Pope Pius V, issued at the request of the Council of Trent. The original title, *Pro sedatione Schismatis* (For the Settling of the Schism), was altered to *Ad tollendum Schisma* (For the Ending of the Schism) and finally, in 1961, was changed by Pope John XXIII to *Pro unitate Ecclesiae* (For the Unity of the Church).

Commentary

THE INTROIT

Save us, Lord, and gather us together from the nations . . .

The theme of this Mass is set by these words of Psalm 105, composed during the Babylonian exile—the great scattering of the Chosen People. They are an urgent and humble appeal to God, who alone can save his people, to end the calamity which has fallen on them. To appreciate the full significance of this text it is necessary to consider briefly the plan of salvation for mankind as revealed to us in the Bible.

The human race according to God's design should have multiplied and spread over all his creation, in perfect union with himself and in perfect agreement within itself. The first fruits of the sin of Adam were his estrangement from his Maker and division between the members of his race, and even between brothers of one family. The inspired authors of the opening books of the Bible, who sketch briefly this downward path towards increasing disorder and division, reveal also God's mysterious plan for restoring all men to friendship with himself—his plan of gathering them again into a unity of charity among themselves. For this purpose the Jewish race was specially chosen and when its unity and existence were threatened God intervened to preserve it so that eventually all other races would be united to it. Finally, he sent his Son, Jesus Christ, as the Messiah, born from Jewish stock, not only to atone for the sins of the children of Adam but to restore the union between men and God by sharing with them the divine life which he himself possessed. The task of Christ was 'to gather into one the children of God who were scattered abroad' (*John* 11:52) by breaking down all barriers between Jew and non-Jew (*Eph.* 2:14). The one call of God to all men is stronger than any human division sprung from race, or language, colour or class.

The fruits of Christ's work are set down in the opening chapters of the *Acts of the Apostles*. His first followers enjoyed the vivid experience of supernatural unity which enabled them to overcome the differences of race and language and the barriers created by centuries of enmity and prejudice. They lived 'with one heart and mind' in a charity so intense that they held everything, even their material possessions, in common. The same *Acts of the Apostles* reveal, however, the pattern of tension between supernatural unity and human divisions which appear in the Church of Christ as it spreads across the world. Although holy in its doctrine and its divine institution, it is a society of men and does not exclude sinners from the number of its members. Even during the lifetime of the first followers of Christ, we can see that each expansion of the Church brought with it the danger of division.

In the small body of Christian Jews in Jerusalem a strain developed between the Aramaic and Greek-speaking sections.[2] The spread of the Gospel by St Paul outside Palestine into the non-Jewish world produced a crisis and clash of opinions in which we see the final victory of the supernatural principles of unity over deeply-rooted national divisions. In the later epistles of St Paul and in the writings of St John appear already the shadows of Gnostic heresies which divide the communities founded by them. Almost by accident we learn in detail the story of a serious schism in Corinth. St Paul was deeply moved by it and denounced it as a scandal and an absurdity in the Church of Christ. His followers can be divided, he teaches, only if there are different Christs, or if Christ himself is divided. All who preach in Christ's name are bearers of a single message, so that divisions based upon these different teachers is nonsense. It is a scandal, unworthy of those who bear his name, that men who are nourished at the same table, eating the same Body of Christ, should tolerate schism in their midst.[3] To meet some similar situation St John sets down in chapter seventeen of his gospel the great prayer of Christ for unity among his followers. Despite the clear teaching of these apostles, both in the Church of Corinth and elsewhere, the seeds of division and discord remained in the Church, sown by the Enemy, and sprouting continually amid the harvest of Christ's planting.[4]

That we may give thanks to thy holy Name, and glory in thy praise

After the appeal to God to gather again into one all who

---

[2] Cf. *Acts* 6   [3] 1 *Cor.* 1:10-18
[4] Cf. The Prologue to the Tridentine Decree on the Eucharist, *Enchiridion Symbolorum*, ed. Denzinger-Schönmetzer, n. 1635 (formerly 873a)

belong to Christ, a second theme is introduced. The ending of schism and disunity among Christians will result in the greater glory of God and the triumph of Christ whose divine mission will be attested.

In the long Collect the same two themes are put explicitly to the people as the content of their common prayer:

> O God, who sets right what has gone astray and gathers together what has been scattered, and keeps together what has been gathered . . . pour down upon the Christian people the grace of union with thee, so that division being overcome, they may join themselves to the true shepherd of your Church and be able to render thee due worship.

The phrase *tuae unionis gratiam* refers to the intimate and inseparable union which exists between Christ and his Father. This idea will be explained more fully in the Gospel.

THE EPISTLE (*Eph.* 4:1-7, 13-21)

To guide and instruct the faithful in their Christian duties concerning the unity of the Church two passages from the Epistle of St Paul to the Ephesians are now read. This Epistle has first set out the great purpose of God for the world—the gathering into one of all things in Christ, and St Paul has shown in the second chapter that the Gentiles are now being welded together with the Jews 'in Christ' to form God's 'New Man'. He prays that they will understand the plan of God more fully, and having been given a share in this unity, work together and increase it.

Worthy of the calling to which you have been called . . . (v. 1)

The vocation of a Christian is not limited to individual salvation, but is to form one Body, filled with one Spirit and one common destiny. Each must be careful to safeguard (the Greek word means: to watch carefully over) this unity.

No true follower of Christ can be indifferent to its break-down.

Bear lovingly with one another . . . (v. 2)

This they will do by great understanding and humility, and with much patience, bearing with one another because of their genuine love for each other. The apostle sets down what they have received in common—'one body, one Spirit, and one calling . . . one Lord, one faith, one Baptism and one God and Father of all". Before examining this magnificent text more closely we can recall that those whose ancestors left the full unity of the Church, and who in consequence are no longer in full possession of its truth and life, may still possess some parts of the common heritage, including sanctifying grace and the Holy Spirit. We can apply to many Protestants and other Christians the words of St Augustine: 'those who born in error, desire ardently the truth, should not be considered as heretics'.[5]

One body, one Spirit . . . one Baptism, and one God (v. 6)

To quote the words of a distinguished Catholic exegete elucidating this dense text:

> Just as, at the final end of all, there is but one God and Father of all, who is over all, pervading all and sustaining all—and just as there is only one means of access to him, the one Lord (Jesus Christ) to whom we attach ourselves by the one and the same Faith, by one and the same Baptism, so also to arrive at that one final end, to walk along that one way, following the same calling and the same hope, there is but one Body and one Spirit given. Here it would be useless and quite false to understand in these words only the

[5] Cf. the words of Pope Leo XIII "With not a few of them dissent is a matter rather of inheritance than of will" in his encyclical 'Longinqua Oceani', *Irish Ecclesiastical Record* 16 (1895), p. 276.

individual body of Christ and his Spirit, or only his 'mystical body' and the Spirit given to Christians. St Paul considers both together, indissolubly united: the individual body of Christ extended by all the Christians who attach themselves to him, through their own bodies, by faith and Baptism; the Spirit penetrating the individual body of Christ and given through him to all the members of his great Body.[6]

To each one of us grace has been given . . . (v. 7)

As in his teaching on the Christian vocation, so when dealing with individual graces, St Paul stresses that they are all directed to a collective work—'until we all attain to unity . . . to the perfect Man, to . . . the plenitude of Christ'. In the present context the 'perfect Man' does not mean the individual perfection of the Christian (although this is necessarily included) but the total Christ, head and members. We are bound to grow in every way towards him, the Head (v. 15); we are bound to work for the increase of his Body, building it up in charity (v. 16) so that the same divine life fills all mankind, bound together in his love— not estranged from the life of God (v. 18).

When we speak of working to establish the unity of the Church it is necessary to maintain the clear distinction as set out recently by Cardinal Bea:

> The unity of the Church desired by her divine Founder is, like holiness and catholicity, one of her essential aspects; but, in reality, *unity is not yet complete and perfect*. It needs our work in order to become even fuller and to surmount victoriously all obstacles and difficulties. . . . We must therefore help to prepare for it by patient labour, full of understanding and charity, according to the viewpoint of true sons of the Church. In the last analysis it will be the work of the Holy Ghost, for he alone can give separated brethren light

[6] P. Benoit, O.P., *Exégèse et Théologie*, Paris, 1961, II, p. 12

and strength to overcome all the difficulties which
delay the decisive step.[7]

Each single member has a role to play in the building up
of the body. St Paul later repeats that 'the body, drawing
nourishment from Christ, *according to the role of each
member*, thus achieves its development and builds itself in
charity" (v. 16).

Doing the truth in charity (*v. 15*)

This famous phrase (so often on the lips of the late Pope
John XXIII) summarizes the attitude of mind and heart
which the Church calls for in her faithful. Truth and charity
—to hate error, yet to love the erring, is the only adequate
expression of the Catholic approach to the ecumenical
problem. As Cardinal Bea has often said: 'truth without
charity becomes intolerant and repels, charity without truth
is blind and does not endure'. Too many are misled by an
unbalanced zeal for truth into an attitude of indifference
towards those separated from full membership of the
Church. By the combined action of these two virtues in
every member the Church grows in unity and 'we will grow
in every respect up to him who is the Head, Christ' (v. 15).
Finally, in the latter section of the Epistle some verses are
included which describe, in sharp contrast, the perilous
condition of those who have not yet been baptized into Christ
and his Mystical Body and which may to some extent be
applied to all those who, either by mortal sin or by formal
heresy, have renounced Christ and his Church: 'tossed to
and fro and carried about with every wind of doctrine', and
again, 'having their understanding darkened, being alienated
from the life of God through the ignorance that is in them
. . .' (v. 14). The unity which is God's will and our vocation
is not only the unity of all Christians but the unity in Christ
of all mankind.

[7] *The Unity of Christians*, London, 1963, p. 35

THE GRADUAL AND ALLELUIA

The original Gradual and Alleluia texts celebrated the joys of unity among brethren, and the verse of the Tract read: ' "I will gather them from everywhere", says the Lord, "and I will make them into one people" . . .'

These texts still survive in those Missals (e.g. the Dominican) which were not affected by the reform of the Roman Missal under St Pius V in 1570. The new texts substituted celebrate the gift of peace and the power of God amid his people. They are taken from the Votive Mass 'For Peace'.

THE GOSPEL (*St John* 18:1, 11-23)

In the Epistle the collective character of our salvation and the eternal plan of God to gather mankind through Christ into a new unity was placed before the faithful in order to deepen and complete their understanding of the Christian vocation and the ultimate purpose for which individual graces are given. The Gospel draws them still further into the mystery. The ultimate explanation of the plan of God lies in the mysterious unity of the three Divine Persons. Man, created in the image of God and re-created in Christ, is to reflect this unity and become a sharer in it.

Holy Father . . . that they may be one, even as we are . . . (v. 12)

These are the mysterious words of Christ to his first followers on the evening before he died. He has promised them a share in his life and in his glory, but he now goes on to pray that God will not take them out of the world with him, but that he will build this mysterious unity in it by making them holy in truth, that is, consecrated to the glory of God in spirit and in truth.

Then looking beyond the immediate circle of those whom he has gathered around the table of the first Eucharist to future horizons he prays for all who 'through their word will believe in Me' (v. 20). He prays that they also may be

brought into this divine unity—THAT ALL MAY BE ONE, JUST
AS YOU, FATHER, IN ME, AND I IN THEE, THAT THEY TOO MAY
BE ONE IN US (v. 21).

That the world may believe that you have sent me (v. 21)

The unity among his followers is named by Christ as the
supreme proof to mankind that he himself and his mission
are of divine origin. We should draw from this statement
both conviction and enthusiasm to carry out the work of
Catholic ecumenism, working for perfect unity among all
who bear the Christian name, because this is the most
powerful argument to the majority of the human race still
outside the sphere of the Christian Gospel that the one,
holy, Catholic Church and its Founder are of divine origin.[8]

Christ prayed not only for his own immediate followers
but for all who through them would come to believe in him.
These words are immediately applicable to all those in the
world today who 'are proud to be called Christians'. They
too have learned to believe in Christ from the word of God
which they treat so reverently and which was set down in
writing by these first apostles.

THE OFFERTORY

We now pass into the central part of the Mass with the
preparation of the bread and wine. Even in these elements
of the Eucharist—each compounded from materials
gathered far and wide—early Christian tradition saw an
image of the 'Many' scattered abroad, but gathered

---

[8] Cf. Cardinal Léger of Montreal: 'But for us the most serious
consequence of division is doubtless that the Catholic Church is, in
the eyes of the non-Christians, but one of the numerous Christian
denominations, even though it be the most important numerically.
Because Christians present in the world the sad spectacle of their
division, the pagan world has not believed in Him whom the Father
has sent, His Son Jesus Christ'. Quoted in *Catholic Mind*, April 1962,
p. 62.

together to form one body of Christ[9]. The Offertory verse does not allude explicitly to this, but considers the effect of this unity—the realization of the apostolic idea of men *concordes caritate* worshipping God with one heart and one voice.

THE SECRET

These gifts offered for the union of the Christian people
. . . through which grant us the gifts of unity and peace
in your Church.

By emphasizing the role of the Eucharist in achieving the supernatural unity of the Church, the Secret introduces the third major theme of this Mass. It is through the sacramental body of Christ that the whole Christ is built up in charity, for by their sharing in the Eucharist the faithful are brought into real living contact with the glorified body of Christ, and the Church is thereby nourished with his divine life and sanctified in truth. Crowning a tradition which we can follow through the early Fathers, St Thomas refers to the Eucharist as the 'sacrament of Church unity' as the efficacious sign 'by which men are gathered into the unity of the Church'. The primary spiritual effect of the Eucharist is the unity of the body of Christ: communion with Christ and with one another.[10]

COMMUNION

The bread is one, and [so] we, the many, are one body.

Apart from the addition in the second half of the words

[9] Cf. *Didache* 9:5; Cyprian Ep. 69:5, n. 2; Augustine, *Tract 26 in Joannem*

[10] *Summa Theologica* III, 67, 2; 73, 4; 74, 1; 83, 4 ad 3. The Eucharist is of course an expression of unity as well as its cause, and participation in the Eucharist thus requires that we are already of one mind and heart by faith; cf. B. Leeming, S.J., 'Intercommunion', *The Heythrop Journal* 3 (1962), pp. 139-51.

'and from one chalice' this verse is taken directly from the first Epistle of St Paul to the Corinthians (10:27). It repeats explicitly the doctrine underlying the Secret—that the body of Christ, like one bread, causes unity among all those who share it. Wherever the Eucharist is celebrated validly, as in every Mass in the Eastern Churches, both Catholic and Orthodox, this bond of unity in Christ is being forged, not only between the members of each local community, but with all other Christians.

POST-COMMUNION

May this your holy communion, foreshadowing the union of the faithful in you, bring about unity in your Church.

The three-fold repetition of 'you' and 'your' in this prayer is remarkable. Christ is the giver of the sacrament and is received in it; union with Christ is the goal of every Christian, the ultimate fruit of this sacrament; and this perfect union is the final term towards which the visible unity of his Church is growing.

Three times during this Mass the celebrant calls on the faithful to pray with him for the unity of the Church. Each time he offers their united prayer—'through our Lord Jesus Christ'. This formula is particularly relevant on this occasion for we know that our prayer is identical with the prayer of Christ at the first Eucharist. If all Christians were in fact fully united to Christ there would be no disunity among them—we would have all arrived at 'the unity of faith, the knowledge of the Son of God, at the Perfect Man, at the full age of the plenitude of Christ' of which St Paul speaks in the Epistle.

The Liturgy and Unity

At the close of their deliberations on the nature of the Eucharist the Fathers gathered at the Council of Trent made the following moving appeal to those of the clergy and laity who were already departing from the path of unity and truth, asking them to return to communion with themselves:

> But finally this sacred synod, with fatherly affection, exhorts and begs, in the name of the merciful heart of our God, that each and every one who bears the name of Christian should now—at last—come together in this sign of unity, in this bond of charity, in this symbol of concord, and be of one heart.[11]

It is at the moment of the Eucharist, as at a family gathering, that one feels most keenly the absence of those who formerly shared in the same table of Christ.

At every celebration of the Mass the Church reminds the faithful of this. As our first petition in the *Canon* of the Mass we ask that God may grant his Church both to spread abroad and still remain in unity: 'grant her, throughout the entire world, peace and unity'. Again after the 'Our Father', in which we ask for our Daily Bread and pledge ourselves before receiving it together to mutual forgiveness, the Church repeats her petition that Christ will, *according to his will*, grant peace and unity to his Church. After this prayer the kiss of peace is given. Of equal importance, although their significance is seldom understood, are two rites which occur at this part of the Mass which precedes the actual Communion—the breaking of the host and the mingling of it with the Blood.

When a group of men share in one meal a natural bond is created among them. This is further developed and transformed into a supernatural union by their receiving together the Body of Christ, which conveys an identical divine life into each. The breaking of the host in order to distribute it was a clear sign to the early Christians of this supernatural unity. Nowadays the gesture is remote from our normal practice, and is emptied of its rich natural significance. There is still a certain modern parallel in the quasi-ritual cutting of a wedding-cake by the united hands of bride and bridegroom, and in the sending of small pieces

[11] Denzinger-Schönmetzer, n. 1649 (formerly 882)

of it to all absent relatives and friends to mark the bond of unity established between them all.

The second gesture of putting a portion of the host into the chalice, although it has acquired a different significance and added symbolism in the course of history, can be traced originally to a gesture of unity. On Sundays in Rome each priest celebrating the Eucharist for his own parishioners received a portion of the host consecrated in the Pope's Mass and placed it in his chalice as a striking proof of his union (*communio*) with him.[12] For the same reason, portions of the host were exchanged between bishops as a sign of their all sharing in the one Bread and forming one Body. The same idea underlies the single Mass now prescribed for Holy Thursday, which gathers priests about their bishops, and the Roman Curia about the pope.

Apart from the texts and ceremonies of the Roman Mass described above, the action of the Eucharist in building up the unity of the Church is frequently mentioned in her prayers.[13]

The care and solicitude of the Church for her unity is found too in the Solemn Prayers of Good Friday, of which no less than four are devoted to this theme. The first echoes the daily prayer of the *Canon*—asking for unity in catholicity; the seventh asks for the return to unity of all heretics and schismatics; the eighth asks for the return of the Jewish people; the ninth for the entering of all the pagan nations into the one flock of Christ—for the praise and glory of God's name.

Similarly in the Litany of the Saints we ask God both for the gift of unity and peace in full measure and in an invocation added by Pope Pius XI for the return of all who have left it and who are straying outside. These petitions are found in many Masses throughout the year.[14]

[12] Cf. Innocent I, 'that they may show, especially on that day, that they are not estranged from our communion' (*PL* 20, 56 ff.)

[13] E.g. (C=Collect; S=Secret; PC=Post-communion) Mass of Corpus Christi (S); of Christ the King (C, S); of Ninth Sunday after Pentecost (PC); of St Augustine of Canterbury (S); of Easter Vigil (PC); of Easter Sunday and Monday (PC)

[14] E.g. Mass of St Robert Bellarmine (C); of St Augustine of Canterbury (C); of Easter Thursday (C)

Of more recent origin are the Novena to the Holy Spirit for Christian Unity before Pentecost, and the Church Unity Week in January. Both are intended to keep this fundamental aspect of the divine plan of our redemption before the minds of all the faithful.

To gather into one flock all the nations of the world is, as we have seen, the ultimate goal for which Christ came on earth. This is set forth clearly in the Gospel of 'Good Shepherd' Sunday, the second after Easter:

> Other sheep I have which are not of this flock; and these also I must bring in and they will hear my voice and there will be one flock and one shepherd (*John* 10:16).

In the Mass of Holy Thursday we have the magnificent Antiphon *Ubi Caritas*, the words of which are from a ninth-century hymn used in Benedictine abbeys:

> The love of Christ has gathered us into one . . .
> And when we are gathered together in one,
> Let us take care that we are not divided in our minds,
> Let all quarrels cease, and all divisions close,
> And in our midst, be Christ, our God.
> Where there is love and charity, there God is.

In some passages of the Liturgy, however, the establishment on earth of this bond of unity is attributed to the Holy Ghost. This corresponds to his role as bond of love in the Blessed Trinity. Many authors, for instance, see this meaning in the closing doxology of the *Canon* of the Mass, where the words 'in the unity of the Holy Spirit' replace the phrase 'in Thy Church' of an older text.

This idea appears frequently during the season of Pentecost[15]—the Church is described as 'gathered together in the Holy Ghost'. This same phrase *in Spiritu Sancto congregati* is placed too at the beginning of the Acts of the great ecumenical Councils of Trent and the First Vatican. An ecumenical Council is the visible manifestation of the

---

[15] Cf. Introit of Vigil; collect of Whit Friday

entire Church 'called together' by God from all parts of
the world, and gathered into one by the Spirit of Christ.[16]
For this reason Pope John XXIII aptly compared the
Second Vatican Council to a new Pentecost. In the words
of an old prayer for the Mass of the Vigil of Pentecost in
the Leonine Sacramentary:

> Grant that the scattering of peoples, by the division of
> tongues, may by the heavenly Gift, be gathered
> together into one acknowledgment of Thy name.

Conclusion

If we wish to learn from the Church's own prayer what
is her teaching on Christian unity we shall find no texts
more pregnant with meaning than those which she has
placed in the special Mass 'For the Unity of the Church'.
In it she has concentrated her teaching on this fundamental
aspect of the mystery of our redemption. Eschewing all
controversies and theological disputes, and speaking only
to her own faithful, the Church inculcates, in various ways,
the following truths which she has derived from her
Founder:

1   Her mission in the world, which continues his own, is to
gather all men into a supernatural unity, and thus prepare
them for their sharing in the perfect unity of the Blessed
Trinity.
2   Schism and division are the fruits of sin and when they
exist among those who believe in Christ they are a scandal
which causes many seeking his truth to stumble and go
astray.
3   Each member of the Church by his Christian vocation
has a role to play in building up her unity. Each should be
concerned for and seek to increase this unity by a life of
greater truth and charity.
4   Christ prayed at the first Eucharist for the unity of all

[16] This statement is based on H. Küng, *The Living Church*, London,
1963, pp. 63-77.

his followers, and it is achieved especially through their sharing in his one, holy Body.

5 To the action of the Holy Spirit in the hearts of all men is attributed the gathering together by God of all those who are dispersed.

These positive truths should stimulate and guide our efforts both for the increase of unity in the Church, as it spreads over the entire world, and for the return to that unity of all our separated brethren. We are not answerable for the beginning of the schisms and heresies which divide the followers of Christ today, but we are bound to work for the restoration of the original unity, and indifference to the plight of our fellow-men places us with the priest and levite condemned by our Lord in the parable of the Good Samaritan. This indifference was, in our own generation, deplored by Pope Pius XII:

> We cease not to pray for them [those not in communion with Rome] to the Spirit of love and truth, and with open arms we await them, *not as strangers but as those who are coming to their own father's home.* . . .
>
> And if there are still many, as unhappily there are, who wander outside the path of Catholic truth, this is due to the fact that not only they themselves *but the faithful also omit to offer to God more fervent prayers for this intention. We therefore earnestly and insistently exhort all lovers of the Church to follow the example of the Divine Redeemer and to offer such petitions without ceasing.*[17]

There is no better way than to offer the Mass 'For the Unity of the Church'.

[17] Encyclical letter *Mystici Corporis* (1943), paragraphs 102-3, CTS edition

Suggestions for Further Reading

B. C. Butler, O.S.B., *The Idea of the Church*, London: Darton, Longman and Todd 1962, chapters 1 and 10

Y. Congar, O.P., *The Mystery of the Church*, London: Geoffrey Chapman, 1960

H. de Lubac, S.J., *The Splendour of the Church*, London: Sheed and Ward, 1956

    Catholicism, London: Burns and Oates, 1950, chapters 2 and 7

J. A. Jungmann, 'The Eucharist in the World', *The Furrow* 11 (1960), pp. 139-50

A. Vonier, O.S.B., *The People of God*, Collected Works, II, London: Burns and Oates, 1952

The Liturgy and Unity in Christ, Washington, D.C.: The Liturgical Conference Inc., 1961

THE WORLD COUNCIL OF CHURCHES

David Thornley

MANY Catholics have long tended to view Anglican, Protestant and Orthodox ecumenical movements, and more especially their most concrete expression, the World Council of Churches, with considerable scepticism if not actual hostility. The reasons for this are not far to seek. The Catholic Church and the World Council can appear to some at first sight to represent opposite poles of, on the one hand, revealed truth and on the other, an all-embracing religious 'liberalism'.

The World Council is not a Church nor even a federation of Churches. It is not a synod; it cannot enact canons or decrees which will be binding on any of its members. It is simply a fellowship of Churches, associated voluntarily without prejudice to the freedom of action of each participant. It does not ordain its own ministers nor has it a eucharistic worship of its own, 'not only because of the practical impossibility of having a service acceptable to all (Baptists, Reformed Churches, Lutherans, Anglicans, Orthodox) but by deliberate choice'. At the same time it has some of the most fundamental characteristics of a Church. 'It fulfils some functions of a Church which are not fulfilled by the separate Churches. For instance, it expresses their universality, as none of the individual member Churches can. It bears a common witness and renders a common service to the world, as no individual Church is in a position to do'.[1] In other words, the World Council

[1] L. Vischer as quoted by J. Hamer, O.P. in *Christian Unity: A Catholic View*, London, 1962, pp. 144-5

must give visible expression to the common claim of all its
member Churches to loyalty to Christ and, besides thus
manifesting their existing unity, help them at the same time
to discover and to realize that fuller unity which is God's
will for the baptized. But all this it must do in such a manner
as to alienate irreparably none of its members' sympathies.

The immense difficulties imposed upon the Council by
this obligation may be left on one side for the moment.
The Churches formally participating in its first Assembly
at Amsterdam in 1948 were asked little more than that they
should affirm their acceptance of 'our Lord Jesus Christ
as God and Saviour'. For the moment it is only by requiring
such limited—but expanding—attestations that Australian
Methodists may be brought together with American
Episcopalians and British Baptists with Dutch Old Catholics.

Membership in the World Council does not however
mean that a Church must reduce its own doctrinal tenets
to this common denominator. It retains intact its distinctive
beliefs but simply agrees to co-operate on this minimal
basis for the furtherance of the Council's aims. The reasons
therefore why it was and is impossible for the Catholic
Church to become a member of the World Council are
'pastoral and practical' rather than dogmatic.[2] There is,
as Cardinal Bea has stated, 'still much ignorance and
confusion of mind about the nature of the World Council'[3]
with the result that the Catholic Church by joining could
easily give the impression that it had renounced its claim
to have preserved all the essentials of Christian unity. But
this and other difficulties do not for a moment make it
necessary for Catholics to adopt an attitude of hostility.
In the words of the 1949 Instruction of the Holy Office,
Ecclesia Catholica:

> The Catholic Church takes no actual part in
> 'ecumenical' conventions and other assemblies of a
> similar character. Yet, as numerous pontifical state-

[2] So the matter was put at the recent Montreal Faith and Order
Conference by the well-known Catholic ecumenist, Father G. Baum,
O.S.A., as quoted in Ecumenical Press Service, 2 August 1963, p. 3.
[3] *The Unity of Christians*, London, 1963, p. 86

ments show, she has, despite this fact, never ceased nor will she ever cease to pursue with deepest concern and promote with assiduous prayers to God every endeavour to bring about what was so close to the heart of Christ the Lord, viz. that all who believe in Him 'may be perfect in one'.[4]

And Cardinal Bea has recently been emphasizing not only the possibility but indeed the desirability that his Secretariat for Promoting Christian Unity should co-operate at least with the World Council; and such co-operation is in fact steadily growing:

> About co-operation [the Cardinal has declared] by the Secretariat with the World Council of Churches, there is no difficulty in principle. In so far as the World Council of Churches does not stand for any doctrine irreconcilable with Catholic dogma, co-operation would in principle be perfectly possible. What come to mind are those fields which do not directly touch on matters of belief, such as social work, *Caritas*, work for peace, assistance to underdeveloped countries. For instance what would it mean for humanity if all Christians could act together in such important matters as nuclear war, general disarmament and the means for preserving and advancing world peace?[5]

It may, then, be stated at the outset that if the Catholic Church cannot in present circumstances formally participate as a member in the labours of the World Council, the individual Catholic may watch them not merely with interest, but with sympathy. And to the history of the ecumenical movement among its member Churches he may fittingly turn, especially on the opening day of a Unity Week, to see how the yearning for Christian unity has worked upon his separated brethren.

The Edinburgh Conference of 1910 is usually seen as the

[4] As quoted in G. Weigel, S.J., *A Catholic Primer on the Ecumenical Movement*, Westminster, Md., 1957, p. 39.
[5] Op. cit., p. 163

historical starting point of the modern ecumenical movement which culminated in the World Council of Churches. But Edinburgh 1910 was not a total novelty. The nineteenth century was a great age of international conferences and commissions in the secular field—about postal and telegraphic conventions, world health, and a host of other subjects. As the world grew effectively smaller and more inter-related, this concern for international order had its natural parallel among the religious denominations. The Evangelical Alliance was founded in 1846 at a conference in London attended by eight hundred delegates from over fifty denominations; the British and Foreign Bible Society had already linked Anglicans and Nonconformists in joint committee. Perhaps most striking was the work of the international youth organizations. 1844 saw the foundation of the Young Men's Christian Association, to be followed ten years later by its female counterpart; in the 1880s the Student Christian Movement was launched. In 1895 common cause was made by the youth of many denominations in the World Student Christian Federation. From this training-ground were to spring many of the great figures of twentieth-century ecumenism, men like the American Methodist John R. Mott, a founder of the W.S.C.F., who was to be chairman of the Edinburgh Conference and a winner of the Nobel Peace Prize.

But if the unsophisticated yearnings of young Christians for fellowship were to provide to some extent a cadre of committed leaders for the later ecumenism, the most pressing impetus to joint action came perhaps from among the missionaries. The official title of the Edinburgh gathering was the International Missionary Conference and the majority of the delegates were chosen by missionary societies. It was not the first such conference; William Carey, 'father of modern missions', had dreamed of regular missionary conferences as early as the beginning of the nineteenth century, and interdenominational missionary assemblies had been held in London in 1888 and New York in 1900. But in the words of one Anglican commentator:

Each of the preceding missionary conferences had come

into being almost by chance; none had taken any steps to perpetuate itself, though it was generally assumed at the end of every conference that another one would take place sometime, somewhere. It was given to Edinburgh 1910 to take the first cautious step forward, and to form that first slender organization, out of which was to grow, in God's providence, the whole of the great worldwide ecumenical movement.[6]

Edinburgh was uniquely a missionary conference in that although only eighteen of its twelve hundred delegates were actually members of the younger, missionary Churches, it was the predicament of these Churches in the light of missionary experience which in a sense overshadowed the deliberations. Nowhere were the divisions of Christianity more painfully evident than in the mission field where the emissaries of rival denominations all too often strove for the soul of the pagan even as they bemused him with the intensity of their own disagreements. From such bitter experience both missionary and convert tended to come away with a burning conviction of the necessity for Christian unity, even more firmly held than that of their brethren who had remained in the older Churches at home. One of the greatest spokesmen of this feeling was the Anglican Bishop Azariah of Dornakal, in India. In 1927 he tersely summed up the predicament of Churches like his:

'I am a Baptist', said an Indian friend to me, 'not because of theology, but because of geography'. Having accidentally become attached to a Church, Indian Christians do not find it difficult, when necessary, to change their ecclesiastical allegiance to a Church other than their own. . . . The feeling of very many Indian Christians is that they were not responsible for the divisions of Christianity, neither would they perpetuate them. Force of habit, financial dependence, denominational training and, above all, loyalty to their spiritual fathers, now keep them in denominational connections.

[6] S. Neill, *Men of Unity*, London, 1960, p. 23

But these circumstances cannot keep them apart for
ever. . . . Fathers and brothers! Be patient with us if
we cannot very wholeheartedly enter into the controversies of either the sixth or the sixteenth centuries.
Recollections of these embitter Church life; they may
alienate the young Churches from all ecclesiastical
connections. Unity may be theoretically a desirable
ideal in Europe and America, but it is vital to the life
of the Church in the mission field. The divisions of
Christendom may be a source of weakness in Christian
countries, but in non-Christian lands they are a sin and
a scandal.[7]

But the enthusiasm of the newer Churches could not of
course undo the reality of the divisions amongst the old.
Indeed, if missionary impetus has been a source of strength
to the movement, it has paradoxically at times been a
source of embarrassment. Not merely to Catholics, but to
members of the Orthodox Churches, the word 'mission' has
often possessed connotations less of evangelical zeal abroad
than of proselytism at home. This was among the motives
—there were of course others—which caused the delegates
of the Orthodox world to refuse to sign all the reports of
the 1927 conference on Faith and Order and to express
severe criticisms of the World Council of Churches as
recently as 1948; they are by no means wholly allayed even
yet. Again, inside the denominations which hesitantly
committed themselves to the Edinburgh deliberations
there were deep rifts as to the legitimate extent of this
bourgeoning ecumenism. Nonconformists might dread a
new surrender to the historic foe of episcopacy; 'liberals'
might condemn as narrowly exclusive a Trinitarian statement of common belief; 'high' Anglicans might hesitate to
expose convictions like their faith in the apostolic succession
of their ministry to dilution by 'liberalism' or derision by
'evangelicalism'.

If the Edinburgh Conference was informed by a rising
missionary spirit it was, then, by no means delivered from
the shadow of historic differences. But Edinburgh faced the

[7] Quoted ibid., p. 56

problem of interdenominational co-operation in two un-precedented ways. In the first place, under the statesmanlike chairmanship of John R. Mott the conference was organized from the outset as much more than an *ad hoc* get-together. In the words of the official history: 'It was felt . . . that the time had now come for a more earnest study of the mission-ary enterprise, and that . . . the first aim should be to make the conference as far as possible a consultative assembly'. But secondly, and still more important, Edinburgh was the first of these conferences to establish before its dissolution the formal basis for the summoning of further meetings, and even for the development of an embryonic inter-denominational organization of Churches. A 'Continuation Committee' was set up under the chairmanship of Mott, its principal task to prepare the ground for a further missionary conference, but empowered also 'to confer with the Societies and Boards as to the best method of working towards the foundation of a permanent International Missionary Committee'.[8] From this committee grew in 1921 the Inter-national Missionary Council, which in turn held five further conferences between 1928 and 1958, until in 1961 at New Delhi it was finally integrated with the World Council of Churches.

Missionary zeal was however by no means the only impulse towards union; indeed, as has been remarked above, some ecumenists viewed it with a more qualified enthusiasm than others. Three strands lead from Edinburgh to New Delhi, of which the International Missionary Council is only one. In 1925 a 'Universal Christian Con-ference on Life and Work' was held at Stockholm, from which developed the 'Life and Work' movement. 'Life and Work' was comparable to the International Missionary Council in its interdenominational character and ecumenical approach; similarly it claimed no formal authority over its subscribing members. The bias of this movement was, however, as its name implies, essentially towards issues of Christian social responsibility. The third strand was that of the 'Faith and Order' movement. This too arose out of the impulse of Edinburgh. It gave, however, expression to

[8] Quoted ibid., pp. 14, 24

some extent to the concern of theologically-minded ecumenists who felt that the necessary concentration of the International Missionary Council upon common missionary experience, and its parallel reluctance to delve into areas of doctrinal disagreement, created a weakness in its effectiveness as a force towards unity. If the road to unity was indeed blocked by such issues, to treat them as unmentionable skeletons in the cupboard was only, it might be argued, to ignore the inevitable. To many in Faith and Order, as to many modern ecumenists, it seemed that the area of agreement might indeed be widened rather than narrowed by the development of a theological dialogue. In this spirit Faith and Order conferences were held at Lausanne in 1927 and Edinburgh in 1937.

The International Missionary Committee may, then, perhaps be seen as most clearly manifesting the specifically missionary impetus of the Edinburgh Conference. Life and Work, on the other hand, expressed the concern of churchmen at the failure of Christianity to leaven the social organization of mankind. It was indeed significant that this particular movement should have been launched in traditionally neutral Sweden, for perhaps more than anything else it stemmed from the shock of the Christian's failure in 1914 to turn men away from the horrors of world war. Faith and Order, lastly, was a monument to the conviction of men like Bishop Brent, first chairman of its committee, and his successor the great Archbishop of Canterbury, William Temple, that ecumenism would wax rather than wane in theological dialogue. The three movements were not as yet integrated nor always identifiable. The zealots of the International Missionary Council might seem at times to some in Faith and Order naïvely unconcerned with theology; to others in the I.M.C. Faith and Order might appear occasionally to enjoy an academic remoteness from reality. To others, the social preoccupations of Life and Work left it dangerously open to unthinking compromise with Unitarianism. But all in the last analysis stemmed from the same Edinburgh spirit; Brent himself was a missionary bishop. And it was from the joint action of Faith and Order and Life and Work that the World Council of Churches was finally born.

The year 1937 was a turning-point in this process. In that year conferences of these two organizations were held at Edinburgh and Oxford. Each passed a resolution calling for the establishment of a World Council of Churches. A provisional committee was set up to prepare for its inauguration. This committee met for the first time in May 1938 at Utrecht. It elected as its chairman William Temple, perhaps the greatest of the architects of the modern movement. The committee decided to call the first Assembly of the World Council together in 1941. But in 1939 Christian Europe was sundered for the second time in the twentieth century by the outbreak of world war. And in 1944 Temple suddenly died at the age of sixty-two.

When the dust of battle had settled the provisional committee met in Geneva in 1946 to pick up the broken threads. It was faced immediately by the same legacy of international bitterness and tension which the first world war had bequeathed to an earlier generation of ecumenists. The tension was allayed to some extent by the tact of the German Church leaders; in turn, however, a new shadow was to be cast over the efforts of the committee as the secular politics of mankind re-formed in the new divisions of the cold war. The committee agreed to press on with its interrupted plans and to summon its first Assembly to Amsterdam in August 1948. At that Assembly the World Council of Churches was at last formally set up. Since then two further conferences have been held, at Evanston in 1954 and New Delhi in 1961. At New Delhi the International Missionary Council was finally merged with the World Council and the movement engendered at Edinburgh may be seen as having crystallized at that point in what will be, at least for the immediate future, its characteristic organizational form.

Perhaps the first thing which it is necessary to repeat about the World Council of Churches is that in the eyes of its own founders it 'is not and must never become a Super-Church'.[9] It is a 'fellowship of Churches'; but by the end of 1961 no less than two hundred and one had given their

[9] The 1950 Toronto Statement of the World Council of Churches; cf. F. Clark, S.J., 'Trends in Ecumenical Ecclesiology', *The Heythrop Journal* 4 (1963), p. 264

adherence to it. They are drawn, geographically, from all
over the world, with China the most notable absentee; they
run almost the entire gamut of the denominations. The
largest and most familiar are the Anglicans, Presbyterians,
Baptists, Methodists and Lutherans, but many tiny Churches
like that of the Dutch Old Catholics are also members.
Nor must it be forgotten that several Orthodox Churches
from behind the iron curtain are full members of the World
Council, the most notable being the Patriarchate of Moscow,
which applied for and gained membership at New Delhi.
The Patriarchate of Moscow was unique among the Orthodox Patriarchates in that it also sent observers to the
first session of the Second Vatican Council.

To retain the support of these disparate organizations the
Council must, then, walk a tight-rope between different
concepts of what constitutes the Church. It does not
'prejudge the ecclesiological problem';[10] that is to say, it
does not impose a distinctive definition of its own. But at
the same time it cannot afford to ignore such issues and
concentrate exclusively upon a unity of sentiment. For a
Church to acquire membership of the World Council
therefore commits it neither to an explicitly 'relative' view
of its own status as a Church, nor to recognition of its
partners' full status as Churches in what it may regard as
the true meaning of the word. What each Church does
accept and what, incidentally, is not unacceptable to
Catholics, is the existence in other Churches and their
members of certain elements of the true Church (e.g.
Baptism) and hence of some positive relationship to it.
From this recognition stems a practical obligation to
converse and co-operate in amity and in humility. It is an
obligation formally recognized in the fact that the members
of these different denominations come together in the
Assemblies of the World Council not, as at Edinburgh, as
individuals or as representatives of missionary societies,
but as delegates of Churches.

[10] The Toronto Statement; cf. M. Hurley, S.J., 'The World Council
of Churches and its Forthcoming Assembly', *Studies* 50 (1961), p.
331. As we shall see however the New Delhi Statement goes beyond
this Toronto Statement and rules out invisible unity as sufficient; cf.
below, pp. 95-7.

Under this umbrella operate the many specialized agencies of the World Council. Some are directly descended from previously autonomous organizations like Faith and Order and the International Missionary Council, which now as sub-sections of the World Council pursue the traditionally primal tasks of theological debate and missionary endeavour. But the organization has branched out in many directions in the last twenty years, both in the acceptance of fresh responsibilities and in the encouragement of area councils among its own members. Perhaps the best known of the former is the refugee service, which from small beginnings has grown to a point where it employs a field staff of about five hundred people in some fifty countries. The British Council of Churches alone raised over a million and a quarter pounds well before the end of Refugee Year —more than a quarter of the national target of the United Kingdom. By 1961 the World Council had found two hundred thousand refugees a home and a livelihood.

Much of the devoted energy of the Council's servants goes into this kind of task. Some critics have felt it to be too much. These are works of mercy but are not specifically ecumenical. In the last analysis the movement must stand or fall by its record in the quest for a better understanding of religious truth which was undertaken so long ago by its pioneers. A benevolent society based upon the sentimental co-operation of various denominations would not necessarily be ecumenical; it might even damage true ecumenism by a neglect of the fundamental issues which divide the Churches.

This fear has provoked scepticism even inside the ranks of some of the member Churches, notably the Anglican and the Orthodox. It is a scepticism often shared by Catholics. Many Catholics in these islands, long attuned to regard individual conversion as the primary channel towards unity, have traditionally seen as the best source of hope those 'High-Church' minorities which sent them men like Newman and Knox. Is there a danger that these more congenial attitudes to worship and to Church authority may suffer dilution in the World Council to a kind of lowest (in a strictly limited sense) common denominator with, for example, non-episcopal Churches like Presbyterianism and Methodism?

This is a question to which it is impossible to give a conclusive answer, since it is still an area of tension inside the member Churches. But some recent events have suggested that the coming together of these disparate elements has tended to advance rather than to halt the return to traditional ecclesiology. There seem to be both practical and theological reasons for optimism. Practically speaking, movements for Church federation like that of South India in 1947 have resulted in the acceptance by Presbyterians and Methodists of institutions like episcopacy, even if their concept of the episcopal role might not always be precisely that of many Irish Anglicans. And if, as seems likely, the current negotiations between the Church of England and the Methodists reach a successful conclusion, we may surely expect the English Methodists to return with even less difficulty to an episcopal form of organization from which, historically, they are not long separated.

Catholic fears of a common 'lowering' of religious attitudes through the World Council are also to some extent allayed by twentieth-century trends in Protestant theology. Without too much simplification it may, perhaps, be argued that the heyday of what many Catholics have regarded as the most characteristic 'Protestant' concepts— individual justification and a parallel aversion to all visible Church organization as superfluous to salvation—passed with the nineteenth century. Under the influence above all of the towering figure of Karl Barth, whose works have been studied with profit and whose stature conceded by many contemporary Catholic theologians, a reaction has developed in a major school of Protestant theology back towards concepts of the Church much closer to those of Catholics.

> The most striking development in Protestant Christianity during the present century has been the return to the idea of objective authority in religion. The pendulum has swung from nineteenth-century religious individualism to twentieth-century religious corporatism. The prevailing trend has turned away from mere

subjectivism and relativism to seek solid and objective authority.[11]

These developments are of course neither precisely a part nor a consequence of the ecumenical movement. But inevitably they have left their mark upon it. When the International Missionary Council was finally integrated with the World Council of Churches at New Delhi, many Anglicans, Orthodox and indeed Catholics feared, for reasons already stated, an excessive emphasis in the central body towards unsophisticated evangelism and away from theological dialogue. But in fact a compensating effort was made to meet these fears by writing in at the same time a deliberate clarification of the confessional basis of the World Council and a fresh statement of common belief. From an original declaration of faith in 'our Lord Jesus Christ as God and Saviour', inherited from previous movements, the Council advanced at New Delhi to the adoption of a fresh Basis:

The World Council of Churches is a fellowship of Churches which confess the Lord Jesus Christ as God and Saviour, according to the Scriptures, and therefore seek to fulfil together their common calling, to the Glory of one God, Father, Son and Holy Spirit.[12]

At first sight the difference is not, perhaps, immediately striking. But in the context of the arguments which have surrounded the ecumenical movement in the last fifty years the new Basis, taken in conjunction with the similarly-drafted New Delhi Statement, represented a real progression towards a concept of belief and of the Church considerably closer to that of Catholicism. The New Delhi Statement on Church Unity just referred to reads as follows:

We believe that the unity which is God's will and his gift to his Church is being made visible as all in each place who are baptized into Jesus Christ and confess him as Lord and Saviour are brought by the Holy

[11] F. Clark, S.J., loc. cit., p. 29
[12] Quoted by J. Hamer, O.P., op. cit., p. 143.

Spirit into one fully committed fellowship, holding the
one apostolic faith, preaching the one Gospel, breaking
the one bread, joining in common prayer, and having
a corporate life reaching out in witness and service to
all and who at the same time are united with the whole
Christian fellowship in all places and all ages in such
wise that ministry and members are accepted by all,
and that all can act and speak together as occasion
requires for the tasks to which God calls his people.

It is for such unity that we believe we must pray and
work.[13]

To Cardinal Bea this Statement showed the results of 'a
deeper study of scripture and Christian tradition'.[14] And
it is significant that as the World Council debated this
issue in plenary session it did so, for the first time in its
history, in the presence of five official Catholic observers
chosen by the Secretariat for Promoting Christian Unity.
The importance of the Statement seems to justify quoting
here at some length from the commentary in which Father
Hamer at the Heythrop Conference in 1962 evaluated it
from the Catholic viewpoint and compared it to a previous
statement drawn up at Toronto in 1950:

From the Catholic point of view we acknowledge that
all the elements mentioned here are quite authentic.
We only claim more. We are looking for what is
missed out. Moreover, we can only appreciate the text
within the framework of a historical development.
Therefore a comparison between New Delhi and
Toronto may be useful. I see progress in the greater
importance given to visibility. . . .

The New Delhi Statement is centred on visible unity.
It is not satisfied with a purely spiritual or invisible
unity, nor yet with a purely federal unity that is, an
external association of autonomous groups. This
visible unity requires one ministry, one body of doctrine, one sacramental life. Toronto, on the contrary,

[13] *New Delhi Speaks*, London, 1962, p. 55
[14] Op. cit., p. 119

declared: . . . 'Membership in the World Council of
Churches does not imply the acceptance of a specific
doctrine concerning the nature of Church Unity. . . .
[The Council] includes Churches which believe that
the Church is essentially invisible as well as those who
hold that visible unity is essential'.

I think that the New Delhi Statement, in relation to
Toronto, is simply a natural development arising from
thirteen years of experience of practical fellowship
within the Council. But at the same time it demonstrates
a real and clear progress. . . .

What are the limitations of the New Delhi Statement?
They are to be found principally in the question of the
ministry. The question of the legitimacy of the ministry
accepted by all is central. . . .

In this context the Catholic theology emphasizes
rightly the apostolic succession, in which it sees the
mission of the apostles, carried on by the episcopacy,
directed by Peter's successor.[15]

To conclude this brief summary on a note of optimism
is not for one moment to underestimate the difficulties
which still attend the process here discussed—the conflicts
of faith not yet resolved, the historical resentments not yet
dissipated. Inside the World Council there are many
churchmen, particularly American Protestants, who bitterly
criticize what they regard as a trend to 'Romanism' in a
body which already in their eyes epitomizes 'bureaucratic
religion'. Indeed, upon many of the American Churches
there are pressures in favour of withdrawal from the Council
which show little sign of weakening. Nor, finally, can there
be any question of 'negotiation' between the World Council
and Rome, for of its very constitutional nature the Council
must insist upon its complete incapacity to act in the name
of its many members upon so vital an issue. Optimism, in
short, must be cautious; no service is rendered to the cause
of unity by a sentimental ignorance of the pitfalls in its way.
One of the leading figures in the work of the Council, the
Anglican Bishop Neill, has indeed praised the clarity of

[15] *Christian Unity: A Catholic View*, pp. 150-2

Catholic teaching upon it as rendering 'a real service to the ecumenical movement. The perpetual danger of such a movement is that it may sink down into the acceptance of a woolly-minded friendliness as its goal'.[16]

Friendliness cannot usurp the place of truth. The road to unity will be long and often bitter; every Christian must approach it with realism. 'If we are to engage in ecumenical activity we must expect to suffer', writes Father Leeming.[17] But realism need not be exclusive of friendliness. The spirit which impelled these men along the path from Edinburgh to New Delhi was the sorrow of the separated Christian at the sundering of Christ's Church. With this spirit certainly we can always be at one. And if we cannot yet associate ourselves directly with all of these men's handiwork, in an age in which little over one-third of humanity subscribes to any form of Christianity, we ought surely watch their progress with prayerful sympathy and understanding. 'We must', in the words of Cardinal Bea, 'fully appreciate the real achievements of such bodies and pray that they may prosper more and more, and not stop short at a half-way point, in a purely practical unity. May they proceed courageously and help to prepare little by little for that full and perfect unity willed by Christ'.[18]

[16] S. Neill, op. cit., p. 173
[17] *Christian Unity: A Catholic View*, p. 164
[18] Op. cit., p. 86

Suggestions for Further Reading

F. Clark, S.J., 'Trends in Ecumenical Ecclesiology', *The Heythrop Journal* 4 (January and July 1963), pp. 25-31, 264-72

P. J. Hamell, 'The Ecumenical Movement', *Christian Unity*, Dublin: Furrow-Gill, 1962, pp. 18-38

J. Hamer, O.P., 'The World Council of Churches', *Christian Unity: A Catholic View*, London: Sheed and Ward, 1962, pp. 140-59

M. Hurley, S.J., 'The New Delhi Programme', *Irish Theological Quarterly* 28 (1961), pp. 303-17, 29 (1962), pp. 52-67

*J. Lawrence, *The Hard Facts of Unity*, London: SCM Press, 1961

B. Leeming, S.J., *The Churches and the Church*, London: Darton, Longman and Todd, 2nd edition, 1963
'Ecumenical Conclusions', *The Heythrop Journal* 1 (1960), pp. 18-33, 285-99; 2 (1961), pp. 129-41

*S. Neill, *Men of Unity*, London: SCM Press, 1960

*Anglican author

BAPTISM

Dermot Ryan

ON the day we pray 'for the reunion of all Christians' it is appropriate to consider what the Bible has to tell us about Baptism, since the Bible and Baptism are common to all Christians.

God's world owed much of its beauty to the waters of paradise (*Gen.* 1-3). When this beauty was spoiled by an ungrateful Adam its restoration was entrusted to God's chosen people. Rescued from slavery by the saving waters of the Red Sea, they passed to the liberty of the Promised Land through the waters of the Jordan (cf. *Exodus* and *Josue*).

The Christian comes from the waters of Baptism as a new creature to live the life of the Risen Christ which these waters have power to give. Just as Christ is the new Adam and head of a new creation, every baptized person is a new creature and part of this new creation (2 *Cor.* 5:17). His new life is to be lived not for himself alone but to carry out the work of total redemption which Christ came to do—to reconcile all things in Christ (*Col.* 1:20), the creation of the new heaven and the new earth (*Is.* 65:17; 66:22; 2 *Pet.* 3:13; *Apoc.* 21:1), the building of the heavenly Jerusalem (1 *Pet.* 2:5; *Apoc.* 21:2). His Baptism gives him entry to the divine family; he becomes a brother of Christ; the joy of his heavenly Father is found in the multitude of Christ's brethren. No baptized person should enter the family circle alone. He should wish not only to be re-created, but to re-create, not only to be restored, but to rebuild, not only to become an heir, but to share the inheritance.

This is the task that confronts the people of God of which we all become members through Baptism. It calls for a united effort if God's plan for creation is to be realized. Inability or failure to communicate is the surest way to prevent progress, as God well knew when he checked the building of Babel (*Gen.* 11:7). The unending vistas of creation's mystery revealed by modern science should be seen with the eyes of faith. It is for the baptized to ensure that men wonder at its divinely-implanted order and not shrink from it in dread of forces which might unwittingly destroy them.

The individual Christian may feel overwhelmed by such a task. But the Christian's Baptism 'into Christ' (*Gal.* 3:27; *Rom.* 6:3) gives him the power of the mysteries of Christ. He is reborn as the son of God (*John* 3:5; *Rom.* 8:15-17; *Gal.* 4:4-7; 2 *Cor.* 6:18). With Christ, he is crucified (*Gal.* 3:20). His old, sinful self is destroyed; he is no longer enslaved to sin (*Rom.* 7:5-6; 6:5-11). The power which gave Christ victory over sin and death is his (1 *Cor.* 15:55-57). Buried with Christ in the waters of Baptism, he rises with him to a new life (*Rom.* 6:2-14), a life of power (1 *Cor.* 15-43), the life of the Spirit (*Rom.* 8:9). By this Spirit, not only does he live, but he is life-giving (1 *Cor.* 15:45). As yet, his 'life is hid with Christ in God' (*Col.* 3:3); 'it does not yet appear what we shall be' (1 *John* 3:2; 1 *Cor.* 15:43).

Such power leaves no room for complacency. The Israelites of old were 'baptized into Moses in the cloud and in the sea' (1 *Cor.* 10:2), 'nevertheless, with most of them, God was not pleased' and they perished in the desert (ibid. v. 5). 'These things are warnings for us'—who have received a more effective Baptism—'not to desire evil as they did' (ibid. v. 6; cf. *Rom.* 6:5-14).

Israel's history sounds another warning for us who are baptized. United in race and homeland, the Israelites should have been united in the practice of their faith. But the North broke away and merited God's reproach for breaking with his Temple (3 *Kings* 12 and 13). He did not, however, abandon the North and some of his greatest prophets were sent to them. In Jerusalem, Samaria[1] and Samaritan were

[1] Samaria was the capital of the Northern Kingdom of Israel.

almost identified with evil and error (*John* 8:48). A 'good'
Jew could scarcely speak of a 'good Samaritan'. Christ was
to show that even though 'salvation was from the Jews'
(*John* 4:22), they could yet learn goodness from the good
Samaritan. Christians whose worship of God is according
to his wishes may yet have something to learn from those
who differ from them in teaching and practice. And, as
Christ was at pains to point out (cf. *Luke* 4:25 ff.), God did
not limit the bestowal of his favours to the members of the
Chosen Race. Our eyes should be open to see God acting
in the lives of all men, baptized and unbaptized.

Baptized in the name of the Father of all, we should reproduce in our lives the justice and love of him who 'makes
his sun rise on the evil and on the good, and sends rain on
the just and on the unjust' (*Matt.* 5:45).

Baptized in the name of the Son who died that he might
draw all men to himself (*John* 12:32), we should draw men
to union in Christ by the practice of Christian love (*John*
13:35). This love is increased by doing and speaking the
truth (*Eph.* 4:15) and unity in the truth of Christian love will
help the world to believe that Christ was sent by the Father
(*John* 17:20).

Baptized in the name of the Spirit, we must ask him to
teach us all things and to bring to our minds all that was
said by Christ (*John* 14:26). We must ask him, the Spirit of
truth, to guide us into all the truth (*John* 16:13; cf. further
John 14:17; *Rom.* 8:14; *Eph.* 4:2-6).

A PRAYER

O Lord Jesus Christ, who didst say unto Thine
Apostles: Peace I leave with you, My Peace I give unto
you: regard not our sins, but the faith of Thy Church,
and grant unto her that peace and unity which are
agreeable to Thy will; who livest and reignest God
forever and ever. Amen.

(*This prayer from the Roman Missal is in regular use
among Anglicans, Presbyterians and Methodists.*)

Suggestions for Spiritual Reading

Psalms 32, 50, 110, 112, 120, 144; *Matthew* 3:13-17; *John* 3:1-21; *Romans* 6:1-11; *Titus* 3:4-7; *Ephesians* 5:25-7; The Easter Vigil Liturgy

P. Th. Camelot, O.P., *Spiritualité du baptême*, Paris: Editions du Cerf, Lex Orandi, n. 30, 1960

J. Daniélou, S.J., *The Bible and the Liturgy*, chapters 2-6, London: Darton, Longman and Todd, 1960, pp. 35-113

C. Marmion, O.S.B., 'Baptism', *Christ the Life of the Soul*, 11th ed., London: Sands, 1925, pp. 151-64

F. Prat, S.J., *The Theology of Saint Paul*, II, 5, 2, London: Burns and Oates, 1957, pp. 254-61

Christian Initiation, Faith and Fact Book no. 50, London: Burns and Oates (publication date not yet announced)

Suggestions for Hymn-singing

Psalm 50 (51) 'Have Mercy on Me' (ecumenical repentance): *Twenty-Four Psalms and a Canticle*, London: The Grail, 1955, pp. 22-4

Psalm 135 (136) 'O Give Thanks to the Lord' (ecumenical gratitude), ibid., pp. 54-6

Psalm 41 (42) 'Like the Deer that Yearns' (ecumenical desire), ibid., pp. 16-18

Psalm 22 'My Shepherd is the Lord' (ecumenical hope), ibid., pp. 10-11

Psalm 8 'How Great is Your Name' (in rite of adult baptism), ibid., pp. 8-9

'The Church', *Westminster Hymnal*, n. 209, London: Burns and Oates, 1947

'On Jordan's Bank The Baptist's Cry', *The People's Hymnal*, Cincinatti: World Library of Sacred Music, 1955, n. A.4

CATHOLICS AND THE COUNCIL

Michael Hurley

THE Catholic Church believes that by God's grace and
mercy it possesses all the essentials of Christian unity.
Notwithstanding this there are various reasons and two in
particular why a Unity Week should include a special day
of prayer for Catholics as for other Christians. The most
obvious reason is that now highlighted by the Vatican
Council and expressed in that prayer from the missal
ordered for its success in the archdiocese of Dublin during
the First Session: 'Purify, O Lord, and strengthen Thy
Church'. Catholics and the Catholic Church need reform
and renewal in order to prepare the way for the reunion of
Christendom. We may begin however by considering a more
fundamental reason, the one which Father Wattson seems
to have partially discerned when in 1912 he included the
conversion of bad or lapsed Catholics among the Unity
Week intentions. Christian unity is a problem not only for
other Christians but for Catholics too because all sin
involves schism and disunity with the Church, because every
baptized sinner needs to be reconciled and reunited to the
Church, to be restored to full communion with the Church;
and sin affects the lives of all of us.

Sin and Disunity

One of the prayers for the dying in the Roman Ritual asks
God 'to join' his departing servant 'to the unity of the Body

of the Church as a redeemed member' and 'to admit him to the sacrament of reconciliation'. In the familiar English version of the prayer our petition is that God would 'make him a true member of the Church and let him partake of the fruit of Thy redemption . . . and admit him to the sacrament of Thy reconciliation'. In either form the prayer is by no means easy to understand; and the Anglican Book of Common Prayer, besides dropping the second part of the petition, makes the first to read as follows: 'preserve and continue this sick member in the unity of the Church'. In fact the prayer contains a whole theology of the sacrament of penance and of sin which needs explaining. It dates probably from the sixth century or earlier and was originally used not just to console but precisely to absolve the dying, for which reason doubtlessly it has been dropped in our new Irish Ritual.

The best way of understanding this prayer is perhaps to open the Roman Pontifical and glance at the prayers and other details of a ceremony there outlined for Holy Thursday and entitled 'The reconciliation of penitents'. On Ash Wednesday these sinners have been solemnly expelled from the Church 'as Adam the first man was ejected from Paradise because of his transgression'. All through Lent they have done penance and stood at the back of the church for Mass and been unable to bring their offerings to the altar or receive Holy Communion. Now on Holy Thursday they present themselves at the church doors in penitential garb, with unlighted candles, and after the Gospel of the Mass the bishop sends a deacon with a lighted candle from which to light those of the penitents and afterwards comes down himself and leads them by the hand into the church and solemnly prays God 'to restore them to the bosom of his Church' 'from whose unity they had strayed by sinning'. The penitents then remove their penitential garb and take their due part in the offering and communion of the Mass.

This is the sacrament of penance as administered in early times and all the prayers and ceremonies make it abundantly clear that the desired immediate effect is not precisely reconciliation with the invisible God but reconciliation with the visible Eucharistic Church. The rite itself may now be obsolete but the thought and theology which underly it and which are also expressed in the prayer for the dying quoted above remain part of the Church's sacred tradition.

According to this theology 'sacramental confession is', to quote a modern scholar,[1] 'the restoration or re-inforcement of ecclesiastical and eucharistic communion'. In other words, to be absolved is to be churched, to be restored 'to the unity of the Body of the Church'. But this churching is also a christening, this reconciliation with the Church is also reconciliation with God: it is an efficacious sign that the Spirit of Christ who is the soul of the Church dwells once again in this person as in his temple. It follows therefore that the baptized sinner, as the ancient Ash Wednesday ceremony illustrated and emphasized in so dramatic a form, is no longer a full member of the Church. He is no longer walking according to the indwelling Spirit and with his divine gifts edifying and benefiting all his fellow-Christians who are the people of God. He is walking rather according to the world, the flesh and the devil. He has saddened and extinguished and expelled the Holy Spirit. He has separated himself by this loss of charity not only from God but also from his fellow-Christians in the Church; he skulks alone in a sectarian cave of selfishness. And by his sinful deeds, however private and unknown, he has made himself an instrument of evil, poisoning Christian relationships, injuring and offending his own consecrated person and God's holy people (of which he is an organic part) and through them God himself. Every sinner is a separatist and schismatic. Every sinner is alienated and estranged from God and from God's people. When therefore God's people in a particular place foregathers to celebrate the Eucharist and to express and consummate their unity with God and with one another by participating in the Body and Blood of the Lord, the sinner who is conscious of a grave fault must stand apart and excommunicate. He may not offer his gift at the altar and receive in return God's gift, the Bread of Angels, until going first he be reconciled with his brothers in the Church as well as with God. He may not receive

[1] P. Anciaux, *The Sacrament of Penance*, London 1962, p. 140

Holy Communion without first approaching the priest who is the accredited representative of God and of God's people. He must first be reconciled and reunited to both through that efficacious sign of repentant love which is confession and that forgiving acceptance of this confession on behalf of God and of his people which is the pardoning absolution of the priest in the sacrament of penance.

The fundamental reason therefore why Catholics must be remembered in praying for Christian unity is because of sin and its nature. It is not only the heresies of Protestants but also the sins of Catholics that injure and disrupt the unity of God's people in the Church. There is of course a very great difference. In the one case it is a question of faith, in the other a question of charity, and the Catholic sinner does not, as the original heretics eventually did, attempt to give himself an anomalously separate ecclesiastical existence on grounds of doctrine. In either case however there is formal estrangement from the Church and exclusion from the Eucharist, and Catholics cannot fail to remember or afford to forget that the sins of their forefathers played a considerable part in the rise of Protestantism and that the 'heresy' of contemporary Protestants who are sincere and in good faith can certainly not be considered a formal sin.[2]

In their relations with other Christians Catholics are often tempted to pride and complacency, those inveterate enemies of truth as of charity. We are very conscious of the defects in faith and order, in the content of religious belief and the form of Church ministry, which flaw the Christian life and witness of our Protestant brethren and separate us from them. If however Christian unity is to be achieved, we must, so we are now frequently told, become at least equally conscious of those other great positive factors which make their life and witness authentically Christian and unite us to them. But will it not also help if we become conscious of the defects and failings—in regard even to the

[2] Cf. John Carmel Heenan, [Archbishop of Westminster,] 'Catholics and the Dialogue', *The Clergy Review* 47 (1962), p. 5: 'No civilized Catholic today would think of describing a sincere non-Catholic as a heretic'.

ideal of Christian unity—which we share in common with
our separated brethren? Is it not salutary for us Catholics
to recall that it is not only Protestants who belong in an
imperfect way to the Church, that we too when in the state
of mortal sin are no longer its full and perfect members?
In particular is it not salutary to remember our common
exclusion from the Eucharist? The tragic fact of Christian
disunity is never more evident and never more agonizing
than when Christians feel obliged in conscience to 'fence'
the Holy Table, to refuse to communicate with their fellow-
Christians. But this, the supremely crucial manifestation of
Christian disunity, involves Catholics as well as Protestants.
We for our part forbid access to the Eucharist not only to
Protestants but also to our fellow Catholics who are in the
state of mortal sin. In either case, though for different
reasons and in different ways, union with Christ's Mystical
Body is too defective to allow union with his Eucharistic
Body. And finally is it not salutary to recall, especially when
we go to confession, that formal reconciliation with the
Church is a spiritual gift we too stand constantly in need of
and that the requisite repentance may sometimes make more
painful demands on us for our sins than on Protestants for
their heresies?

Reform and Unity

The second main reason why Catholics and the Catholic
Church should be remembered in praying for Christian
unity is the plain fact that without Catholic reform there
can never be true and full Christian unity according to
God's will.

It is, to say the least, simply unrealistic to imagine that
the problem of Christian disunity can be solved by inten-
sifying our efforts to reconcile individuals. Precisely
because they reach only individuals and leave the institutions
intact, such efforts must leave the basic situation unchanged:
the plurality of Churches will remain. Individual reconciliation for all its excellence is by itself just as inadequate to
solve the ecumenical problem as charity is to solve the

social problem. In either case institutional reform is also needed.

It is by no means scandalous to suggest that the Catholic Church is subject to reform. Those whose theology and piety are tinged unconsciously with monophysitism, for whom the Church is almost exclusively the glorious Church without spot or wrinkle, may indeed jib at the suggestion. But, besides being indwelt by the Spirit and thus secured infallibly against error, the Church is also very human, composed of weak sinful men who tend to resist the Spirit and to kick against the goad. This is one reason why it stands permanently in need of reform.

Catholic reform is however something much more than the negative correction of abuses and its true *raison-d'être* lies deeper than the endemic fragility of human nature. The early medieval councils, the first to be attended by Irish bishops, were councils of reform but their work was to a large extent a positive work of creation and adaptation. They devised new rules for papal and episcopal elections, regulated the spirit and forms of lay-investiture, instituted the Truce of God and (a significant precedent for today?) condemned as a thing 'detested by God' the new military weapon of the catapult.[3] The Council of Trent was also a reform council, and contemporary abuses, in so far as they stemmed from the inadequacy of clerical formation, were initially dealt with in 1546 by merely reinforcing the existing legislation which demanded that in each cathedral church there be an endowed post for a master of theology. Ultimately however in 1563 they were dealt with by a decree which discarded the old inadequate medieval institution and created the new modern institution of the seminary.

To reform therefore is not always merely to correct abuses by restoring and re-establishing what already exists. As happened in that period of rapid social change which took the Church unawares and unprepared in the aftermath of the barbarian invasions, abuses may also arise from new situations and new problems which have not been foreseen

[3] This condemnation was made at the Second Council of the Lateran in 1139. Cf. P. Hughes, *The Church in Crisis*, London, 1961, p. 173

and provided for. To reform in these cases is to introduce new rules and usages, to create new laws and institutions or refine and adapt existing ones in order to meet the apostolic needs of the day and enable the Church to preach the Gospel to a changed contemporary society.

Here then is the ultimate reason for Catholic reform and it lies in the very nature of the Church's divine purpose. Christianity is essentially missionary. Like Christ and the Twelve we are all of us apostles, 'sent' by God to spread the good news which is the Gospel of salvation. And we are 'sent' in this way not only in virtue of an external command but also in virtue of an inner dynamism which is the enabling grace of baptism and of confirmation. We are sent however not to colonize but to become incarnate, not to beat the air with vapid unintelligible esoteric discourse but to communicate, to reach men's minds and hearts, 'to make disciples' (*Matt.* 28:19), to enable each people to achieve that enhancement and ennoblement of their whole being and of their whole culture which since Calvary is their destiny and their right. Granted the great diversity of conditions obtaining in different places at any one given period and in the same place at different periods, this divine mission of the Church is quite impossible without constant change and adaptation, without reform.

That such reform is needed in the Church today, and precisely though not exclusively as a necessary preparation for Christian unity, was the whole burden of Pope John's message to us in his life and in his death. It is not that the world is too much with us, that there are widespread abuses as a result to correct but rather that the world is too little with us, that there are widespread abuses to prevent, that we lack the attitudes, or at least the institutions to express and strengthen them, which the religious situation of our day and the Church's divine mission seem to demand. We have, for example, persisted in thinking that the cause of Christian unity is still today best served as it was in the past: by the traditional refusal of all intercourse with our separated brethren, forgetting that the situation now is scarcely comparable to the situation then, forgetting that a lack of intercourse with us is no longer an obvious anomaly or a salutary punishment but rather an added obstacle in so far as it strengthens and perpetuates mutual ignorance and antipathy. Or if our thinking in this respect has changed—as indeed it has under the guidance of the Holy Spirit—it still remains hampered by old norms and regulations and has yet to find the institutions which will canalize its energies. Again, to take another example, we have gone on as in the past demonstrating our possession of the whole truth, emphasizing the errors of the Protestant heretic and inviting him to 'return' to the fold which he abandoned. We have forgotten that this understandable post-Tridentine attitude can with the passage of centuries have little meaning and less pastoral value. We have failed to realize that the modern Protestant who has never been in full communion with us can never in any very meaningful sense 'return' to us; and that the modern Protestant who is ordinarily in good faith and proudly aware of what Pope Paul has called 'the very great riches of his religious inheritance' can never in conscience allow himself to renounce these but only to have them 'enhanced with new splendour'—as Pope Paul assured him he would and will in the Catholic Church. Or if we have in fact begun at last to realize all this we still lack a theology and a catechism to embody such insights and secure their transmission to our clergy and laity.

Finally, the persistence of this negative, defensive, isolationist attitude has gravely affected the due development of the Church's discipline and the due manifestation of its catholicity. An inbred Catholicism has perpetuated and propagated not only its divine evangelical essentials but also its human Latin accidentals. We still go on trying to latinize the Oriental Christian and the African pagan, and the only Church we can present to our separated brethren as supposedly their real home is one in which their rightful demands have not yet been satisfied: in which, for example, the vernacular is not yet the language of the liturgy, in which the laity has not been accorded its proper role, in which authority is still embarrassed with the trappings if not to some extent with the spirit of temporal power. Or if we have at last awakened to the fact that the Catholic Church cannot, and in virtue of its divine mission to the world, be

simply a Latin Church or a clerical bureaucracy or a
juridical monolith, we are hamstrung by a code of canon
law which both for East and for West is biased in principle
as well as fact towards centralization and latinization, in
so far, for example, as it renders practically impossible the
rightful development of customary law and gives no real
legal standing to regional episcopal conferences.[4] For these
and other reasons it would appear obvious that, as Pope
John so clearly saw, Christian unity is an impossible goal
without an institutional reform in the Catholic Church
which, while safeguarding the divine deposit of faith as
infallibly handed down through the centuries, allows once
again that diversity of rite and usage and human tradition
which is the authentic and due manifestation of true
Catholic unity.

The Vatican Council

The most dangerous illusion we can have about the
Second Vatican Council is not (as some appear to think)
that it will re-establish Christian unity but rather that it
will achieve of itself this reform of the Catholic Church.
To expect such a result from the Council is theological as
well as practical nonsense. The Council is not the Church
and the Council's immediate aim is not to reform the Church
but to enable the Church to reform itself. This work of
reform will begin only when the work of the Council has
ended and it will be a long and laborious process; as Rome
was not built in a day so neither will it be reformed in a day.

The great problem facing the Vatican Council is the disagreement and division existing within the Church as to
the mode and measure of reform it needs in order to remain
faithful to its divine mission of preaching the Gospel to
every creature. As the liturgical movement, the biblical
movement, the movement of the lay-apostolate and the
ecumenical movement amply testify, a movement for reform
and renewal, for what Pope John called *aggiornamento*

[4] Cf. L. Oersy, 'Some Reflections about the Renewal of the Legal
Life of the Church', *The Clergy Review* 48 (December 1963)

(bringing-up-to-date), has long been in existence in the Church. Our response to this movement has however been very disparate and uneven. The Pope and his brother bishops, who together are the divinely-appointed mediators of Christ's truth and life and authority to his Church, had not yet reached that one common mind and outlook which the individual bishop (who is primarily a member of this episcopal college) could and should reflect in serving and ruling the Church in his particular diocese. The unfortunate result (all the more tragic because of the peculiar challenge or opportunity of our times) was confusion and frustration, and indeed disunity in so far as a contrast has steadily emerged among us between developed and under-developed dioceses, between 'haves' and 'have-nots'—a contrast which no distinction between unity and uniformity, no emphasis on differing circumstances can alone adequately explain or justify.

The immediate aim of the Council is therefore to enable the collective episcopate to reach at last this common mind and outlook on the widespread movement for reform which in varying degrees has been manifesting itself throughout the Church. By means of sustained direct contact, discussion and dialogue under the guidance of the Holy Spirit the bishops in Council are forging a common spirit and policy and giving it solemn expression in general statements on certain issues of major importance. The practical elaboration of this policy will begin only when the Council is over and will be the concern apparently of international commissions and regional or national conferences of bishops. The actual application will finally be the concern of each diocese acting under the guidance of its bishop. It seems inevitable therefore that, even were there no resistance to change to be overcome, a considerable interval of time must elapse before the new spirit of Vatican II seeps down among us all in each place and finds its appropriate institutional expression at every level: before its principles of reform come to modify the constitutions and rules of religious; before its theological outlook is fully reflected in all seminary teaching and catechetical instruction; before its liturgical principles are everywhere embodied in a reformed ritual of the Mass;

before its ecumenical directives for co-operation with our separated brethren become a reality at the local as well as the international level.

And yet until all this and more is accomplished the Council has not been a success and in its own way will lie open to much the same criticism we Catholics tend to make of the Assemblies of the World Council of Churches and the Conferences of its Faith and Order Commission when we ask to what extent their statements have been everywhere accepted. If our separated brethren are not now in their turn to embarrass us with a similar question, the Church in each place must be purified and strengthened in the spirit and truth of Vatican II. To pray for the success of the Council is to pray precisely for this; and it is undoubtedly a consummation most devoutly to be prayed for because it cannot but severely tax the spiritual resources of us all.

The sobering fact is that a council of reform can be a failure as the Fifth Lateran Council was or succeed as Trent did but take almost a century to achieve its aims. Vatican II may not in fact take quite so long but it is surely Trent with its vital disciplinary decrees rather than Vatican I with its exclusively doctrinal decrees that provides the most helpful parallel with the present Council. There may at first sight appear to be no real basis of comparison between a Council to correct abuses such as Trent was and a council to prevent abuses such as Vatican II is. In either case in fact the fundamental task is exactly the same: to change the face of the Church, and to think that this task is easier in the case of Vatican II because it envisages a change from good to better rather than from bad to good is unfortunately to forget that it is not the bad but the good which is the enemy of the better and that the resistance to change of the high-principled and holy is notoriously more obstinate than that of the lax and the sinful; and on that account therefore Vatican II may take even longer than Trent to achieve its aims. In any case we too like Trent will have our difficulties and disappointments. The fact that in our day the winds of change have already been blowing a long time and accomplishing a considerable measure of reform does not, as we might think, improve our situation by comparison with that of Trent. The same was true in the pre-Tridentine period. There arose indeed in those years what a modern historian calls a 'tidal movement towards reform', and Ignatius Loyola and the Society of Jesus represented no more than its 'high-water mark'.[5] And yet the same historian does not hesitate to write that 'round about 1600 the situation in many countries seemed not very different from what it had been in 1500. Numerous facts, taken in isolation, would almost entitle us to say that no serious result had yet been obtained'.[6] Will some future historian have something similar to say of the year 2000? A negative answer which is not just wishful thinking is suggested by the fact that the modern bishops who must be the main instruments of conciliar reform are so vastly superior in every way to their sixteenth-century brothers. Not, as the Council has already shown, that a large number do not need that change of outlook from good to better which corresponds to the change from bad to good so sorely needed at the time of Trent, but that those who do need it seem relatively fewer in number and not only cannot evade the change by political entanglements as many sixteenth-century bishops did but will not wish to do so in their consummate loyalty to the Church and the Pope. In any case even if the Vatican Reform be as slow in permeating the whole Church as the Tridentine was we can take courage in the fact that Trent did eventually become the very 'flesh and blood of Catholicism', and in this fact we can found our hope that Vatican II will, with our prayer and co-operation, be in its own very different task a still more splendid success.

[5] H. Daniel-Rops, *The Catholic Reformation, 1500-1622*, London, 1962, pp. 1-64, 62
[6] Ibid., p. 360

Suggestions for Further Reading

P. Anciaux, *The Sacrament of Penance*, London: Challoner Pub-
lications, 1962

J. A. Jungmann, 'Baptism and Penance', *The Early Liturgy*,
London: Darton, Longman and Todd, 1960, pp.
240-52

The Community of Saint-Séverin, *Confession*, London: Geoffrey
Chapman, 1959

H. Daniel-Rops, *The Catholic Reformation* (History of the Church
of Christ, vol. 5), London: J. M. Dent and Sons
Ltd., 1962

P. Hughes, *The Church in Crisis*, A History of the Twenty Great
Councils, London: Burns and Oates, 1961

H. Küng, *The Council and Reunion*, London: Sheed and Ward,
1961

T. F. O'Dea, *American Catholic Dilemma*, New York: New
American Library, 1962

L. and A. Rétif, *The Mission of the Church in the World*, Faith
and Fact Book 101, London: Burns and Oates,
1962

X. Rynne, *Letters from Vatican City*, London: Faber and Faber,
1963

PETER

Enda McDonagh

THE wise man, Christ reminded his audience, built not on sand but on rock (*Matt.* 7:24), for only a rock-foundation could provide stability and continuity. Israel had depended for survival on the fidelity and constancy of the Rock that was Yahweh (God) (2 *Sam.* 23:3; *Ps.* 18:3-32). This same durability was characterized by the use of the rock image in both the Old and New Testament.

This makes it all the more surprising then that it should have been chosen by Christ himself as the name for the lovable and generous fisherman from Galilee, lovable and generous in his impulsiveness but hardly constant and unshakeable as a rock. After the first confident steps on the water in response to his Master's invitation his faith began to fail (*Matt.* 14:28 ff.). And this was no isolated example: the braggart words at the last supper of being ready to die for Christ (*Matt.* 26:35) were but a prelude to the cowardice of the denials (*Matt.* 26:69 ff.); and even when the Holy Spirit had come to strengthen and confirm the mission of the apostles, the same weakness of character showed itself at least once again in yielding on the vital question of submitting the Gentile converts to the rites of Judaism (*Gal.* 2:11 ff.).

It was clearly not for his personal character then that Christ had given Simon the name Peter, meaning rock. And yet in the light of his characteristic failings his choice as the rock-foundation on which Christ would build his church was all the more mysterious. Its real significance was revealed in the promise (*Matt.* 16:18 f.) and bestowal (*John* 21:15 f.) of the supreme authority in his Church for which Christ had chosen him. It was the office not the man, the prayer and promise of Christ and not the human qualities of Simon, Son of Jonah, which would provide firmness and durability in Christ's Church.

This distinction between the office and the man reassures us today when we consider some of the grosser weaknesses into which individual successors of Peter have fallen. And these abuses were not peculiar to the papacy but were widespread in Christ's Church. Even if the Church is not a democracy, yet its head must reflect to some extent the condition of his Church and of his time.

The first among the disciples was to be the servant of all. For this exacting role Christ chose Peter only after he had prayed for him that his faith should not fail and had been reassured of his love. And in the exercise of this service of feeding Christ's sheep Peter would model himself on the Good Shepherd who laid down his life for his sheep.

But not all of Peter's successors were to follow their model. It was not easy at all times to discern at the heart of Christendom this service of the faith in fidelity to Christ's word or this personal love for the sheep after the example of Christ. And as a result of such human failure in faith and love at the centre and throughout the Church, many have been prevented from recognizing in Peter the Vicar of Christ.

For this failure there is need of repentance, so that the friendlier eyes which today have turned to a John or a Paul may discern there the successor of Peter presiding with the apostolic college of the bishops in service of Christ's flock.

A PRAYER

Almighty God, we entreat thee, let no manner of storm shatter us, whom thou hast firmly established on that rock, the testimony of thy apostle.

(*Collect for the Votive Mass of St Peter in the Roman Missal.*)

O God, who on this day didst give blessed Peter to
be head of the Church after thyself when he truly
confessed thee and was by thee worthily preferred, we
humbly beseech thee that, as thou didst give a pastor
in order that none of the sheep should be lost and that
the flock might be preserved from error, so thou
wouldst save by his intercession the flock thou didst
form.

*Collect for the Mass of St Peter's Chair in the
Tallaght (Stowe) Missal which dates from the eighth
or ninth century.*

Suggestions for Spiritual Reading

Matthew 16; *John* 1:35-42; 21; *Luke* 22:24-62; *Acts* 1-5
Letter of St Clement of Rome to the Corinthians and Letter of
St Ignatius of Antioch to Rome in *The Epistles of St Clement of
Rome and St Ignatius of Antioch*, ACW vol. 1, London: Long-
mans, 1946
O. Karrer, *Peter and the Church*, Edinburgh: Nelson, 1963
H. Küng, 'The Chief Obstacle to Reunion', *The Council and
Reunion*, London: Sheed and Ward, 1961, pp.
188-214
B. Leeming, S.J., 'The Papacy', *Christian Unity*, Dublin: Furrow-
Gill, 1962, pp. 116-39
P. Mailleux, S.J., 'Eastern Churches and Primacy', *Problems
Before Unity*, Graymoor Symposium, Dublin:
Helicon, 1962
K. Rahner-J. Ratzinger, *The Episcopate and the Primacy*, Edin-
burgh: Nelson, 1962

Suggestions for Hymn-singing

Psalm 22 (23), 'My Shepherd is the Lord', *Twenty-Four Psalms*,
pp. 10-11
Psalm 71 (72) 'O God, Give your Judgment to the King', *Thirty
Psalms*, pp. 38-9
'Christians at Peter's Throne Unite', *Westminster Hymnal*, n.
214
'Holy Church', *Holy Ghost Hymnal*, n. 102

THE SEPARATED EASTERN CHURCHES

Patrick O'Connell

THE purpose of this article is not to enquire into the historical origins of the divisions which cut off the Eastern Churches from union with Rome, nor to discuss the theological questions involved or thought to have been involved. Certainly historical causes and theological differences may not be ignored, but if these are mentioned here the aim is to clarify the actual situation today. It has been said that the main reason for the present division between Rome and the Orthodox Churches is that the schism has always been there, at least for a thousand years or so. This statement touches the essential, and may be applied to all the divisions which separate the various Eastern Churches, whether Orthodox or not,[1] from Rome. Whatever causes there were in the beginning have been aggravated by the passing of the centuries to the point where the original differences though rather anachronistic now, as Pope Paul has recently commented, and paradoxically reduced to almost empty quasi-ritual formulae, have produced the worst fruit of schism— the acceptance of separation, with all the prejudice involved, as an immutable fact with which one must learn to live. This is the scandal of the relations between the Eastern Churches and Rome.

[1] The term 'Orthodox' is used throughout this article in a purely historical sense to denote all those Churches whose separation from Rome stems from the break between Rome and Constantinople. Other Eastern Churches, although they describe themselves as 'Orthodox', are here described as 'non-Orthodox'. This is merely for the present purpose a matter of terminology.

The first step towards mutual charity which in God's providence will heal the divisions of past centuries is mutual understanding and respect, as Pius XI pointed out forcibly in his encyclical letter *Mortalium Animos* in 1928. This article is an effort to deepen and make more widespread an understanding of the Eastern Churches, to make this knowledge more concrete and vivid, so that prayer for reunion may be seen to be something actual and urgent.

I

The Eastern Churches are called 'Eastern' because their main centres were originally situated in the Eastern part of the old Roman Empire, or were founded outside the Empire by those Churches. This part of the Roman Empire, which was to have a continuous history as the Byzantine Empire up to the year 1453 when Constantinople was taken by the Turks, corresponded to the Mediterranean countries which stretch from Greece eastward and to the south in a great crescent to Egypt. Originally the language and liturgy of these countries was Greek, but gradually earlier languages and cultures, which pre-dated the centuries of hellenistic civilization, asserted themselves, just as in the West the earlier Greek liturgy was translated into Latin. Outside the Empire, in Persia, Armenia and Ethiopia, non-hellenistic cultures dominated from the beginning, but in Georgia under the influence of Constantinople, Greek became the liturgical language. Later still, in the ninth and tenth centuries, the Slav nations received Christianity from the East, but through the pioneering work of Saints Cyril and Methodius and their disciples, the liturgy and the sacred books were transmitted in the old Slavonic language. The conversion of Russia, for many centuries under the influence of Constantinople, brought the equivalent of a new continent within the fold of the Eastern Churches. Indeed the term 'Eastern' is misleading nowadays when many members of these Churches are to be found in the United States, Canada, Brazil, Argentina and Australia, and more recently even in Uganda.

In the Western Roman Empire, Rome had an unchallenged position as the great ecclesiastical centre, but in the East there were many centres. Alexandria in Egypt, Antioch in Syria and from the fourth century on, Constantinople, the capital of what became increasingly a Greek or Byzantine Empire as distinct from the more universal thing which had been the Roman Empire, were the three main ecclesiastical centres of the East. Outside the Empire, the Persian Church early tended to become isolated, as in the continuous wars between the Byzantine Empire and the Persian Empire, the Persian Christians soon found themselves regarded as a fifth column. For a similarly political motive the Armenian Church situated in a country which was the object of Persian and Byzantine ambitions acquired very distinctive characteristics. Liturgically, as the earlier forms of the liturgy became more regulated, Alexandria and Antioch, whose liturgies derive from the early liturgy of Jerusalem, became the centres of influence and later Constantinople emerged as the third liturgical centre of the East. All Eastern liturgies derive from these three but in Persia and in Armenia considerable variations took place. Further developments were to emphasize the gradual emergence of what are described as five rites, which comprehend not merely liturgical matters but also matters of Church discipline. In all of this diversity there was originally no disrupting of Church unity. However once this unity was broken diversity of rite served to facilitate the continuance of separation.

Two of the great ecclesiastical sees of the East, Alexandria and Antioch, not merely enjoyed what were later described as patriarchal rights, recognized by the Council of Nicea in 325, but also were centres of Christian learning. Important differences of terminology as well as different interpretations of theology led to two mutually opposed Christologies early in the fifth century. Those trained in the school of Antioch, in order to combat the heresy of Apollinaris, whose theology led to a denial of complete human nature in Christ, tended to stress the completeness of the two natures, divine and human, to the point where some seemed to state that there were two persons in Christ. The first to assert this openly was Nestorius, who was condemned at the Council of

Ephesus in 431, and there the heresy should have died. However the anti-Antiochene polemics of the Alexandrine school provoked a reaction and the Church of Persia which had already declared its autonomy soon adopted the doctrine of Nestorius. This was largely an assertion of independence and a guarantee to the Persian government of political loyalty in the struggle against the Christians of the Byzantine state. But the division remained permanent. On the other hand, Alexandrine terminology which had long been suspect to the school of Antioch and which stressed the unity of Christ's Person soon gave rise to the suspicion that the Alexandrines held that the two natures in Christ were united by a kind of fusion, where the human was absorbed by the divine or vice versa, or else a new nature was produced. Apart from some few who may have held these views, the vast majority of the Church of Egypt, as Pius XII stressed,[2] were by no means heretics. The ensuing struggle is to be seen rather as a cultural and partly national struggle against the central government of Constantinople, and more specifically as a duel between the old ecclesiastical centre of Alexandria and the rising star of the bishop of Constantinople. The tessera of orthodoxy became the acceptance of the Council of Chalcedon, which in 451 had condemned the new heresy. This council also condemned Dioscorus, bishop of Alexandria, the nephew of the famous St Cyril who had opposed Nestorius. Skilful propaganda, allied to the anti-Constantinople feeling in Egypt, represented the struggle as a defence of the faith of Cyril. Mutual charges of heresy were levelled. But the result, in spite of governmental attempts to restore unity by persecution and compromise, was that the Monophysites, as they came to be called, were cut off from the rest of the Church. Thus a great part of the Church of Egypt, as well as very many in Syria, known as Jacobites after their main inspirer, were lost to the Church. The Armenians were also drawn into the Monophysite party and the Church of Ethiopia followed the lead of Alexandria from which it depended. A small remnant in Egypt and in Syria remained staunch supporters of Chalcedon and thus were in union with Constantinople. They soon became known as 'Melchites' or 'Imperialists'.

[2] *Acta Apostolicae Sedis*, 43 (1951), p. 636

The old titles and trappings of power were retained by the Melchite patriarchs of Alexandria and Antioch, but they had little influence. Constantinople became the effective head of all the Orthodox, that is, of all those in the East who stood by the Council of Chalcedon. This was reflected in the gradual byzantinization of the Melchite Churches, as also of the Patriarchate of Jerusalem, all of which eventually adopted the Byzantine rite and used Greek as their liturgical language.

Then in the seventh century an event of capital importance occurred. Into the power vacuum created by the exhaustion of the Byzantine and Persian Empires after a long drawn out war, came the Arabs bringing with them the new religion of Islam. In a remarkably short time they succeeded in overrunning Syria, Egypt and Persia. Then they occupied Armenia, and remained an ever-present threat to the Byzantine Empire. From this time on the Eastern Churches in those countries occupied by the Arabs were isolated from the rest of Christendom, and the Nestorian and Mono-physite schisms became definitive. The city of Constantin-ople remained the capital of an Empire, but it was a Greek Empire now, the outpost of Christendom in the East, and at the same time cut off from the West not merely by the Lombard invaders of Italy, but also by the intangible though no less real differences of language, culture and political ambitions. The bishop of Constantinople was for all practical purposes the ecclesiastical ruler of the Christian East outside the Arab-occupied countries, and even in those countries the Christians who remained faithful to Chalcedon looked to him for help and guidance.

It may be said with some truth that no definite event caused the schism between the Byzantine Church and Rome, that it was the gradual estrangement wrought by political environment, cultural background and language, manifested rather than caused by occasional theological or personal disputes, which almost imperceptibly led to disunion. This estrangement is very apparent in the period of the Crusades, so well described by Runciman in his book on the Eastern schism, but even in the centuries which preceded the Patriarch of Constantinople's break with Rome in the mid-eleventh century the same mutual ignorance, prejudice and perhaps more than anything else the all too human desire to cut a fine figure and to make one's career, instead of patient dedication to consolidating unity, had gradually induced the official break between the Byzantine Church and Rome. The Orthodox Churches which had received their faith from the Byzantine Empire followed Constantinople into schism, though not all at the same time nor for the same reasons. The Russian Church indeed did not secede formally from communion with Rome until the fifteenth century, when it declared its independence, because of the heresy of the Church of Constantinople, which, it was declared, had betrayed the faith at the Council of Florence by signing the Act of Union with Rome.

2

In the years which followed the consummation of the schism in the mid-eleventh century, many attempts at reunion were made. For various reasons all these efforts failed, although at the Second Council of Lyons in 1274 and again at Florence in 1439, formal acts of Union were drawn up and signed. The reasons for failure are not easy to summarize, but it may be said in general that the West was very slow to appreciate the different environments and ritual traditions of the East, and recent memories of attempts to recast the Eastern Church after the Latin model did not inspire confidence. Sufficient to say now that the faults were not all on one side. Ignorance and prejudice found theological differences and heresy where real difference did not exist. Minor ritual differences were exaggerated out of all proportion. Without denying a certain amount of ill-will and obstinacy, perhaps the real fault lay on the one side in a readiness to interpret past history with a view to preserving the state of schism, without much regard for the many elements in past tradition which showed that this attitude was a gross over-simplification and exaggeration, and on the other side there was the attitude of mind which saw in the solution of purely theological difficulties a successful termination of the whole affair, and did not grasp the importance of the legitimate and traditional differences of liturgy, and above all of discipline. In particular it may be said that the Western concept of a 'Patriarch' had been modified considerably by the appointment of Latin 'Patriarchs' to the main Eastern Sees at the time of the Crusades and did not correspond at all to the Eastern idea. Of the two notions, the Eastern view corresponded more closely to the older practice of the Church.[3]

Even though the West was suspicious of the implications read by polemical theologians into the institution of Patriarchs, in the period which saw the consummation of the schism, the reaction went too far, so that 'Patriarch' was regarded in the West as purely an honorific title and the bishops of the East, including the Eastern Patriarchs, were regarded as though they were members of what in older times was the Roman or Latin patriarchate, with the minor difference that they celebrated Mass in a different language and a little understood rite.

This was particularly unfortunate for the future, as through the force of circumstances the Patriarchs, even though the multiplicity of Eastern Churches tended to obscure the importance of their office and the principle of regional or national autonomy multiplied their numbers even in the Orthodox Church, acquired an importance which was more than ecclesiastical. They became leaders, in symbol perhaps more than in reality, of the old Christian nations which were subject to the Mohammedans.

After the fall of Constantinople in 1453, not merely was the Union of Florence brought to an end, but all the Eastern Churches, with the sole exception of the Church of Russia, passed under the control of the Mohammedans. Their life was for the next few centuries lived in isolation, and the cultural world of Islam which surrounded them and which had dominated the Churches of Egypt, Persia and Armenia

---

[3] Cf. Wilhelm de Vries's articles: 'La S. Sede ed i patriarcati cattolici d'Oriente', *Orientalia Christiana Periodica* 27 (1961), pp. 313-361; and 'Die Entstehung der Patriarchate des Ostens und ihr Verhältnis zur päpstlichen Vollgewalt', *Scholastik* 37 (1962), pp. 341-369

for much longer cut them off even more definitively from Rome. They lived in general the life of martyr Churches, in a non-Christian environment, which was often actively anti-Christian and always hostile. In such an atmosphere learning all but perished, ecclesiastical standards declined and all that remained in the continuous struggle against discriminatory taxation and legislation was tradition, which while it preserved the Mass and the sacraments, though practice declined, also kept alive the tradition of schism, fed on ignorance and prejudice. Under the continuous pressure and isolation many of the faithful fell away especially in those countries which had been subject to Islam for many centuries, but the thing to grasp is that the faith survived. The heroism of the Eastern Churches during these long years of trial, which for those in Mohammedan countries have not yet ended, is surely one of their glories. But martyr Churches tend to a certain narrowness and exclusiveness and if the martyrdom be prolonged may lose the wider vision of the Church universal, and replace it by the idea of the local Church, associated more or less vaguely with those Christians in other parts who have preserved the faith. When the criterion for judging the orthodoxy of other Christians is itself vitiated by lack of learning and also by the tradition of schism, it is small wonder that those Churches, such as the Church of Greece, which emerged in the nineteenth century from under the Turkish yoke, were more than ever confirmed in their schism from Rome.

As regards the Church of Russia, the isolation of this Church until comparatively modern times from the main current of West European life, with the suspicion which accompanied such isolation, justified to an extent by the sixteenth century ambitions of Catholic Poland and Lithuania, forms an interesting parallel to the more rigid and oppressive isolation of the Greek branch of the Orthodox Church and of the other Eastern Christians. Latin influence in theology, entering Russia through the great school of Kiev, balanced the more rigid and prejudiced Greek theology which derived from Constantinople, but later North German and rationalist philosophy and theology again widened the gap, until in the nineteenth century Russia returned once more to the early tradition, although this time in a rather anti-Western and more anti-Latin spirit. The Russian government, which dominated the Russian Church sought everywhere to suppress any groups which had returned to union with Rome, while Catholic Poland for a long time strove to latinize these groups, so that the distinction between Eastern and Western Christian became for both sides a distinction between Orthodox and Catholic.

With the break-up of the Byzantine Empire the example of Russia was imitated by other national groups among the Orthodox and each national group claimed autonomy or autocephaly, often setting up a patriarchate of its own, while at the same time recognizing the primacy of honour of Constantinople followed by Alexandria, Antioch and Jerusalem. In spite of apparent multiplicity, unity was maintained among the various Orthodox Churches, as it is today, by unity of faith and by official letters between the various 'sister' Churches.

After the great struggle of the Protestant Reformation the Latin West became again interested in the Eastern Churches, and here the invaluable protection afforded to Latin missioners in the Near East by the French government must be recognized. By the eighteenth century the Christians of the Turkish Empire, outside Europe and Egypt, had been driven by their desire to escape molestation to the highlands of Syria and Kurdistan, and especially the Lebanon. There the proximity of different schismatic groups made the scandal of disunity very apparent, and many groups from different rites returned to union with Rome. The policy of Rome was naturally aimed at the return of a complete Church, so that many of the attempts at reunion were made when a patriarchal see fell vacant, and a pro-Roman candidate was available, but in not a single case was complete success achieved. These attempts at reunion continued throughout the nineteenth century and there is practically no group of Eastern Christians now which has not a smaller or larger number reunited to the Holy See. Unfortunately the Iron Curtain which now has shut off most of Eastern Europe has meant that the reunited Eastern Christians in

Communist countries have been forcibly amalgamated with the various national Orthodox Churches. Perhaps in time they will be seen to have worked as a leaven through the great mass of Orthodoxy.

3

With the gradual pressure of the Mohammedan occupation which isolated the Eastern Churches of the Mediterranean regions, schools of theology eventually ceased to exist, or continued as mere shadows of their former selves. In Russia, on the other hand, especially in the great revival of the nineteenth century, the highest standards were maintained, and there is still a great deal of work to be done in making available to Western scholars the results of Russian investigations in patrology, history and canon law. But in the Mediterranean countries and in the Near East generally Christianity was preserved by an heroic insistence on tradition, centred particularly around the liturgy of the Mass. The great monasteries, where they were allowed to continue in existence, notably on Mount Athos, played a great part in this. In spite of persecution and isolation, the Mass was retained, with a validly consecrated hierarchy and duly ordained priests. The sacraments were also maintained, although the enforced ignorance of the clergy meant that the practice of Penance and of other sacraments was infrequent, and in some places died out. In the Orthodox Churches a rigid three-day fast before receiving Holy Communion, with absolute fast on the last day, was the custom. Obligation of attendance at Mass was enforced canonically at least to the extent that one was excommunicated for missing three consecutive 'Liturgies'. However, because of the length of the services, it became the custom to substitute attendance at any sacred function, such as Vespers, to satisfy this obligation and in many places it was not taken too seriously. For one thing, in the older Christian lands the churches were small, nor was it easy to repair or enlarge existing churches. That so much religious knowledge survived at the popular level in the

absence of a well-educated clergy who could preach and
hear confessions is due not merely to the liturgy of the
Mass which worked powerfully on the imagination, but
also to the popular cult of icons or Sacred Images which,
as it stressed the Communion of Saints and the role of the
saints as intercessors, also kept before the mind the great
truths of tradition, of which these saints were witnesses.

For the liturgist and the patrologist, as also in general for
all those interested in investigating early Christian tradition,
all that pertains to the Eastern Churches is of the greatest
interest. One may however have the suspicion that this
interest is somewhat akin to the interest taken in the natural
sciences in the fossilized remains of once-living creatures.
That is to say that interest in the Eastern Churches is
unfortunately all too often merely a form of antiquarianism.

Modern interest in the Church tends rather towards the
mission field. Notably in the last hundred years the Church
has spread its Gospel throughout the world. Yet this period
is rapidly passing and the Church is now entering on the
post-mission period, if one understands 'mission' in the late
nineteenth-century sense. In the new countries of Africa
foreigners are becoming increasingly unwelcome, because
behind the missions of the past lies the bogey of 'colonial-
ism'.

In the countries of the Near East this is equally true.
The salvation of these countries depends on the Churches
which are indigenous and which work there. Nor may
anyone imagine a situation in which a group of missioners
in the old sense might be sent into even a post-Communist
Russia, unless they came not to create a Church from the
beginning but to complete and reunite the Church already
there. For this work a great deal of understanding and
prayer is needed. To treat the Eastern Churches as pathetic
survivals which should be swept aside in the cause of
greater apostolic efficiency would be worse than a crime.

A great amount of work remains to be done. As against
the 111 million members of the Eastern Churches who are
separated from Rome (the numbers in Russia and Georgia,
for example, being estimated on the basis of taking one-

third of what the natural increase of population would have amounted to since the Communist Revolution), there are only eleven millions of the Eastern Christians united to Rome. Some of the Eastern Churches still separated from Rome are not at all considerable in numbers. For instance, the Nestorians, who once counted 27 metropolitans and 200 dioceses, now number barely 80,000, and are in a wretched condition; but the work of union has progressed to the point where about 200,000 from the old Nestorian Church now are united to Rome; and in India, those Christians in Kerala who had received their liturgy from this Church and who are in union with Rome, number 1,349,360. In Egypt the Coptic Church amounts to barely one-eight of the total population, but the number of other Christians is inconsiderable. It is in the Coptic Church, now separated from Rome, that the hope of the future lies.

Among the Orthodox, apart from the Patriarchate of Constantinople, which governs directly some million and a third members scattered throughout the world, there are some 50 millions in Russia, about 8 millions in Greece, 16 millions in Rumania, 6½ millions in Bulgaria, and 7 millions among the Serbs of Yugoslavia. It has been estimated that there are some five million Orthodox in the United States, though they pertain to different jurisdictions, and they now have their own chaplains in the United States Armed Forces. It may not be amiss to point out that many of the Orthodox in the United States were once in union with Rome, but returned to Orthodoxy because of the difficulties put in their way by the Latin clergy. This is not likely to happen today but it should serve as a reminder that the Eastern Churches are not a collection of cranks who persist in considering themselves different. Their traditions in liturgy and discipline, as in most of their theology, derive from the early Fathers of the Church and from the early Councils. They have as much right as Latin Christians to insist on respect and full equality.[4]

[4] The statistics given are taken from *Oriente Cattolico*, Vatican City, 1962

4

Outside the confines of Islam and the Communist world
the most considerable Orthodox Church is the Church of
Greece. This Church, while it honours the Patriarch of
Constantinople as first among the Orthodox Patriarchs,
declared its autonomy in 1833, admitted by the Patriarch
in 1850. The Church is administered by a Synod under the
King. Ever since the liberation from the Turks in the nineteenth century the Church's close association with the
government has caused great difficulties. A further upheaval
which hardened into a schism led by three bishops developed
when the modern reformed calendar was adopted by the
Synod in 1924 instead of the old Julian calendar. This
schism still remains and conveys an idea of the power of
conservative traditionalism among the lower clergy and the
people. It also gives an insight into the difficulties facing
all attempts to break down anti-Latin prejudice. This task
has not been made easier by the Italian invasion of Greece
during the Second World War. The work of reconstructing
the Church after the liberation of the last century has been
further hampered by the fact that during the Second World
War many parts of Greece were devastated, and the clergy
especially suffered, 350 priests being killed at the hands of
the Germans, the Bulgarians and later the Communists.

The main problem facing the Church is the education of
the clergy, because many of the priests were incompetent
to hear confessions or to preach, confining their activities
to the celebration of the liturgy of the Mass and the various
liturgical Offices. There are now a dozen seminaries engaged
in the education of clerical students, and centres of higher
ecclesiastical learning have emerged, especially in Athens,
Salonika, Khalandri and Thessalonika. The seminary of
Halki, situated on the Turkish island of the same name
near modern Istanbul (formerly Constantinople) is also
improving the standards of the clergy and many Greeks
study there. Some students are sent abroad to foreign
Christian universities in France, Germany, the United
States and even Rome.

A good general idea of the practice of religion in Greece

is given by P. Hammond in *Waters of Marah*, and the atmosphere of popular Greek religious feeling is excellently conveyed by Nikos Kazantzakis in his novel *Freedom and Death*. There it is made clear how closely the Orthodox Church has been associated with the survival of the Greek nation.

On the more popular, apostolic level, new life is stirring in Greece. In Athens the parish of Zoödochos Pege is a great centre of activity and publishes many popular religious magazines. At the Apostoliki Diakonia a school has been set up to train confessors: it is worth noting that in the whole of Greece there were, a few years ago, only about 500 priests recognized as competent to hear confessions. At the Monastery of Pandeli there is a school of catechists for all the dioceses of Greece. Eighty per cent of the children now study the catechism, in some parishes one hundred per cent. The great apostolic organization of theologians and laymen, *Zoe* (Life), has had enormous influence. This was a movement set on foot towards the end of the nineteenth century by a monk in imitation of St Dominic, and in 1911 the Brotherhood of Theologians, *Zoe*, was founded. The group called *Sotir* (Saviour), which broke off from this movement, works in harmony with it. The Apostoliki Diakonia, which dominates apostolic activity, combines very well with these two movements. The members of *Zoe*, who come from every social background and profession, specialize in street preaching and also preach every Sunday in the churches. The old monasteries which had fallen into popular disfavour seem to have been revitalized in recent years, and new monasteries are replacing the old, with new ideas and a more practical grasp of the needs of the times.

On the popular level there is great devotion to the Mother of God, nor would any theologian or bishop dare to express doubts about the Immaculate Conception in public, although they oppose the Vatican definition of 1854. The island of Tinos has become a great centre of pilgrimage to honour the miraculous Icon of the Mother of God. On 15 August 1962 over 25,000 pilgrims visited the shrine and took part in the ceremonies.

All of this gives great hope for the future, for with the

revived spiritual force of the Greek Church is linked the
hope of ultimate reunion.

5

Once schism becomes a *fait accompli* a theology to justify
schism comes into being. Various points of difference may
be listed, but fundamentally it is the theology of the constitution of the Church which is at stake. The Eastern
Churches separated from Rome, especially the Orthodox
Church, have always held that divine revelation is contained
in Scripture and Tradition, but they also assert that all
patriarchs are equal, the primacy of honour being given to
the Bishop of Rome (once he retracts his errors). The
ultimate authority in the Church which is competent to
decide matters of faith is an Ecumenical Council, which, in
the absence of the Bishop of Rome, is technically impossible.
The multiplication of patriarchs and the rise of autonomous
Churches have somewhat obscured this doctrine, and a more
general line now is a decrying of all manner of juridical
authority in the Church as being something entirely secular
and untraditional. Stress is laid on the primacy of charity
and the spiritual life of the Church, and indeed it must be
admitted that at times post-Tridentine polemics did tend
to obscure the more interior and mystical aspect of the
Church.

The attack on juridicism became very popular in the last
century, largely through the influence of the Russian
theologian, Khomiakov, who evolved his rather obscure
Sobornost theory to reject all juridical authority in the
Church, Christ alone being Head of the Church. Under the
guise of a 'eucharistic' doctrine of the Church this theory has
been revived in recent years.

Yet signs are not lacking that Orthodox theologians
realize the insufficiencies of their positions and recent
studies on the Primacy of Peter indicate a less polemical
and more critical approach to the problem of authority as
related to Church unity. While we pray during the Church
Unity Week for a deeper understanding on the part of the

separated Churches of the East of what the Primacy of Peter implies, prayer may also be directed usefully towards a deeper realization on our part that unity does not necessarily imply uniformity of practice. The words of St Irenaeus written to Pope St Victor during an earlier controversy with the East on the subject of the date of Easter and the Lenten fast, may be applied in a wider sense and are still valid: 'Yet all of these lived none the less in peace (i.e. past generations in East and West), and we also live in peace with one another; and the difference in regard to the fast confirms the agreement in the faith'.[5]

[5] Eusebius, *Hist. Eccles.*, V, xxiv

Suggestions for Further Reading

Donald Attwater, *The Christian Churches of the East*, vol. II, London: Geoffrey Chapman, 1961

‡Timothy Ware, *The Orthodox Church*, Pelican Books, 1963

Walter Kolarz, *Religion in the Soviet Union*, London: Macmillan, 1961

Yves Congar, *After Nine Hundred Years*, New York: Fordham University, 1959

‡N. Zernov, *Eastern Christendom*, London: Weidenfeld and Nicolson, 1961

*P. Hammond, *The Waters of Marah* (on the Greek Church), London: Rockliff, 1955

*S. Loch, *Athos: The Holy Mountain*, London: Nelson, 1957

*S. Runciman, *The Eastern Schism*, Oxford University Press, 1955

‡J. Meyendorff, N. Afanassieff, R. P. A. Schmemann, N. Koulomzine, *The Primacy of Peter in the Orthodox Church*, London: The Faith Press, 1963

‡Orthodox author
*Protestant author

THE EUCHARIST

Pól Ó Súilleabháin

Of all the major Christian confessions separated from the Holy See of Rome, the Oriental Churches alone possess validity of sacred orders and the Eucharistic Sacrifice. Despite the thousand-year-old breach in doctrine and obedience, this fellowship in the Table of the Lord reminds Catholics and Orientals every day that they are brothers who are nourished by the same heavenly Bread.

ABOUT 150 A.D. Polycarp of Smyrna came to Rome to discuss with Pope Anicetus the problem of the date of Easter. They failed to agree. But the historian Eusebius writes (*Ecclesiastical History*, v, 24) they 'communicated each other', that is, the Pope allowed Polycarp to celebrate and distribute the Holy Eucharist to the Roman clergy in his presence. This was accepted as public testimony that Pope and bishop, though divided on a disciplinary issue, were one in faith. Holy Communion was the seal and symbol of communion with the Catholic Church.

The word Communion originally meant Christian fellowship or membership of the Church. This fellowship, which fused the faithful into the Body of Christ, demanded a common faith; but its clearest expression was revealed in the sharing of the Eucharistic Sacrifice and Sacred Meal. This rite was more than a symbol of unity: it was conceived as the effective cause of unity. And soon the rite became synonymous with membership of the Church. It was called Holy Communion.

The early Christians insisted on doctrine and the Eucharist as the two pillars of fellowship: 'These occupied themselves continually with the apostles' teaching and with their fellowship in the breaking of bread . . .' (*Acts* 2:42). In his letter to the Ephesians (20:2) Ignatius describes Church unity as 'one faith . . . one obedience . . . one bread'. For Cyprian the crime of a heretic lay in his refusal to offer sacrifice in the Catholic Church: 'He is a rebel against the Sacrifice of Christ; he dares to set up another altar'. Excommunication meant exclusion from Holy Communion; reinstatement meant simply readmittance to the Sacred Mysteries.

This ancient conception of fellowship has governed the practice of the Catholic Church until now. And in this sphere the Orthodox have been no less faithful to tradition than we: they too demand a common faith and sacrifice for membership of their Churches. For many of their modern theologians, it is true, exterior jurisdictional unity is of less importance; and the indefiniteness of their doctrines allows considerable latitude in interpretation. To be 'divinized', to be made alive and ruled by the Holy Ghost, to become one with Christ and the brethren in the Holy Eucharist: for them that is Christian life. We deny none of this, though our emphases differ. They and we are at one in believing that there can be no 'breaking of bread' without community of faith.

They, like us, are heirs to the teaching of the Greek Fathers, which evokes a longing for unity, for a 'living together'. The first meaning of *Convivium* (Banquet)—which we often use of the Eucharist—is 'living together'.

The Fathers love to comment on the phrase of St Paul: 'For we, being many, are one bread, one body' (1 *Cor.* 10:17). The theme of the grains of wheat kneaded into one bread is already in the *Didache* (about 100 A.D.): 'As this bread, which we break, was at one time dispersed over the hills, then collected and made into one thing; so may Thy Church be gathered together from the ends of the earth into Thy kingdom' (9:4). Chrysostom frequently develops this theme: 'As this bread, composed of many grains, was so kneaded into one that nowhere do the individual grains

appear—for though they still exist, their identity is hidden
. . .; in the same way we are joined together with Christ
and with one another'.

In their Mass the Orthodox Christians repeatedly pray
in the words of Basil and Chrysostom that all believers may
be united through the celebration of the Eucharist:
'Beseeching unity of faith and communion of the Holy
Spirit . . .'; 'That all who partake of this one bread and
chalice may be united with one another in the communion
of the Holy Spirit . . .'; 'Lord, preserve the fullness of Thy
Church . . .'. Though they apprehend the notion of Church
unity in a manner different from ours, they have always been
sustained by this faith in the ultimate achievement of unity
through Holy Communion.

When one enters a church in Athens one perceives despite
the unfamiliar icons and the strange gestures of the wor-
shippers that here is the Real Presence we know so well. It
is the memorial of his Passion, the pledge of our resurrection,
and the force that will draw all believers to one altar. In
that Presence we dare to pray that some day soon doctrinal
differences may be resolved, and the Pope and Patriarch
may 'communicate each other'.

A PRAYER

Remember, O Lord, Thy Church: deliver her from all
evil, perfect her in Thy love, and from the four winds
assemble her, the sanctified, in Thy Kingdom which
Thou hast prepared for her. Amen.

From the Didache, *a very early Christian manual.*

Suggestions for Spiritual Reading

Isaiah 42, 49, 53; *John* 6; 1 *Corinthians* 10-13; *Ephesians* 2;
1 John 3

Epistles of St Clement of Rome and St Ignatius of Antioch,
Ancient Christian Writers, Vol. I, London:
Longmans, Green, 1946

L. Cerfaux, *The Church in the Theology of St Paul,* London and
New York: Herder-Nelson, 1959, esp. pp. 228-286.

I-H. Dalmais, O.P., *The Eastern Liturgies,* Faith and Fact Book
no. 111, London: Burns and Oates, 1960

H. de Lubac, S.J., *The Splendour of the Church,* London: Sheed
and Ward, 1956, esp. pp. 87-113

Suggestions for Hymn-singing

Psalm 42 (43) 'Defend me, O God', *Twenty-Four Psalms,* pp.
20-1

Psalm 115 (116) 'I trusted even when I said', ibid., pp. 36-7

Psalm 116 (117) 'O Praise the Lord', ibid., p. 19

Psalm 150 'Praise God in His Holy Place', *Thirty Psalms,* p. 68

'Sancti venite', *Laudemus,* pp. 54-5

'O Bread of Heaven', *Westminster Hymnal,* n. 84

'Fáilte romhat, a Rí na naingeal', *Holy Ghost Hymnal,* n. 109

ANGLICANISM

The Earl of Wicklow

THE Anglican Communion, of which the Church of Ireland is a member, is the most interesting of all the Christian bodies which may be described as 'reformed', but also the most puzzling; while it has preserved far more of the Catholic heritage than any other, at the same time it presents us with a bewildering variety of outlooks. An acute Anglican writer has summed this up very strikingly: 'There is no Anglican theological system. . . . Anglicanism is not a confession: and it is not permanently interested in Anglicanism'.[1] The last sentence may seem bewildering, but at this stage ecumenically-minded Anglicans are prepared for a time when their parent body may lose its identity as it becomes merged with other denominations.

This note of paradox is to be found from the earliest days of the Elizabethan Settlement. The reformed English Church retained, despite vigorous Puritan opposition, the threefold order of bishops, priests and deacons, but on the other hand the new hierarchy was definitely Calvinist in belief, with the exception of Cheyney, Bishop of Gloucester, and perhaps one other; Cheyney was at one time in serious trouble with his colleagues on the bench because of his avowed Lutheran views. Calvinists rejected in particular any real objective presence of Christ in or with the Eucharistic elements, thus striking at the foundations of the Catholic doctrine of the Sacrifice of the Mass. This meant that

[1] David M. Paton, *Anglicans and Unity* (Mowbray, 1962), p. 20

England was exposed to the full force of Calvinist iconoclasm.[2]

The state of affairs in those days has been convincingly described by one of the most learned and generous of Anglican historians, Dr W. H. Frere, C.R.:

> If the Puritan, repressed and imprisoned for conscience' sake, deserves pity, even more so does the Recusant who shared his prison. The one merely had his reforming zeal checked, while the other had all his cherished traditions outraged that had long been a sacred part of his inner life. . . . They had heard much of a restoration of purity in faith . . . what they actually saw before them as the immediate consequence of the change was the desecrating of the churches by iconoclasm, the destruction of altars, the burning of the sacred ornaments and the derision of the holy ceremonies. The blasphemous parodies of the Eucharist were not merely a momentary excess of the first days of reaction, but were held to be the right sort of entertainment wherewith to amuse the Queen and her court when she visited Cambridge in 1564. . . . The Recusant in his youth had seen the churches thronged every day by worshippers; now he saw the doors beginning to be closed from Monday to Saturday, the people giving up their daily worship and coming down to a mere attendance on Sundays and a rare reception of the Sacrament for conformity's sake.[3]

---

[2] In this article which is, I hope, irenic and ecumenical in its intention, I do not propose to discuss the Bull *Apostolicae Curae*, dealing with the question of Anglican orders. Much of value has already been written on this subject by experts. Needless to say, I accept Pope Leo's judgment absolutely but one knows what a painful subject this is for some Anglicans.

[3] W. H. Frere, C.R., D.D., *The English Church in the Reigns of Elizabeth and James I* (Macmillan, 1904), p. 130. The author was a renowned liturgical scholar as well as a historian, and a member of one of the monastic communities which are such a remarkable feature of present-day Anglicanism. He was Bishop of Truro from 1923 to 1935.

I quote from this depressing picture in order to show
later how the Catholic influences at work in Anglicanism
can revive, and did revive after this century of gloom.
Unfortunately these Catholic revivals have tended to be
followed by periods of recession, but still these revivals have
been most remarkable and have had lasting results. In
spite of a determined and at times a fanatical opposition
from the Puritans, the Church of England has become
something quite different from Continental Protestantism,
for the episcopate remains the basis of its Church order and
government and Holy Communion, not the sermon, is the
centre of its worship.

The Church of England was not submerged, then, by
the new doctrines which were finding their way over from
the Continent, and early in the next century the Catholic
elements in her reasserted themselves, in spite of further
Puritan opposition. This turn of the tide showed itself with
the rise of a High Church movement under Archbishop
Laud (1573-1645) and Bishop Andrewes (1555-1626), but
it must be owned that they both fell into the prevailing error
of the age by relying on political power in order to enforce
religious order and conformity, while Laud seriously under-
estimated the conviction and driving power of the Puritan
party in the young national Church; for this miscalculation
he paid with his head. After the short, bitter winter of the
Commonwealth the High Church strain flowered again with
added lustre in the Caroline divines, who were for a period
to have a marked influence on Newman and his young
friends. This withered prematurely, however, after the
victory of William of Orange and his Whig supporters,
followed by the noble secession of the Non-Jurors. These
sincere, devout, inflexible men who represented the best in
Anglicanism, having protested strongly and indeed courageously against James II when he tried to improve the lot
of his much-tried Catholic subjects, nevertheless, after he
had been supplanted by his son-in-law, renounced their
benefices and went out into the wilderness rather than break
the oaths of allegiance which they had taken to him.

For nearly a century and a half, with a promising but
abortive religious revival under Queen Anne, there followed

a strangely arid period which, with a certain number of notable exceptions, was given over to the Latitudinarians, Liberals,[4] call them what you will. Through these stagnant waters there flowed however a clearer stream of something far nearer Catholic belief which never quite dried up and produced such fine Christians as Dean Swift[5] (who belonged partly to the reign of Queen Anne), Dr Johnson, William Law, Bishop Butler[6] and the Wesley brothers. The two latter were well-grounded in a number of Catholic principles by their father who was an admirable but financially unfortunate country clergyman. There were also the Evangelicals, who figured prominently in the eighteenth century and numbered some devoted men in their ranks; they shared the Wesleys' love of souls and their opposition to the latitudinarian tendencies of the age, but in doctrine they were far further from them than is usually imagined. Devout men they were and very effective philanthropists, largely through whose efforts the slave trade was abolished, to say nothing of Lord Shaftesbury's and 'Parson Bull's'[7] constant struggle in the next century on behalf of the unfortunate victims of the Industrial Revolution, but as far as they had a theology[8] it was more closely allied with the Calvinism of the Puritans.

[4] I use the word Liberal in Newman's sense: 'My battle was with Liberalism; by Liberalism I mean the anti-dogmatic principle and its developments." (*Apologia pro Vita Sua*, Part IV)

[5] See the interesting account of the great Dean's spiritual and pastoral life in Robert Wyse Jackson, D.D., LL.D., *Jonathan Swift, Dean and Pastor*. Swift established a weekly Communion Service in St Patrick's Cathedral, Dublin, which has continued ever since. He had many deeper and gentler qualities than his *saeva indignatio*: he is said to have known the Anglican liturgy by heart.

[6] We may, I think, include the author of the celebrated *Analogy*, who was also an exemplary bishop. He was thought by quite a number to have died a Catholic.

[7] A good biography of this stalwart Evangelical clergyman has recently appeared, *Parson Bull of Byerley*, by Canon J. C. Gill (S.P.C.K., 1963).

[8] Lest these words sound offensive, may I quote once again from Newman's *Apologia*. In Part V he refers to an article he wrote for the *British Critic* in April 1839: 'As regarded what was called Evangelical religion or Puritanism there was more to cause alarm. I observed upon its organisation; but on the other hand it had no intellectual basis, no internal idea, no theology'.

The Evangelicals and the Methodists were intent on the
conversion of souls, and the state of the Church of England
as a whole did not greatly concern them. A Victorian writer,
Dr Jennings, has described this very aptly:

> Under the influence of the Methodist and Evangelical
> movements, the Church here and there recovered
> vitality . . . many philanthropic schemes were carried
> out, but it was ever the inspiration of detached units,
> not of the mass. For corporate action the Evangelical
> system offered no scope. It was a purely subjective
> religion, to the exclusion of creeds and means of grace
> . . . and it attached no value to accessories of worship.[9]

During the first thirty years of the nineteenth century, in
spite of John Wesley's words in his last charge, 'In God's
name stop there—Be Church of England men still', his
followers were gradually slipping away from the national
Church. In the *Methodist Magazine* for April 1834 they
declared that they accepted 'the utility, nay, under present
circumstances the *necessity* of an established religion', but
all the same, the drift continued. Their attitude was however
in marked contrast to that of the original 'Dissenters', who
not only protested against the Popish ways of the Established Church, but were opposed to its existing at all. The
Evangelicals thus continued for a quarter of a century to be
the most active party in the Church of England, and while
undistinguished in theology, their philanthropic work was
of high quality. There was also what was known as the
'High and Dry' school, few of whose members held what
would now be called Anglo-Catholic views. There were
eminent churchmen among them, notably Dean Hook of
Leeds, who in 1835 preached what became a celebrated
sermon in the Chapel Royal defending the Apostolic
Succession, but in general they were solid rather than
dynamic. The Liberalism against which Newman was to
wage war was widespread, but not organized as a party.
. . The future did not look hopeful and in 1832 Dr Arnold,

---

[9] *Ecclesia Anglicana*, p. 469. Quoted in G. H. F. Nye's *The Story
of the Oxford Movement*, pp. 38-9.

the well-known headmaster of Rugby, declared that the Church of England, as it then stood, 'no human power could save'. This was the view of a Liberal who became a strangely bitter opponent of the Tractarians. Writing forty years later Mr Gladstone, a devoted son of the Oxford Movement, thus describes the conditions prevalent in those days:

> The state of things as to worship was beyond all parallel known to me. . . . Taking together the expulsion of the poor and labouring classes (especially from the town churches), the mutilation of the fabrics, the baldness of the service, above all the coldness and indifference of the lounging congregation, our services were possibly without a parallel for their debasement. . . . They would have shocked a Brahmin or a Buddhist.[10]

This was the milieu in which Keble preached his historic sermon on national apostasy. 'I have ever considered and kept that day', wrote Newman, 'as the start of the religious movement of 1833'.[11] Some have said that the men who rallied to Keble at that time were trying to put the clock back, and it might with justice be urged that he and his friends were far too conservative in their politics, compared, for instance, with Manning's magnificent radicalism both as Archdeacon of Chichester and Archbishop of Westminster. In religious matters, however, their view was that the Anglican clock had run down and must be wound up without delay. Certainly the political reasons for Keble's sermon seem scarcely valid now: he spoke against the government's intention to reduce the number of Anglican bishoprics in Ireland, where there were far too many in proportion to the size of the flock that they served. There was, however, a deep spiritual motive for the sermon, the Catholic elements in the Church of England were once again asserting themselves and doing so with increasing force.

The years which followed may be divided roughly into

[10] Article in the *Contemporary Review*, October 1874
[11] *Apologia pro Vita Sua*, Part III

two parts of unequal length, the Oxford period, lasting till Newman's reconciliation with Rome in October 1845, and then the period of expansion which has lasted down to our own day during which the forces set in motion have gradually spread their influence over a large part of the earth's surface, both civilized and uncivilized. After Newman and Ward had gone the movement came under a cloud at Oxford, where its influence declined in the university and men like Jowett and Mark Pattison came into their own; as has been said, 'scepticism and rationalism were added to Protestantism'.[12] 'In 1860', we are told, 'Jowett was attempting to construct a *via media* between Atheism and Athanasianism'.[13] Younger men joined the movement, but they did not remain at Oxford. They went out with the Tractarian doctrines to the rural parishes as Keble and a number of others had done, but also to the industrial areas and the slums of the great cities; no longer were the working people neglected as Mr Gladstone would one day describe in his article. It was symbolic of this fresh and powerful trend that Dr Pusey with his own money built a fine church at Leeds (St Saviour's). Valiant work was done in areas where the Gospel had never been heard, and it still goes on.

The influence of the Oxford Movement has certainly permeated the Anglican communion at home and abroad, but there are dangers in this; during the last thirty years, perhaps for rather longer, the doctrine taught has in many cases tended to become more accommodating and less virile, through the acceptance of prevalent views that are not in accordance with Catholic teaching. As a recent and very well informed chronicle of Anglo-Catholicism in this century tells us, speaking of the years before the first World War: 'In those days the wearing of vestments meant Catholic teaching about the Mass and the confessional; in these days the guarantee is not so sure'.[14] The conviction

[12] Outram Everett, article in *The English Catholics, 1850-1950* (Burns and Oates, 1950)
[13] C. E. Mallet, *History of the University of Oxford*, Vol. II, p. 378
[14] Anselm Hughes, *The Rivers of the Flood* (Faith Press, 1961), pp. 34, 100. The author has for forty years been a member of an Anglican monastic community. With shrewdness and mordant wit he tells the story of twentieth-century Anglo-Catholicism from within.

seems to be lacking which in the nineteen-twenties packed
the Albert Hall at the great Anglo-Catholic Congresses,
and when the aged Lord Halifax, in spite of the weight of
years and failing eyesight, laboured so gallantly with his
friend Cardinal Mercier for a reconciliation between Rome
and Canterbury. As the same author has written: 'Though
he was the oldest of the old men, he was also the youngest
in spirit. Whom the Gods love, die young'. In the case of
Halifax we might well paraphrase: 'Who loves God, dies
young'.

The President of the first Anglo-Catholic Congress at the
Albert Hall in 1923 was Frank Weston, Bishop of Zanzibar,
a missionary of dynamic and indeed heroic character who
died in his diocese the following year at the age of fifty-three.
He seems to have had a prophetic sense of the dangers
lying ahead and his words to the Congress are most interesting to recall:

> We Anglo-Catholics have need to stiffen our backs,
> lest, with an eye to easy victory, we bow our heads in
> modern houses of Rimmon. We must not sacrifice
> Catholic truth to success. Nor must we lean on their
> patronage and sympathy who in their hearts are
> opposed to our ultimate aim. We are definitely called
> by God to end party spirit in the Anglican Communion
> and to lead British Christians to love the Catholic
> Church. We shall never do this by compromise of
> principle; brotherly charity does not require the
> betrayal of principle.[15]

An interesting letter recently appeared in the *Church
Times*, the leading Anglican weekly, which, written forty
years later, bears out Bishop Weston's warning:

> Conviction can only come from a spiritual life based
> on Christian discipline and fortified by Catholic
> worship and devotion. There is little conviction in the
> Church today, but plenty of opinions. . . . The fire
> has gone out of the Catholic movement, smothered

[15] H. Maynard Smith, *Frank Weston, Bishop of Zanzibar* (S.P.C.K.,
1926), p. 298

by a false catholicism. The Communion rails are full,
but confessionals are empty of priest and people. . . .
Liturgical experiments are exciting, but the doctrine of
the Sacrifice of the Mass is a point to be avoided. . . .
There are plenty of priests in vestments who only
possess opinions . . . are we to drown in the flood
of this self-opinionated, respectable religion of the
Englishman?[16]

I quote this letter from the industrial North of England
in no spirit of controversy, but because a number of letters
to the same effect have been appearing in the papers, both
secular and religious, and similar views have been expressed
in public speeches, showing the distress that is felt by many
loyal Anglicans at this time. Are the Catholic influences
in the Anglican Communion on the decline? We must hope
that once again they will show their remarkable powers of
recovery. Meanwhile, we shall do well to remember the
courageous example given by Lord Fisher, when as Archbishop of Canterbury he visited Pope John XXIII and the
valuable work which many Anglicans are doing in the
ecumenical cause.

During the last century and a half another striking change
has come over Anglicanism, for the insular Church of
England has become the world-wide Anglican Communion.
As Mr Paton has said in his book from which I have already
quoted:

That which began as simply the extension of the Church
of England, so that the jurisdiction of the Bishop of
London at one time included all North America and
India too, is now something quite different. The
Anglican Communion is not merely the Church of
England projected on a wide scale; it has an indepen-
dent life, and it is itself in a process of rapid
development.[17]

The change may be said to have started as far back as the
year 1784. In November of that year, in an upper room in an

[16] Letter from the Rev. A. G. Alderson, St Francis' Vicarage, South
Shields, Co. Durham (*Church Times*, 2 August 1963)
[17] Rev. David Paton, *Anglicans and Unity* (Mowbray, 1962), p. 7

Aberdeen back street, three bishops of the Scottish Episcopal Church did what their English colleagues had lacked the courage and initiative to do, and consecrated Samuel Seabury as bishop for the Anglican Church in North America, now known officially as the Protestant Episcopal Church. The process of expansion had begun and has since then continued with increasing momentum in a variety of ways, most of all through the labours and sacrifices of missionaries.

The Lambeth Conferences are a significant result of this transformation. They are held roughly every ten years and each time are attended by a larger number of bishops; the first of these was held in 1867 and the most recent in 1958. We have travelled far from the comfortable insularity of the eighteenth century as expressed by Mr Thwackum in *Tom Jones*: 'When I mention religion I mean the Christian religion; and not only the Christian religion but the Protestant religion; and not only the Protestant religion but the Church of England'. At the time of writing this essay a Pan-Anglican Conference was being held in Toronto, attended by clergy and laymen representing forty million Anglicans in seventy-three countries, and also by Catholic guests. The *Church Times* thus described the effect it gave: 'It was a moving and impressive sight to see these visible representatives from the ends of the earth, with their different coloured skins symbolizing the world-wide nature of the Anglican Communion'.[18] What would Mr Thwackum have said?!

Shortly after the first Lambeth Conference an event took place which, while it was brought about by Parliament, nevertheless gave an impetus to the centrifugal tendencies that were stirring in Anglicanism. The disestablishment of the Church of Ireland had about it a note of paradox, for while Keble's historic sermon was a protest against the proposal to abolish a number of Anglican bishoprics in Ireland, this was the work of one of his most loyal followers, Mr Gladstone. Even while he was an Anglican archdeacon, Manning had been convinced this should be done, and though to the end of his life he remained most friendly

[18] *Church Times*, 16 August 1963

towards Anglicans, he had been urging this measure on
Gladstone for some time, as essential for the pacification
of Ireland. On 24 March 1868 he wrote to him: 'It is no
question of religion but of political justice', and on 4
December of the same year, five days before Gladstone
became Prime Minister, he wrote: 'So you are at the end
men live for, but not, I believe, the end for which you have
lived. . . . I take much consolation from the fact that what
has made you so is a cause in which my whole heart can go
with you'.[19]

The Irish Church Bill was introduced by Gladstone on
1 March 1869, in a speech which his biographer, Morley,
described as the highest example of his oratory and, though
there was some bitter controversy at the time, it has in the
long run been greatly for the benefit of the Church of
Ireland; she is, in consequence, no longer regarded as the
representative of an alien power, but has, ever since Ireland
gained her independence, been accepted as a thoroughly Irish
body, and in her turn has with splendid loyalty accepted the
rule of the Dublin governments. Neither have the various
Irish governments which have held power since the Treaty
was signed ever departed from a consistently tolerant and
liberal religious policy, and the Church of Ireland fulfils a
valuable role in the life of the country; in her schools and
in all matters of this sort, she receives the same terms as the
Catholic Church.

It was unfortunate that at the time when the disestablishment took place the disputes over the adoption of
Catholic doctrines and practices in the Church of England
were flaring up. After the passing of the Bill a General
Convention was set up in Dublin to legislate for the Church
of Ireland in her new situation, and this met in February
1870; it consisted of her hierarchy, with clergy and laity in
the proportion of one to two. A number of alterations were
made in the Prayer Book, directed against the sacramental
teaching of the Anglo-Catholic school, and special 'Canons

[19] Shane Leslie, *Cardinal Manning, His Life and Labours*, new
and abridged edition (Clonmore and Reynolds, Dublin, 1953), pp.
86-7. See also Vincent McClelland, *Cardinal Manning, his Public Life
and Influence* (Oxford University Press, 1962), pp. 171-3.

Ecclesiastical' were passed to forbid 'Romish' practices. These were clearly the work of those who knew and understood very well what the disputes in England were about. These regulations are however faithfully obeyed by the clergy, rather in contrast to the policy of some in England who have produced a state of affairs that at times approaches liturgical chaos. A brilliant Church of Ireland clergyman, whose early death we all mourn, headed an article on his branch of the Anglican Communion with the words: '1870 Ecclesiastical Fashions, but a Law-abiding Clergy'.[20]

It is often imagined, but erroneously, that the Church of Ireland is a sternly Protestant body rejecting all that could connect it with the medieval Church. Certain facts support this view even to the extent of misleading Anglicans from other countries: the most popular service on Sunday morning is still that of Morning Prayer, an adaptation of the traditional Matins and Lauds with the addition of a sermon, rather than Holy Communion, which is an adaptation of the liturgy of the Mass, but which is certainly celebrated far more frequently than used to be the case. When celebrating Holy Communion the minister is definitely forbidden to wear the Eucharistic vestments, to use wafer bread or to mix water with the wine, and he is ordered by the Canons to stand at the north side of the Communion Table, on which no cross is allowed nor lighted candles except when these are required for the purpose of giving light. These liturgical practices are often mistaken as evidence of a general 'Low Church' mentality.

There is, in fact, a strong tradition of High Church doctrine in the Church of Ireland and the emphasis on continuity with the past, familiar to us all now from the celebrations of the Columban Year, goes right back to Archbishop Ussher, its first Caroline Primate who, so declared Dr Johnson, 'was the great luminary of the Irish Church, and a greater no Church could boast of, at least in modern times'. Today members of the Church of Ireland are sharply distinguished in many ways from their Protestant brethren, Presbyterians, Methodists and others. They are

[20] *Addresses and Papers of Michael Lloyd Ferrar* (S.P.C.K., 1962), p. 180

fully committed, as are indeed all members of the Anglican Communion, to the threefold order of bishops, priests and deacons, so fully that the views on episcopacy of the late Dr Gregg (Church of Ireland Archbishop of Armagh) would be slightly modified by such a distinguished Anglo-Catholic scholar as Dr Mascall.[21] They firmly hold that the ordained minister possesses a priesthood different in kind from that of the baptized laity and would strongly reject lay celebration of the Communion which the Methodists at least allow in principle. They also almost all hold the doctrine of Baptismal Regeneration, according to which Baptism signifies and effects a cleansing from sin and new birth to spiritual life through incorporation into Christ. Again, the belief in the Real Presence is widely held, though the doctrine of Transubstantiation is certainly rejected. Finally, as their sincere and truly religious interest in the Vatican Council and their fine tributes to the late Pope John XXIII amply testify, anti-Roman views are on the decline. May the Caroline High Church tradition[22] prosper and the hopes of the present distinguished and friendly Church of Ireland Primate, Dr George Simms, as expressed at the Toronto Congress, be fulfilled.[23]

[21] E. L. Mascall, *Corpus Christi* (London, 1953), p. 16
[22] Cf. F. R. Bolton, *The Caroline Tradition of the Church of Ireland* (London, 1958)
[23] *Irish Times*, 22 August 1963

Suggestions for Further Reading

F. Clark, S.J., 'Anglicanism', *Christian Unity*, ed. K. McNamara, Dublin: Furrow-Gill, 1962, pp. 57-73
*A. Hughes, *The Rivers of the Flood*, London: Faith Press, 1961
H. Johnson, *Anglicanism in Transition*, London: Longmans, 1938
*S. Neill, *Anglicanism*, Pelican Books A421, Harmondsworth: Penguin Books, 1958
*J. W. C. Wand, *The Anglican Communion*, London, 1948
    The Church Today, Pelican Books A471, Harmondsworth: Penguin Books, 1960
    Anglicanism in History and Today, London: Weidenfeld and Nicolson, 1961
*Anglican author

EPISCOPACY

Kevin McNamara

Among the Churches of the Reformation the Anglican Church is unrivalled in the emphasis it places on the office of bishop. Perhaps Catholics do not appreciate sufficiently the Anglican fidelity to the ideal of episcopacy and staunch defence of it in re-union discussions. In this meditation on Episcopacy and Unity, Catholics and Anglicans are invited to leave aside for the moment controversial questions and to meet together in prayerful reflection on the truth which they hold in common.

LET us begin by giving thanks to God for our joint witness to the indispensable role of episcopacy in the life of the Church. At the same time let us ask God's pardon for the imperfection of that witness, for the many sins, inadequacies and distortions which in the course of our history have obscured the full significance of the episcopate as Christ conceived and willed it. May God cause the episcopal ideal to shine out more clearly in our Churches. If it be his will, may he use our common witness to episcopacy to lead those Christians who, partly through our fault, have been led to abandon this doctrine, to look upon it in a new and more favourable light.

Let us now ask God to renew and deepen our understanding of the episcopacy in relation to Church unity. And as we pray for the light of his Holy Spirit, let us reflect on the message of St Ignatius of Antioch in his letters to the Churches of Asia Minor at the beginning of the second

century. 'It is proper for you', he writes, 'to act in agreement
with the mind of the bishop; and this you do. Certain it is
that your presbytery, which is a credit to its name, is a credit
to God; for it harmonizes with the bishop as completely
as the strings with a harp'.[1] Elsewhere he warns: 'Let us
take care not to oppose the bishop, that we may be sub-
missive to God'.[2] In this way there will be not only unity of
hearts in charity but also unity of minds in faith: 'Shun
division and bad doctrines. Where the shepherd is, there
you, the sheep, must follow'.[3] There will be unity, too, in
worship: 'Let that celebration of the Eucharist be considered
valid which is held under the bishop or anyone to whom
he has committed it'.[4]

The bishop, in other words, ensures visible unity because
he is Christ's representative. By his presence and his office
the bishop ensures that our unity will not be merely interior.
It will not be ill-defined, uncertain, fragile. Around the
bishop it will have visible and stable form. Let us pray that
God will restore a lively understanding of this unifying role
of the bishop to all Christians.

The bishop however does not stand alone. 'The episcopate
is one', says St Cyprian, the great third-century champion
of Church unity, 'and all bishops are partners in it with
joint and several responsibility. The Church also is one,
which is spread abroad far and wide. . . .'[5] Through communion with his fellow-bishops the bishop of the diocese
must preserve the unity of the Church of God. The one
Lord, the one faith, the one baptism, the one altar, the one
bread of which we partake and the one Body which we all
become—all these scriptural realities[6] find their full expression in the undivided unity of the universal Church. Let us
pray that God will speedily re-unite all Christians in such a
unity, presided over and guaranteed by a single, undivided
episcopate.

[1] *Ephes.* 4:1
[2] *Ephes.* 5:3
[3] *Philad.* 3:1
[4] *Smyrn.* 8:1
[5] *On the Unity of the Catholic Church*, c. 5
[6] Cf. *Ephes.* 4:5, *Hebr.* 13:10, 1 *Cor.* 10:17

A PRAYER

O Almighty God, who hast built thy Church upon the foundation of the Apostles and Prophets, Jesus Christ himself being the head corner-stone; grant us so to be joined together in unity of spirit by their doctrine, that we may be made an holy temple acceptable unto thee; through Jesus Christ our Lord. Amen.

Anglican Book of Common Prayer, Collect for Feast of Saint Simon and Saint Jude (28 October).

Suggestions for Spiritual Reading

Acts 15; 20:17-38; 1 & 2 *Timothy*; *Titus*

St Cyprian, *The Unity of the Catholic Church*, ed. M. Bévenot, S.J., Ancient Christian Writers, vol. 25, London: Longmans, Green, 1957

St Ignatius of Antioch, *Epistles*, ed. J. A. Kleist, S.J., ACW vol. 1, 1946

H. de Lubac, *The Splendour of the Church*, chapter 4, London: Sheed and Ward, 1956, pp. 87-113

H. Küng, 'The Petrine Office and the Apostolic Office', *The Living Church*, London: Sheed and Ward, 1963, pp. 333-69

J. Lécuyer, C.S.Sp., *What is a Priest?*, Faith and Fact Book 53, London: Burns and Oates, 1959

F. Van der Meer, *Augustine the Bishop*, London: Sheed and Ward, 1961

Suggestions for Hymn-singing

Psalm 71 (72) 'O God, Give your Judgment to the King', *Thirty Psalms*, pp. 38-9

Psalm 22 (23) 'My Shepherd is the Lord', *Twenty-Four Psalms*, pp. 10-11

'The Eternal Gifts of Christ the King', *Westminster Hymnal*, no. 124

PRESBYTERIANISM[1]

Denis Faul

To restore all things in Christ (*Eph.* 1:10): this was the motto of St Pius X and it sums up the vision that lies behind the Catholic Social movement and the calling of the Second Vatican Council. It is a call to bring creation, technology and above all man into conformity with the will of God so that the universe may say the Our Father: Hallowed be Thy name, Thy will be done on earth as it is in Heaven.

An attempt to get at the leading thought behind the Presbyterian Churches in Ireland leaves one with this same text and vision. It reads in *The New English Bible*:

> He has made known to us his hidden purpose—such was his will and pleasure determined beforehand in Christ—to be put into effect when the time was ripe: namely that the Universe, all in heaven and on earth, might be brought into a unity in Christ.

This vision of the sovereignty of God, of his universal dominion, his absolute right to rule and carry out his own will in all his dominions implies the seeing of God in every sphere of life and is very characteristic of Presbyterianism.

[1] I wish to thank ministers of the three Presbyterian Churches in Ireland for their help in composing this article and for their kindness and hospitality

Government and Worship

According to Presbyterianism all members of the Church share in the 'Royal Priesthood' of Christ and all therefore share in the ministry of implementing the sovereign will of God in and to the world. Everyone is not his own priest but is a priest to everyone of his fellow men.[2] However, certain men are set apart for a distinctive ministry within the Church. The pastors or ministers serve the Church in things spiritual especially in preaching the Word and administering the Sacrament of the Lord's Supper and Baptism. The ruling elders are representatives of the people elected to take part with ministers in the government of the Church.

The actual governing of the Church is done by four courts, the Kirk-Session, the Presbytery, Synod and Assembly. The Kirk-Session corresponds to the parish and consists of the minister who is ex-officio moderator and of the ruling elders who have been ordained by Presbytery in congregation. The Presbytery corresponds to the diocese and this court might have jurisdiction over twenty-five congregations or even more. A Synod would be a grouping of Presbyteries (corresponding to an archdiocesan province). An Assembly is the highest court of a country and has jurisdiction over the whole Church in its area. It consists of representative ministers and elders from the whole Church in roughly equal numbers. It is presided over by a Moderator elected annually.

In Irish Presbyterian churches a communion service is usually held about twice a year after a great deal of special

[2] Catholicism also fully accepts this doctrine of the priesthood of all the faithful and is endeavouring to give it clearer expression in the liturgy and life of the Church. In Catholicism however the ordained minister, the priest, is considered to receive from God through the sacrament of orders, a further, special participation in the priesthood of Christ which enables him to do what the ordinary faithful cannot. Protestantism, on the other hand, tends to consider all, both ministers and people, as participating equally in the priesthood of Christ: ordination is a non-sacramental rite by which the Church authorizes certain persons to perform functions which belong to the whole Body. Cf. J. Lécuyer, C.S.Sp., *What is a Priest?*, Faith and Fact Book no. 53

preparation. It is now becoming common however in cities
and towns to hold a communion service four or six times
in the year. Many of the prayers in this communion service
are paraphrases from the canon of the Mass. We shall see
later what doctrine about the Eucharist Presbyterians hold.

The ordinary service in Presbyterian churches on Sunday
mornings and evenings consists of prayers, bible-readings,
singing and sermon, and usually lasts about an hour. The
congregational singing is the most prominent feature of the
service. They choose from versions of the 150 psalms along
with 67 paraphrases of Scripture passages and about 700
hymns. The centrepiece of the service is the sermon, the
proclamation of God's Word, which is written and prepared with a very deep sense of its part in the saving purpose
of God.

History and Divisions

Due to historical reasons there are three Presbyterian
Churches in Ireland. The principal one is the Irish Presbyterian Church which, with its 400,000 members served by
470 ministers, is fifty times larger than either of the others
and naturally possesses a great deal more influence in
public life. The other two are the Non-Subscribing Presbyterian Church and the Reformed Presbyterian Church each
of which has about 7,000 members.[3]

The formation of the first Presbytery in Ireland came in
1642 with the landing of the Scottish army of General
Munroe (defeated in 1646 at Benburb by Eoghan Ruadh
O'Neill). Cromwell did not like the Irish Presbyterians and
attempted to interfere with their Church life, but they found
themselves in a much worse position when Charles II
restored the Church of Ireland as the established religion
of the country. He did grant the small sum of £600 per

[3] The Irish Presbyterian Church has publicly dissociated itself (in
October 1962) from the Paisleyites who call themselves the Free
Presbyterian Church of Ulster but whose founder was not ordained by
the Irish Presbyterian Church. The other two Presbyterian Churches
likewise dissociate themselves from the Paisleyites

year to their funds—the first *Regium Donum*—in 1672 but by his death in 1684 persecution of Presbyterians was being encouraged. The arrival of James II on the throne brought immediate relief for he suspended the penal laws against Catholics and Dissenters. However, fear of losing religious liberty and of losing their relative positions of ascendency drove Episcopalians and Presbyterians together against James who was favouring Catholics. The Treaty of Limerick however proved a boomerang to the Presbyterians for the Church of Ireland took up a dominant position and persecuted Catholics and Dissenters alike.

During this century divisions in Presbyterianism appeared in Ireland. The Reformed Presbyterian Church was formed from Scottish roots in 1763, and reorganized in 1792. In the early years of the eighteenth century an attempt was made by the Synod of Ulster to impose subscription to the Westminster Confession of Faith of 1644 as a condition of taking up a benefice, but a number of zealous ministers centred around Belfast (The Belfast Society) refused to accept this condition.

The history of Presbyterianism in Ireland in the eighteenth century was a struggle for religious liberty in which they tried to help their downtrodden Catholic neighbours. Presbyterian agitation and the Volunteers brought about the Religious Relief Acts of 1781 and 1793 and their attitude to their Catholic neighbours at this time is summed up in a declaration of the Synod of Ulster of 1793 in support of the Catholic claims:

> That impressed with that goodwill and brotherly love which is inculcated by their religion towards good men of all religious denominations and trusting that this spirit will always be cherished by the people under their care, they congratulate their Roman Catholic countrymen on their being restored to the privileges of the constitution, that the time may never more return when religious distinctions shall be used as a pretext for disturbing society, or arming man against his neighbour—that intolerance of every kind may be trodden under foot; and every good subject shall be equally cherished and protected by the State.

One hopes that with the increase of goodwill these words shall soon be true of Northern Ireland.

The 1798 rebellion in the North was largely led and fought by Presbyterians and names like Henry Joy McCracken, William Orr, Jemmie Hope and the Rev. James Porter of Greyabbey are immortal in Irish history. Many others played a notable part in the land troubles of the nineteenth century and the Rev. J. B. Armour of Ballymoney is remembered as a far-seeing thinker on the Home Rule question and one who worked unceasingly to promote good relations among all creeds and classes in a truly Christian way.

Irish Presbyterian Church

The doctrine of the Irish Presbyterian Church might be described as mitigated Calvinism with an evangelical flavour. If one takes Justification by faith alone and Predestination by the divine foreknowledge regardless of good works as the distinctive Calvinist doctrines, Irish Presbyterians maintain the position of the Reformer on Justification. They hold that the word means 'being acquitted' or 'made right' with God rather than 'being made just'. Similarly they reject the idea of merit understood as implying that sinful man can of himself alone make any real positive contribution towards his salvation.[4] The doctrine of absolute predestination is not however held by Irish Presbyterians with the same force as formerly. In their view the initiative in man's salvation comes from God and Christ's election or approval of a man reaches its climax when a man knows himself to be claimed by Christ, but at the end God will judge him by his works and by the way he responded to the call of Christ and the

[4] A leading modern Presbyterian theologian, T. F. Torrance, gives an excellent presentation of their view on grace in his essay "Justification" in *Christianity Divided* (ed. D. J. Callahan, H. A. Oberman, D. J. O'Hanlon; Sheed and Ward, London, 1962), pp. 283-303. This same volume (pp. 309-33) contains a companion article on the same topic contributed by the Catholic theologian Hans Küng, and entitled 'Justification and Sanctification according to the New Testament'.

attraction of Christ. A majority of Presbyterians do not claim to be converted (or 'saved') at a particular day and date by an intense religious experience, although this may sometimes happen.

The Church, they hold, is the chosen instrument for the building of the Kingdom of God on earth, to bring all things into conformity with the will of God. It is both visible and invisible and membership of it is the ordinary means of salvation. The marks by which the true Church can be known are, firstly, the true preaching of the Word of God, secondly, the right administration of the sacraments of Christ Jesus, thirdly, ecclesiastical discipline rightly administered. The ordinary act of worship is the service on Sundays culminating a few times a year in the Communion service. This whole service, according to Presbyterian belief, is used by Christ to make the people realize his presence; the Elements in the service are the points which most effectively make this presence felt. It is believed that there is the real presence of a spiritual being along with the Elements of bread and wine, especially at the moment of reception.

But Christ is also present in the total act of worship and the preaching of the Word, which takes primary place every Sunday, is considered to be the most important point of contact with the presence of Christ. As the Scriptures are explained and borne witness to, the hearers realize that God is speaking to them and the Word comes alive through the Holy Spirit influencing the hearers. While the Bible for Presbyterians is the supreme authority in doctrine and Church tradition has only secondary value, yet the Word of God which teaches is something more than the written words of Holy Scripture; it is the written message interpreted by the inner persuasion of the Holy Spirit— aptly called the Spirit-given Word.

In its moral teaching the Irish Presbyterian Church allows divorce on two grounds, adultery and long desertion, but only the innocent party is re-married in church. Marriage is not a sacrament, the only two being Baptism and the Lord's Supper. Human life is held sacred and hence a very rigorous attitude is taken against abortion and euthanasia, following closely the civil law of Britain. There are differences of opinion about contraception, but most authorities believe it can be used conscientiously. Catholics can see at once that whereas one can discuss terminology and theology in dogmatic matters with a certain amiable aloofness, moral matters bring denominational differences out sharply into the realm of everyday living. But it clears the air to know each other's point of view and one must pay tribute to some scholarly efforts being made by Presbyterian medical men to appreciate Catholic teaching on medical ethics.[5]

The necessity of religious education in weekday schools (as distinct from Sunday Schools where much excellent work is done) is insisted upon by Presbyterians in Northern Ireland. But one feels that they allowed the initiative to pass from their Church when they transferred their schools to State control in the twenties. A certain amount of legislation has been secured to ensure that religious instruction of a non-denominational type, Bible-reading in fact, can be given in State schools, but this is a poor substitute, one feels, for a theological system based on the Bible and the theological insights of John Calvin. The training of youth in their religion is a very real problem for the Presbyterian Church and one to which they are giving considerable attention.[6]

Obedience to civil law is taught and passive resistance permitted only when the State makes unjust demands; armed rebellion is permitted only as a last resort. It is considered to be the duty of the Church to advise the State on legislation and to criticize the laws but only if they appear contrary to the revealed will of God.

Presbyterianism fears what it considers to be the totalitarian nature of the Catholic religion. Presbyterians object to the authoritarian note in Catholic teaching. They reject the Pope as visible head of the Church, holding Christ to be sole head. They also reject the doctrine that apostolic succession is of the essence of the Church and hence reject

[5] Notably by H. I. McClure of Queen's University, Belfast. Cf. *The Ulster Medical Journal*, November 1954, p. 57, on Difficult Childbirth; *Biblical Theology*, September 1958; January 1959 on Human Artificial Insemination

[6] Cf. *Presbyterian Herald*, July-August 1963, pp. 212, 216, 218-220

episcopacy in the full Catholic sense.[7] They express fears of the Catholic Church in a dominant position. In common with Catholics they have great zeal for the glory of God and the doing of his will on earth, an independence of State control in their government, love of the Bible, interest in foreign missions and a vast scheme of works of charity.

A glance through the monthly journal, the *Presbyterian Herald*, will show quickly the support given to these many enterprises by the people, a practical proof of the vitality of their belief. Likewise they have a fairly satisfactory supply of vocations to their two theological colleges: Assembly's College, Belfast (30 students in 1963) and Magee College, Derry (11 students in 1963), and they do not need to obtain many from Scotland, the motherland of Irish Presbyterianism. They have foreign missions in Africa, Jamaica and India and these are very well supported by their people. These indications plus the steady Sunday church attendance point to a vigorous Church life and help to allay rumours of growing indifference, especially among the young.

The Non-Subscribing Presbyterian Church of Ireland

This Church is concerned more with moral and ethical excellence than with precision of dogma. The main principles of its teaching are simple and clear and are expressed even in the design of their churches. Where Catholics are accustomed to see the altar, they have the pulpit, according to the ancient Presbyterian tradition emphasizing the primacy of the Word and its function of helping the people to make

[7] In the recent Anglican-Presbyterian conversations which failed but are to be resumed shortly: 'On the Presbyterian side there was a willingness to consider the functions of a bishop, as they are recognized by the Anglican Communion, so long as the office was duly integrated with the Presbytery and the whole Church. The concept of a presiding "Bishop in Presbytery" exercising functions in relation to ordination and pastoral oversight as a Father-in-God to ministers and congregations with authority given to him by consecration at the hands of bishops as well as with the authority of the collective Presbytery appeared to be a possible modification of the Presbyterian polity'. *Relations between Anglican and Presbyterian Churches* (London, 1958), p. 12

correct judgments in their everyday life. The Communion
service is held every six months, the communicants seated
at tables placed in the aisles. In taking the Elements of
bread and wine the Presbyterian communicant endeavours
to take the life of Christ into himself and go out to live it
in the world among his fellow-men. The Communion is
prepared for with great seriousness and its community and
social aspects are stressed; it is the acting-out of the faith
declared in the sermon. The presence of Christ is felt not
only in the reception of the Elements but in the whole
service, especially in the preaching of the Word. The Bible
is the Rule of Faith and Duty and the Word is the Bible
explained to help the hearers to make informed private
judgments; the Word and the Church cannot be separated.

Among the Non-Subscribers there is no official view on
divorce, but the question does not arise as in this group the
divorce rate is nil. The method of birth control is a matter
for the individual to use his personal responsibility guided
by his worship. And the same solution would be given to
doctors faced with serious problems in medical ethics,
namely that they must use their informed moral judgment
in the discharge of their profession.

Non-Subscribing Presbyterians are against segregation
in education, which they regard as an activity embracing
the whole community. They leave education to the educa-
tionalists as their personal responsibility and do not feel
any need for their own schools or teachers of their own
denomination. This is chiefly because of their broad liberal
view of other Christian religions: their pulpits are open to
any Christian minister and they do not seek to impose a
theology on any member of their Church. They are free to
search the Bible for divine truth and their doctrine of
the Blessed Trinity is imprecise. One result of this
liberal attitude has been that they have always preached and
fought for tolerance and freedom of worship for themselves
and for other Churches. They consider themselves as owing
the State allegiance in all morally lawful matters but having
the right and duty to oppose it if it violates Christian
principles; traditionally they have espoused the cause of the
exploited and the underdog. Sincerity and charity make

them opposed to any kind of pretentiousness, cant or hypocrisy in religion.

Their feelings towards the Catholic Church have traditionally been benevolent. They feel that they would resent any traces of a paternalistic approach which might restrict the liberal atmosphere they desire for religious and civil development. Minority views might not be effective in a Catholic atmosphere and they are prepared to fight for the liberty that they love. They admire the social teachings of the Popes but they feel they are not being implemented very efficiently by the Catholic Church and that in fact they might be realized more quickly and effectively in a Protestant ethos.

One senses a unity and vitality—to be seen for one thing in their strong financial support—in this group of thirty-four congregations. One might hardly expect this considering the very liberal and free nature of their teaching, but their strength may be attributed to the primacy of charity, neighbourliness and good works in their life and to a vivid sense of a colourful historical past.

The Reformed Presbyterian Church of Ireland

After the Revolution settlement of 1690 which they refused to accept, the Covenanters existed in Scotland until 1743 without any organized Church, keeping their faith alive by group or society meetings. During these years some small groups had come over to the North of Ireland in the Scottish emigrations and they settled in Antrim, Derry and Down. In 1757 a minister, William Martin, was set over them and when a second minister was appointed in 1763 they formed a Presbytery. There was one Presbytery until 1811; then they divided and made a Synod. They have just completed two centuries of organized existence.

These Reformed Presbyterians accept the Presbyterian form of government with the small difference that the Kirk-Session has power to ordain Elders. They are called Covenanters because they stand by the National Covenant of 1638 and the Solemn League and Covenant of 1643, both of which were theocratic. They hold that Christ should be King and Lord in the constitution and administration of the nation: his Word should be the guide of the nation: Christian qualifications are necessary for legislators. Since these qualities are lacking in Britain's law and constitution, members of this Church do not vote, stand for Parliament or take the oath of allegiance, declaring that loyalty to Christ must take precedence over allegiance to Crown and constitution. They are opposed to the Erastian principle of Church government, but keep all civil laws and vote in local elections. They accept the Constitution of the Republic as it recognizes God's overlordship in its preamble.

In contrast to the Non-Subscribing Church, where the emphasis was on moral or ethical doctrine, the emphasis in the Reformed Presbyterian Church is on dogmatic teaching and it keeps close to the teaching of Calvin in doctrine and to John Knox in its pastoral outlook.

Marriage for the Reformed [Presbyterian Church] is not a sacrament but a serious ordinance of God and divorce is allowed only on the grounds of adultery or irremediable desertion. Birth control is not allowed except by abstinence and self-control or the use of periodic continence (safe period). It is emphasized that the purpose of marriage is the procreation of children: if circumstances prove difficult, then self-control must be used. Abortion and euthanasia are regarded as murder, and in compassionate cases (such as the widowed mother of ten dying in a difficult child-birth, a nonagenarian dying of incurable cancer in insanitary conditions or the thalidomide baby) they will say 'these things happen within the permissive will of God: they are mysterious to us, but they do not give grounds of sympathy or compassion for going against the known Will of God, which is "Thou shalt not kill" '.

In education the Reformed Presbyterian Church would have liked to preserve John Knox's idea of the Church and the Church school in each parish, but that was not possible in the North after 1922. Now they use Sunday schools and youth classes and ensure the proper teaching of the Bible in day schools, but they would like to control their own schools and appoint teachers of their own denomination.

The vitality of this small group of Irish Presbyterians is proved by very good Church attendance, by an adequate supply of vocations to their Theological College in Belfast, and by their activity on the foreign missions which are always to the Mohammedans, formerly in Syria, now in the Lebanon and Ethiopia. Another proof of vitality is the fact that the people furnish the full financial support for their clergy. True to their principles they never accepted the *Regium Donum* or the salary offered by the government and today they are generously supported by a weekly free-will offering from the people and also from endowments left in wills to the Church. Special collections for their missionary enterprises are eagerly subscribed to.

Whatever suspicion of Catholicism exists is anti-papal rather than anti-Catholic, if one accepts this as a factual and not a doctrinal distinction, i.e. their horror of Erastianism makes them opposed to any visible human head of the Church. They find Mariology difficult to understand. They cultivate friendship and good relations with Catholics. They admire the consistency and clarity of Catholic teaching, our authority, our independence of the State, our main-tenance of our own schools and our thoroughness in instructing the young.

The Presbyterian Church in Ireland met for the first session of the 1963 General Assembly on 3 June at 7 p.m. At 8.50 Pope John XXIII died. The newly-elected Moderator, Dr W. A. Montgomery, immediately paid a warm and sincere tribute to the late Pope as follows:

> The death of Pope John is matter for sincere regret to all Christian people. In him the graces of a Christian have been made apparent to all. By his personal attitude it has been made clear that without abatement of principle men of all Churches can share a common understanding of Christian charity and enjoy a friendly interchange of ideas. He has taken a leading part in the counsels of men concerning matters of social and political importance, and his recent lead concerning world peace has given new hope to the people of all lands. The world is poorer for his passing.

The congregation then stood for a moment in silence.

The sequel to this tribute was dramatic. On the following day the Rev. Warren Porter, sincerely speaking for a more old-fashioned view of Christian relations than that of the majority of his confrères, asked that the tribute be recorded in the minutes as only the personal opinion of Dr Montgomery and not as the opinion of the Assembly and he wished to dissociate himself from it. The Clerk of the General Assembly, Dr A. G. Gailey, replied that he was as staunch a Presbyterian as Mr Porter but one aspect of his Presbyterianism was not churlishness; this remark was greeted with the applause of the Assembly.

At the 1963 General Assembly the subject of ecumenical relations was discussed by Very Rev. Dr J. C. Breakey, a former Moderator. He suggested that when a hand was stretched out from the Roman Catholic Church they must grasp it in a spirit of Christian faith and love:

> What a change might take place in Ireland were a better spirit to obtain between our Churches [he declared]. Too long we in Ireland have stressed the evils of the Roman Catholic faith. Is it not time we had a look at the other side? What has been said by the late Pope John during his lifetime indicated a softening of the attitude of the Roman Church towards the Protestant Churches. There are those who would refuse to have any contact with Rome or even with any Church until that Church is prepared to accept our principles and admit that it is wrong and we are right. What folly! Surely that is the way to stultify from the outset any hope of progress. The desire to dominate is found not only on the Roman side, but at times on the Protestant side. Domination will not get us anywhere.[8]

A similar statement was made by the Rev. Dr H. J. McLachlan, Moderator of the Non-Subscribing Presbyterian Church, in accordance with the tradition of that

[8] *Irish Times*, 7 June 1963

Church for moral and ethical Christianity rather than dogmatic:

> We need to get out of the dangerous cul-de-sac of ecclesiastical complacency and affirm our unity with the life of the other Churches in the twentieth century and, not least, our concern with the tide of public affairs which is sweeping around us. Is it not high time that the Christian Churches, and notably our own, should speak out against religious bigotry and racial and national intolerance, wherever they are found? We have moved out of a theological age when men were interested in religious dogmas and logomachies into an age when humanity and charity are of paramount importance. The impression that Pope John has made upon mankind was due entirely to his deep humanity and his essential charity. These are the factors that more and more influence men today and I could wish that our Churches would play a more active part in the work of creating more unity among men and breaking down the divisions that cause so much harm and distress.[9]

Charity is indeed the great Christian virtue. We Catholics still remain deeply divided from our Presbyterian brethren on certain essential matters of the Christian faith, notably on the need for apostolic succession, on the nature of the priesthood, on the meaning of the Eucharist as sacrament and sacrifice. And truth too has its imperious claims. But if the truth is to be seen and done it will be seen and done in charity and mutual love.

[9] *Belfast Telegraph*, 12 June 1963

Suggestions for Further Reading

*J. M. Barkley, *Presbyterianism*, Belfast: The Publication Board of the General Assembly of the Presbyterian Church in Ireland, 1958

L. Bouyer, *The Spirit and Forms of Protestantism*, London: The Harvill Press, 1956

*R. McAfee Brown, *The Spirit of Protestantism*, Oxford University Press, 1961

L. Cristiani and *J. Rilliet, *Catholics and Protestants*, London: Sands, 1960

A. Dulles, S.J., *A Testimonial to Grace*, New York: Sheed and Ward, 1952

*J., McNeill, *The History and Character of Calvinism*, Oxford University Press, 1957

S. O'Riordan, C.SS.R., 'Protestants in Ireland', *The Furrow* 8 (1958), pp. 90-101
   'Catholic-Protestant Relations in Ireland', ibid., 12 (1961), pp. 15-20

*J. K. S. Reid, *Presbyterians and Unity*, Star Books on Reunion, London: Mowbray, 1962

*A.-M. Schmidt, *Calvin and the Calvinistic Tradition*, Men of Wisdom Books, London: Longmans, 1960

R. Walls, *The One True Kirk*, London: Burns and Oates, 1960

*Presbyterian author

GRACE

Wilfrid Harrington

'FOR the law was given through Moses; grace and truth came through Jesus Christ', St John tells us (1:17). But he speaks of fulfilment and already grace was present, as a promise and as a hope. God is ever lavish with his gifts, always mercifully forgiving: 'Yahweh, a God merciful and gracious, slow to anger and abounding in steadfast love and faithfulness' (*Exod.* 34:6). The great proof of God's generosity was his choice of Israel, a choice not prompted by anything in the people, an utterly free choice, the outcome of his love (*Deut.* 7:7 f.).

The generous grace of God was not poured out blindly; its end was the covenant, the alliance of his people with their God; it called forth a response of thanksgiving and love. But the Old Testament covenants, with Noah, with Abraham and with Moses did not lead to fulfilment, and the prophets looked to something different, to another covenant: the forgiveness of sin, a new law, a new heart, a new breath of the Spirit (*Jer.* 31:31-34; *Ezek.* 36:26; *Ps.* 50:10-14).

The coming of Jesus Christ was the supreme manifestation of God's generosity and the assurance of its range: 'He who did not spare his own Son but gave him up for us all, will he not also give us all things with him?' (*Rom.* 8:32). Grace is a free gift of God, not a reward earned by our own efforts (*Rom.* 4:4; 11:16), and if faith can enable us to perceive this gift, faith itself is a fruit of grace (*Eph.* 2:8). But God sent his Son to save the world (*John* 3:16

ff.); grace is redeeming grace. It is God's saving commerce with men, it is God at work (2 *Cor.* 12:9; 1 *Cor.* 15:10). God's grace not only brings salvation, it is salvation.

For us men the comforting truth is that this grace of God is the grace of God-made-Man, and to speak of grace is to speak of Christ. Grace is 'the grace that is in Christ Jesus' (2 *Tim.* 2:1), it is 'the grace of the one man Jesus Christ, (*Rom.* 5:15). This must be so since grace has come through him (*John* 1:17) and the promise of the Old Law was 'the grace which he gave us in Christ ages ago' (2 *Tim.* 1:9). If grace is saving grace it is because 'in him we have redemption through his blood, the forgiveness of our sins' (*Eph.* 1:7). If we are justified by faith, it is by faith in Christ (*Rom.* 5:1 f.). And those whom God has so justified he has predestined to bear the family likeness of his Son, that he might be the eldest of a family of many brothers (*Rom.* 8:29). As head of this family of God Christ prayed—it was his last prayer—that all whom the Father had given him should become perfectly one (*John* 17:20-23).

We Catholics might take a step towards that longed-for unity if we were to realize that our Presbyterian brethren can teach us, many of us, a deeper appreciation of the absolute necessity and utter freedom of grace; for it does happen that our outlook is sometimes clouded by an uncertain grasp of merit and its place. We should pray that Presbyterians, in their turn, may come to recognize that authentic Catholic doctrine is not a travesty of New Testament teaching. At very least we can, all of us, strive that Christ our Lord may become more surely the centre of our thought and of our life—that from his fullness we may receive grace upon grace (*John* 1:16).

A PRAYER

Lord we pray thee let our doings be prompted by thy inspirations and furthered by thy help, so that every prayer and work of ours may begin from thee, and through thee be accomplished.

From the Litany of the Saints in the Roman Missal.

Suggestions for Spiritual Reading

Deuteronomy 6, 8; *Psalms* 35, 50, 61; *Isaiah* 54-5; *Jeremiah* 31:31-4; *Ezekiel* 36:22-32; *Hosea* 11:1-9; *John* 15:1-11; 1 *John* 5:11 f.; *Romans* 8:31-9; *Ephesians* 1-2

C. Howell, S.J., *The Work of our Redemption,* Oxford: The Catholic Social Guild, 1962, pp. 17-24

B. Jarret, O.P., *The Abiding Presence of the Holy Ghost,* London: Burns, Oates and Washbourne, 1935, pp. 74-6

H. Küng, 'Justification and Sanctification, according to the New Testament', *Christianity Divided,* ed. D. J. Callahan, H. A. Oberman, D. J. O'Hanlon, London: Sheed and Ward, 1962, pp. 283-303

C. Marmion, O.S.B., *Christ the Life of the Soul,* London: Sands, 1925, pp. 58-91

F. J. Sheed, *Theology and Sanity,* London: Sheed and Ward, 1948, pp. 295-308

Suggestions for Hymn-singing

Magnificat, *Twenty-Four Psalms,* pp. 57-9

Psalm 126 (127) 'If the Lord does not Build the House', ibid., pp. 48-9

Psalm 130 (131) 'O Lord my Heart is not Proud', *Thirty Psalms and Two Canticles,* London: The Grail, 1957, p. 21

Psalm 26 (27) 'The Lord is my Light and my Help', ibid., pp. 18-20

'Veni Sancte Spiritus' (Sequence of the Mass for Pentecost)

'Hail Redeemer King Divine', *Westminster Hymnal,* no. 100

THE PEOPLE CALLED METHODISTS

Leon Ó Broin

A WRITER in *Studies* recently said that 'the best of the
Protestant Anglo-Irish tradition has much to offer us in its
concern for civic responsibilities, for the virtues of truth-
fulness, honesty and hard work, and for its concern for the
appreciation and cultivation of art and letters. Our national
ideal would be a poor one without these qualities'.[1] He was
not thinking specifically of Methodists but they, more than
any other section of Irish Protestants, exemplify the truth
of the first part of the statement. They have no particular
achievements to their credit in the cultural sphere,[2] but in
other respects they are just what the writer says. They stand
out in the community as men and women who are indus-
trious, conscientious and truthful. They have built up for
themselves a reputation for integrity in business and this
has made them a solid influential element whom Catholics
admire. And as might be expected, their virtues have also
brought them financial rewards. 'Seek ye first the kingdom
of God and his justice and all these things shall be added
unto you'.

The evolution of the Methodists is a most interesting
story. They came originally from the so-called working class
or from the ranks of small shopkeepers. They learned from
the pursuit of holiness and from its accompanying asceticism

[1] R. Burke Savage, S.J., *Studies* 52 (Summer 1963), p. 118
[2] Their well-known educational establishments however deserve
mention: Wesley College, Dublin; Methodist College, Belfast; Gurteen
Agricultural College in Tipperary which has pioneered this kind of
work among Irish Protestants.

love of the natural virtues which they practised in a rather strict, 'puritanical' way, emphasizing sabbatarianism, frugality and a hatred of drink and gambling. These habits have persisted among them. Methodists in Ireland today are as much identified with total abstinence as are Pioneers and they have a holy horror of race meetings and sweepstakes. The story is told of one of their ministers who was given a present of a Sweep ticket and spent the weeks before the draw praying that he would not draw a horse. He must have been the only man who ever did. There was a time too when investment was regarded by them as a form of gambling. So much so that they sold Great Southern Railway shares when somebody pointed out that the company was drawing some of its profits from the bars on the railway stations. The trouble, as we Catholics know too well, is the danger of undue or misplaced emphasis. In Belfast, among Methodists and other Protestants, a Sabbath Day is kept (or used to be kept) as if it were the central theme of the Gospel. Catholic Dublin, on the other hand, tends to be careless about it.

When I think of Methodists a formal Civil Service boss of mine, Arthur D. Codling, comes into my mind. He was English, very much so, and politically a Liberal Radical with a strong sense of the need to undo the evils of English rule in Ireland. It was this, I believe, that brought him to Ireland in the first instance where, first as a specialist in housing in the Local Government Board, and later as an all-purposes senior official in the Department of Finance he won the highest reputation for industry, probity and kindliness. He arrived at his office early in the morning, worked unremittingly a long day, and such free time as he had in the evenings, apart from rose-growing, he devoted to his Church. He was a lay-preacher—I can almost see the fastidious preparation that would go into one of his sermons —and a prop of the Stranger's Friend Society ('I was a stranger and you took me in'), visiting the poor of all denominations in their homes like a brother of the Society of Saint Vincent de Paul. He would have fitted splendidly into the original group in Oxford to whom the term Methodists was first applied derisively.

This group consisted of the friends of Charles Wesley. They had organized themselves in 1729 as a Holy Club, meeting regularly to read the Bible and pray together, and attending a Communion service once a week. This was unusual; their very *methodical* approach to the practice of religion drew attention to them. John, Charles's brother, joined them a little later and became their leader. Besides the natural gifts that singled him out for this role he was an ordained minister of the Church of England and the son of one. But the effective originator of the revival was not John Wesley but another member of the Club, George Whitefield, who had discovered he was the possessor of quite extraordinary oratorical powers and who appealed urgently to Wesley to help him with the 'field-preaching' on which he had almost too successfully embarked.

Both these men had recently undergone similar 'conversions'. Whitefield had the spirit of mourning taken from him and in its place he knew what it was to rejoice in God his Saviour. Wesley, who had been unsure and scrupulously introspective, felt his heart strangely warmed. ('I felt I did trust in Christ, Christ alone, for salvation; and an *assurance* was given me that he had taken away my sins, even mine, and saved me from the law of sin and death'.) The psychological effect of these 'new births' supplied the driving power for a revival which spread rapidly through the British Isles as they were then called, particularly in the expanding industrial areas where the Established Church had made little or no impact. Everywhere the converts and 'seekers' were grouped together in Societies and, as these became too large for effective fellowship, in Classes for whom lay-preachers and Leaders provided continuous guidance and pastoral oversight. The whole 'Connexion' was linked together by John Wesley's organizing genius, while Charles provided in his hymns, with tunes found here, there and everywhere, both inspiration and a solid grounding in the faith as the brothers knew it. 'Why should the devil have all the good tunes?' The tunes have been changed since then but the words continue to be sung and constitute not only valuable meditation material but also a chief source of Methodist belief. Indeed, an experienced Methodist minister has humourously confessed to me that the singing often does more good than the preaching.

At an early stage Churchmen began to frown on these developments and the emphasis the Methodist preachers laid on 'experience' or the working of the Holy Spirit in the souls of individuals. What affected them mainly, understandably, were the strange stories that reached them from the revival meetings of men and women discovering their sinful state and falling trembling and shrieking to the ground where they lay until the prayers offered for them had brought them joy and tranquillity. Wesley was warned away from the parish pulpits, his people were spoken of as 'nasty and numerous vermin', but the more he was despised and frustrated the more his work prospered. He was convinced he was responding to divine prompting in trying to revive the religious spirit of the Church. In 'spreading Scriptural holiness throughout the land' he could not see he was doing anything inconsistent with the doctrines and practices of the Church of England for which he had a holy regard, and this he manifested by breaking with Whitefield and others when they diverged from Anglican teaching. He looked upon such trouble as he had with the Church as being due not to the newness of what he said but to the zeal with which he said it, and to the distinction that he and his friends inferentially drew between the profession of godliness and the enjoyment of the power it conferred on the clergy. The Classes that came into being as a result of his exertions could read the Bible and pray together and exchange religious experiences, but Wesley always counselled them to attend the formal services in the parish churches. His idea was that they were to be little groups of people, evangelical societies or communities, within the Church of England, keeping the religious spirit alive; but the pastors usually saw them as a noisy hymn-singing crowd who had for the most part never been seen in church before and who at any moment might be led by their enthusiasm into dangerous paths. The Church therefore criticized the Methodists and made difficulties for them and would have liked to have seen the end of them, but never actually went so far as to condemn them formally; and it is probable that these same Methodists would have been welcomed and esteemed in the circumstances of later times. 'But the Anglican Church of that day was not the Church of today: had it been alive then as it is now the story would doubtless have been a very different one. The Methodists . . . grew more and more apart from the unfriendly Church of England, which made no attempt whatsoever to keep them, and indeed often tried to suppress them, until a separation became inevitable'.[3]

It was Wesley himself, however, who precipitated the break. This was in 1784 when at the age of 81 he made two extraordinary moves under the pressure of what has been called 'evangelical necessity'. Seeing death not far off, and no outstanding person among his followers to take over from him, he appointed by deed poll a Conference of a hundred men (a 'Legal Hundred') to succeed him and with power to reproduce their number. This in effect was setting up the 'Connexion' of Methodist Societies as a separate Church. In the same year and without consulting this body, he began the practice of ordaining preachers, and consecrating superintendents to take the place of bishops when he could get nobody else to do it. His brother bitterly criticized this action; for him ordination was separation. But John would not admit this and continued to argue against separation for the few years that were left to him. He died in 1791 and shortly afterwards the Conference redressed the situation by deciding that the ordination of preachers should not take place by the laying on of hands but 'by reception into full connexion' with the Conference by a formal vote. 'It was thought by those who did not want to break all links with the Church of England that subsequent re-union would be easier if Methodist preachers had not had hands laid on them'.[4] This decision remained operative until 1836. The Rev. Rupert E. Davies who has written a splendid account of Methodism in a book of that title ends his account of the separation of the Methodists from the Church of England by saying that the various

[3] S. B. Frost, *The Pattern of Methodism*, London, 1948, p. 81
[4] R. E. Davies, *Methodism*, Penguin Books, 1963, p. 130

degrees of blame incurred must be left to the decision of the Last Judgment:

> Meanwhile it can fairly be said that the choice facing first of all John Wesley, and after his death, the Methodist Conference, was this: is the work of spreading Scriptural holiness assigned by God to the Methodists, to be continued, in defiance of the laws of the Church of England, at the cost in the last resort of separation from her? Or are her laws to be kept and separation avoided, at the cost of stopping this work of God? This was a harsh dilemma, and the first request of those who wish to heal the breach between Anglicans and Methodists is that they should recognize how harsh it was.[5]

After the Wesleys had passed from the scene, various disagreements arose over matters of Church government, and these gave rise to many offshoots from the parent stem. Indeed the fragmentation was on such a scale that the development of Methodism has been described as the saddest tale of all Protestant dissension. But the divisions appeared to have little effect on Methodist zeal, because their numbers continued to increase down through the nineteenth century. In time a strong current in the opposite direction manifested itself, and in 1857 an association was formed of the United Methodist Free Churches including the Wesleyan Methodist Association, the Wesleyan Reform Union, the Protestant Methodists, and several smaller connexions. In 1907 the United Methodist Church was formed of the United Methodist Free Churches in association with the Methodist New Connexion and the Bible Christians. A larger grouping still was created in 1932 when this United Methodist Church joined the Primitive Methodist Church and the Wesleyan Methodist Church to form the Methodist Church of Great Britain. The names alone, without further detail, give an idea of how far the fissuring had gone. In 1939 a similar movement resulted in the one Methodist Church of the United States of America, which

[5] Ibid., pp. 130-1

is the largest Protestant body in that country with, in 1955, over 10 million members and more than 42,000 ministers of all grades. Its property was valued at more than 1,335 million dollars and its annual expenditure nearly 250 million dollars. The American Methodists, incidentally, were pioneered to some extent by emigrants from Ireland.

Today in Britain, the mother country of Methodism, there are found only the Methodist Church (1932) and the Independent Methodists (1805) who, with a remnant of the Wesley Reform Union (1849), still maintain independence from the Annual Conference on the plea of greater congregational government by the laity and of an unpaid ministry. Elsewhere in continental Europe, in the Americas, West Indies, Asia, Africa and Australasia there are still many Methodist communities, some of them quite small, independent or linked. In round figures, active Methodism was estimated in 1955 to be in touch with about 51 million souls. The corresponding Irish figure would be about 95,000 (the active membership is much smaller), the bulk of these in the North where the Methodists continue to flourish especially in the industrial area around Belfast. In the South, a decline is in progress as a result of emigration.

Methodism is a Church of fellowship, but the practice of fellowship is becoming increasingly difficult. The Class meetings which were occasions for the making and strengthening of friendships as well as for the exchange of religious experiences have practically disappeared and so has the Love Feast, a revival of the New Testament *Agape*.[6] Evangelical Revivals are being replaced by Conventions for the deepening of spiritual life. Fewer people come to the Evening Services; television is taking its toll. But the Sunday morning Preaching Service and monthly Communion Service are well attended; and the Church endeavours to meet changing habits by requiring the Class leaders to visit their members in their homes and by encouraging members

---

[6] In many places in England however the Classes meet frequently and in Ireland there has been a tendency in one form or another to re-develop them. In quite a number of places, I am told, the Love Feast is still held but in a modified form.

to enrol in various works as for instance those of the Women's Department for the overseas missions.

The Methodist Church in Ireland is separately organized from that of Great Britain but along exactly similar lines; its constitution is enshrined and its property vested by legislation passed simultaneously in 1928 by the Parliaments of Saorstat Éireann and Northern Ireland. A link is maintained with Britain by having the President of the British Conference preside over the annual Irish meeting which itself sends a delegation of ten members to the annual British Conference. There were already pockets of Methodism in Ireland by the time Wesley came in 1747 on his first visit, and by the time he returned on his twenty-first forty-two years later, Methodism was solidly established despite severe opposition from the Church of Ireland. At that time the state of that Church was so deplorable that it was said that a score of really pious men among the clergy could only be found with difficulty, and Dean Swift, admittedly a biased witness, accounted for the bizarre bishops by saying that they were really highwaymen who had robbed the real prelates of their surplices and credentials as they made their way to take up their appointments.

The first Irish Methodist Conference which organized the country into Circuits, was held in Limerick in 1752 under Wesley's chairmanship. He had an extraordinary affection for Ireland, which however did not prevent him from speaking about the Irish in uncomplimentary terms at times. He doubted if they were civilized before the British came on the scene. They were more wanting in discipline than any other nation. They were as unstable as water; so soft and delicate that the least slackness utterly destroyed them. Ninety-nine per cent of them, he said, had remained Roman Catholics and he was not surprised that the figure was so high when the Protestants could find no better ways of converting them than penal laws and Acts of Parliament. Often the English preachers complained of the amount of time he spent here, but Wesley's reply was: 'Have patience and Ireland will repay you'. In his lifetime he saw Irish Methodism grow in numbers, wealth and influence; but what a later generation could see even better than he could

was the persistent influence which Methodism wielded on
other branches of Protestantism in Ireland. 'It is not an
unfair estimate', adds a Methodist historian, 'to say that
it was Methodism which awakened the Irish Church and
the Presbyterian Church out of their lethargy, and resus-
citated them in many parts of the country. No province of
the Anglican Church is freer from ritualism and more alive
to the evangelical work of the Church than the Episcopalian
clergy in Ireland. It is perhaps not too presumptious to
suggest that the intimate associations that existed between
Methodists and Churchmen have left a definite impress on
the Church of Ireland. During a period of more than half
a century the Primitive Wesleyan Methodists carried their
evangelistic fervour into the parish churches and left their
stamp on Irish Episcopalianism during the critical years
when across the Irish Sea Tractarianism was infecting
Anglicanism'.[7] In the beginning of the nineteenth century
some of the leading English Methodists were working for a
rapprochment with the Church of England but the Tractarians unable, it was said, to distinguish between historic
Dissent and the new-fangled Methodism, drove the Methodists to adopt a more consciously non-conformist position,
so that Methodists proceeded to evolve as both an ex-
Anglican body and a Free Church.
   According to its Constitution

> The Methodist Church claims and cherishes its place
> in the Holy Catholic Church, which is the body of
> Christ. It rejoices in the inheritance of the apostolic
> faith, and loyally accepts the fundamental principles
> of the Historic Creeds and the Protestant Reformation.
> It ever remembers that, in the providence of God,
> Methodism was raised up to spread Scriptural Holiness

[7] R. Lee Cole, *History of Methodism in Dublin*, Dublin, 1932, pp.
127-8. There is, however, as Lord Wicklow points out elsewhere in this
book, a strong tradition of High Church doctrine if not ritual in the
Church of Ireland. And it may also be worth mentioning here that
there is now a notable tendency among British Methodists to criticize
nineteenth-century Methodism for having effectively lost the Wesleys'
rich legacy of Anglican doctrine and that efforts are being made to
revivify it.

through the land by the proclamation of the Evangelical
Faith, and declares its unfaultering resolve to be true
to its divinely appointed mission.

The Methodist Church, in Ireland as elsewhere, sees
itself therefore within the one holy, catholic and apostolic
Church as a communion that was brought into being by
the Holy Spirit at a specific time and that continues to
'witness to the universal grace of God, *to the gift of assurance
by the Holy Spirit*, and to the power of the Holy Spirit to
make us perfect in love'. It is a particular, Protestant,
Church, one of the many, they say, within the Universal
Church, the Church of Christ, and its characteristics are
that it revives 'the witness to the Supreme Authority of the
Scriptures, salvation by Faith, the Priesthood of all Believers
and the Ministry of the Whole Church'. Under God it
attributes its beginnings to John Wesley.

Its notable doctrines are (*a*) the Universality of Atonement ('Christ died for all mankind'); (*b*) the Witness of the
Spirit ('We are enabled to repent by the Grace of the Holy
Spirit who gives us to know *and feel* that we are sinners'.
'We may know that we have been born again by the sure
word of God, *by the witness or inner convictions of the Holy
Spirit in our hearts* and by the fruit of the Spirit in our lives');
(*c*) Sanctification ('the state in which we love God with all
the heart and mind and soul and strength and our neighbour
as ourselves') and (*d*) the necessity for continued faith to
final salvation ('Believers are kept in the state of salvation
by the power of God through faith in Christ', but 'Believers
may fall from faith and watchfulness; they may cease to be
diligent in duty and lose the blessings of salvation for ever').
At the judgment Christ will open heaven to the righteous
and condemn the wicked—those who finally refuse to
repent—to hell, the eternal fire.

Most of these are recognizable as the parts of Christian
belief accepted by the reformers, but the passages—from
the Methodist Catechism—which I have italicized echo
Wesley's doctrine of assurance. This at first sight seems to be
an accretion to the Anglican formularies which Wesley
always held were adequate. And it is true that for a long

time he asserted that unless a man had the assurance of 'saving faith' such as he believed had been vouchsafed to himself, he was simply not pardoned by God at all. However, he came to see the extravagance of this notion. God might sometimes give peace and tranquillity to souls who sought to love him but the only test of genuine assurance was a changed life.[8]

In doctrine Methodists are generally distinguished from Anglicans because they do not hold that those who exercize pastoral care or oversight ('episcopacy'[9]) in the Church must be successors of the apostles; because they do not hold that ordained ministers possess a priesthood differing in kind from that of the laity; because they allow in principle lay celebration of Holy Communion and, besides using unfermented wine, have no rule about the disposal of the consecrated elements which remain after Communion. It was on this issue of the Ministry that representatives of the Methodist Church and of the Church of England concentrated in the six years of corporate thought and discussion that ended recently in the issue of a joint report now being studied at all levels by both Churches. The Report indicates agreement between the Anglican representatives and eight of the twelve persons who represented the Methodist Church and contains precise proposals for bringing the two Churches together in two stages, which allow for a

[8] The gift of the Holy Spirit which Methodists call 'assurance' will be more familiar to Catholics as 'spiritual consolation'. In its final modified form Wesley's doctrine on assurance has been found quite acceptable by such Catholic writers as Mgr H. Francis Davis and J. M. Todd; cf. the latter's *John Wesley and the Catholic Church*, London, 1958, pp. 120-36

[9] Here and in the following pages I use the word 'episcopacy' in this generic sense and put the word in this sense in inverted commas because it is a sense not very familiar to most of my readers. In this sense it is possible to speak of 'episcopacy' in a corporate form and of 'episcopal' functions distributed among various officers. A bishop on the other hand is a successor of the apostles and I use the word in that sense. By the historic episcopate I mean that traditional ecclesiastical institution in which the apostolic succession is maintained. Anglicans, it may be added here, accept the historic episcopate 'as vital to the fullness of the life of the Church' but the Catholic Church does not accept its claim to have in fact preserved the apostolic succession unbroken.

period within which they will grow together and learn how to achieve the goal of reunion by consultation, common action and common devotions at all levels. A special reconciliation service is proposed to provide for the integration by reciprocal action of the existing ministries. This envisages the acceptance by the Methodists of 'episcopacy' in continuity with the historic episcopate (of bishops in other words) as well as the practice of episcopal ordination for its ministers in the future.

The Methodist representatives who approved the report recognized that the historic episcopate could be used for the preservation of the unity and continuity of the Church, that a ministry related to it would have the widest possible acceptance, and that the growing unity thus achieved would be of incalculable value for the evangelization of England. Having examined the form of 'episcopacy' in British Methodism they believe that the proposals in the report can be adopted without the absorption of one Church by the other or the loss of the prophetic or teaching emphasis in the Methodist concept of the ministry. 'Episcopal' functions are distributed among various officers in the Methodist Church but they believe that there is no objection in principle to the coalesence of these functions in a single person.

The four dissenting Methodist representatives declare their belief that the proposals will divide their Church and may also lead to division in the Church of England. The Methodist Church had entered into the Conversations, they say, with a view to considering how it might 'take episcopacy into its system'—an unfortunate phrase in their view—for it transpired that the only 'episcopacy' the Church of England had in mind, and what the majority of their own colleagues was accepting, was the historic episcopate. This 'episcopacy' they believed was historically incapable of proof and completely without support in the New Testament; it had also failed to act as the safeguard it was claimed to be. Methodists had consistently claimed that their Church was one with the Church of the Apostles, without the aid of any material succession, the Christian heritage being in faith and life and not in institutions. Most Methodists would prefer to be visibly one with the Churches

of the Reformation than with medieval and un-reformed
Christendom. If the hope of further union, on the basis of the
historic episcopate, was canvassed, it had to be remembered
that the largest episcopal Church in the world, the Catholic
Church, believed that the Church of England did not have
and therefore could not impart the historic ministry. And
there is much more in this minority report, as for instance
on the question of the office and functions of a priest, that
reveals Methodism widely divided. And yet it has been
wisely said by the Anglican Bishop of Winchester that if
the Church of England and the Methodist Church cannot
be reconciled and reunited there can be no hope of reunion
between the Church of England and any of the Free
Churches in Great Britain. And the bishop replied to the
suggestion that the organic unity of the Church throughout
the world would not really be furthered by piecemeal uni-
fication in particular countries by saying that anyone who
believed that the wit of man could ultimately produce one
vast scheme for the reunion of Christendom in one fell
swoop was living in a fool's paradise.

What about the position in Ireland? The impression one
gets is that there is little doctrinally between the Church of
Ireland and Presbyterians and Methodists except with
regard to the form of 'episcopacy' and the nature of priesthood. On these latter issues Methodists and Presbyterians
do not seem to differ greatly and in fact they did before the
last war hold conversations and found no theological
differences of any consequence but there was failure to
agree on what has been described to me as a practical
administrative question affecting the status of ministers.
The Presbyterians now desire to renew these conversations
and the Methodists have 'warmly welcomed' the approach
but reminded the Presbyterians that they might soon be
involved also in conversations with the Anglican Church
of Ireland. When these latter conversations take place the
starting point will probably be the position reached in
England. The evangelical Protestant character of Irish
Anglicanism will doubtless facilitate these talks but on the
other hand the Church of Ireland, for all its Protestantism,
is deeply committed to the historic episcopate and to a

difference in kind between the priesthood of the minister and that of the laity. Besides the majority viewpoint in Irish Methodism would seem at least to reflect that of the English minority Report. The status of ministers will in these conversations certainly be much more than a 'practical administrative question'.

Irish Methodists present an impressive ecumenical front. The Rev. Frederick Hill was probably speaking for the bulk of them when in his induction speech in 1963 as President of the Methodist Church in Ireland he mentioned the impatience of the younger Churches overseas who can see no point in maintaining divisions which they did not create and had no desire to perpetuate. They, who were subject to the constant pressure of the great non-Christian religions, were sure that this fragmentation and division which characterized the Church today was not the ideal that Christ prayed for. The fundamental reason for unity was that it was the will of God. Unity that was sought after because it could better resist Communism, or save men and money, or close redundant churches, was not going to succeed. He continued:

> Perhaps here in Ireland in our very limited but praise-worthy attempts at co-operation we are beginning to find that co-operation is no substitute for corporate unity. . . . Our fear here in Ireland, as with some in Great Britain, is fear of absorption and of losing our identity but if I could organise the 32,000 full members of the Methodist Church in Ireland into vital living class meetings, demonstrating in their life and fellow-ship the riches of our Methodist heritage, then it would be other Churches that might fear absorption. If, on the other hand, our Methodist inheritance has become such a diluted colourless sort of thing that when poured into a bigger Church even the colour is lost, it is hardly worth clinging to. And do not let us judge others by the worst they can produce, but by their best.

Suggestions for Further Reading

*J. L. Cairns, 'A Methodist's View of Unity', *The Furrow* 14
          (Jan. 1963), pp. 44-9
*C. H. Crookshank and R. Lee Cole, *History of Methodism in
          Ireland*, Belfast 1885-1960
*R. Lee Cole, *A History of Methodism in Dublin*, Dublin, 1932
*R. E. Davies, *Methodism*, Penguin Books, 1963
                    Methodists and Unity (Star Books on Reunion),
                    London, 1963
R. A. Knox, *Enthusiasm*, Oxford 1950, pp. 422-548
M. Piette, *John Wesley in the Evolution of Protestantism*, London,
          1937
J. M. Todd, *John Wesley and the Catholic Church*, London, 1958

   *Methodist authors

CHARITY

Joan Sweetman

'THAT they may be one'. It was a request both simple and sublime, as befits Godhead, something humanly unattainable, something so vast that it has not yet been fully granted to his prayer. 'That they may be one in us'. It was not a desire to see those he loved out of pain and comfortably settled. It was a longing to fulfil God's plan by introducing them into the very pattern of the Triune Life. There is a divine virility in this prayer, based as it is on a supernatural reality, on a fact rather than a feeling however noble. *Ut unum sint,* not because it is sad to see good people fighting but because we have been created to reflect the unity of the Three Divine Persons and to be partakers of their beatitude.

Modern theologians underline the objectivity of divine love by their exciting distinction between *eros* and *agape*; *eros* standing for subjective, emotional love, tainted with self-interest, and *agape*, an almost new word for an entirely new thing, the gift of the Spirit. This is a love not of the earth, but supernatural, the love which constitutes the innermost life of God. It does not belong to the human order and is largely independent of psychological climate, temperament and emotion, like the daffodil flaunting its gold in contradiction of the grey March weather. Charity does not postpone its blossoming till faith and feelings are in tune. Our Lord himself suggests that *agape*, the overflow of his love in us, begins only where the suavity of natural affection fails. 'If you love them who love you, what reward shall you have?' Even a naturally unloving temperament need be at no disadvantage where charity is concerned.

A love that triumphs over such formidable obstacles is certainly something new. 'A new commandment I give unto you'. Its novelty never wears off. With what awesome delight young people will watch two tired teachers, whose vibrations do not really agree, nodding together amicably over a change in the timetable. This is the light that never was on sea or land, the miracle flower that never blooms on earth unless Christ sets it there. As a sign of his presence, it is as unmistakable as a thunderclap.

So beautiful and wonderful is Christian charity for those who watch others practise it. But when our own turn comes, self-love, faced with its destruction, cries out: 'Impossible!'. This is the moment to cast aside all psychiatric dodges and rely on the great truth of Christ's indwelling. Let his Spirit take over in us and fulfil his own impossible precept by his own power.

Truth, in Chesterton's immortal metaphor, keeps her whirlwind course between extremes. It is well to stress the objectivity of *agape*, to avoid sentimentality in our love for God, but God became man and as such he loves us passionately as well as creatively, with interior words of affection, as well as with deeds of might. He asks for a return of love, even on the emotional level. By all means give priority in the spiritual life to intellect and will, but catastrophe is predicted for those who send their emotions underground. Devotion to the Sacred Heart, says Father Stierli, S.J., helps man to be completely human in his most fundamental relationship, his dealings with God. Everyone, however self-forgetting and objective in outlook, needs the security of being loved, valued for his own sake, in the give and take of friendship. The bravest cannot rid themselves of a child's need for understanding and compassion, and an ever-available confidant. Many of our separated brethren are enjoying already this fully human companionship with Jesus, in a faith and love which Pope Paul VI, in his coronation address, called 'the powerful bond' which unites them with the Catholic Church.

In union with them we practise this week the charity of prayer. Direct efforts to remedy family dissensions sometimes go wide of the mark, or even aggravate the trouble, whereas in prayer, and especially at Mass, we can apply the balm of Christ unerringly to the wound.

Today we are praying especially for the Methodists, choosing for our meditation that love of God and neighbour which is so central to their concept of Christianity. Here already is a broad ground for agreement. We ask them to join us today, praying with us and for us, as we make our petition for deeper insight into the truths that already unite us, humility to regret the divisions that separate us, and a more effectual desire to see the consummation of our unity.

A PRAYER

O God of love, O Giver of concord, who hast given one counsel for our profit, with a new commandment, through Thine only-begotten Son, that we should love one another, even as Thou didst love us, the unworthy and the wandering, and gavest Thy beloved Son for our life and salvation; we pray Thee, Lord, give to us Thy servants, in all time of our life on earth (but especially and pre-eminently now), a mind forgetful of past ill-will, a pure conscience and sincere thoughts, and a heart to love our brethren. Amen.

Part of the prayer before the Pax *in the Coptic Liturgy of St Cyril. E. Renaudot,* Liturgiarum Orientalium Collectio, *Paris 1716, I, pp. 39-40. This English version is taken from the 1959 Unity Week leaflet prepared by the Commission on Faith and Order of the World Council of Churches.*

Suggestions for Spiritual Reading

Matthew 5:20-4; 22:35-40; 25:31-46; 1 *John* 4:7-21; 1 *Corinthians*
    13:1-13; *Ephesians* 4:1-6

A. Brunot, S.C.J., *St Paul and his Message*, Faith and Fact Book
    70. London: Burns and Oates 1960

W. Grossouw, *Revelation and Redemption*, Westminster Md.:
    The Newman Press, 1955

J. Stierli, S.J. (ed.), *Heart of the Saviour*, New York: Herder and
    Herder, 1958

C. Tresmontant, *St Paul*, Men of Wisdom Books, London:
    Longmans, 1957

Suggestions for Hymn-singing

Psalm 22 (23) 'My Shepherd is the Lord', *Twenty-Four Psalms*,
    pp. 10-11

Psalm 99 (100) 'Cry out with Joy', ibid., pp. 32-3

Psalm 121 (122) 'I Rejoiced', ibid., pp. 42-3

Psalm 32 (33) 'Ring out your Joy to the Lord', *Thirty Psalms*,
    pp. 24-5

'Sweet Heart of Jesus', *Holy Ghost Hymnal*, n. 80

'Jesus, the very Thought of Thee', ibid., n. 82

'Gile mo Chroi', ibid., n. 110

'Ubi caritas et amor, Deus ibi est' (Holy Thursday Liturgy)

PROTESTANTS OF OTHER DENOMINATIONS

Geoffrey Hand

EARLIER contributions have concerned the Anglicans, Presbyterians and Methodists. If to the numbers of Christians of those denominations in the world today we add the Lutherans and the Calvinists of the 'Reformed' Churches—known in Ireland only in the persons of visitors and immigrants—we have accounted for about seventy per cent of those whose tradition of separation from Rome dates from the Reformation. Most of the remainder are Baptists of some kind, but there are numerous other denominations, presenting a bewildering variety of origin, doctrine, church life and government. To consider origin alone for a moment; some—the Baptists and the Congregationalists, for example —emerged early from the turmoil of the Reformation and may even have derived something from the subterranean streams of medieval heresy. Others grew out of pious discontent with an existing denomination. Thus, one of the reasons for the breach of the 'Plymouth' Brethren with the Established Church was the wish for a weekly communion. Others, such as the Pentecostal 'Elim Church', have in part sprung from the urge to keep together those 'converted' in a 'revival', rather as if, *mutatis mutandis,* a successful mission in one of our parishes led to a new confraternity amongst those who had taken a fervent part in it. To find common elements in these bodies is not easy. Certain broad general characteristics, though certainly not valid for every case, do provide some guidance nevertheless, and an attempt will

be made here to examine some of them. But first two
warnings are perhaps needed.

Firstly, there are some bodies which many Catholics may
think of as vaguely 'Protestant', but which are not really
Protestant or Christian at all. They have merely drawn upon
the Protestant culture in which they grew, rather as Islam,
centuries ago, drew upon Christian and Jewish sources.
Christian Science is a gnostic cult, promising to the initiate
the secret of a happiness at least as much temporal as
eternal, and expounded in the sacred writings of a founder
exalted almost to the level of the Founder of Christianity.
As for the Mormons, 'Christ is to them merely a forerunner
of Joseph Smith', their prophet.[1] The fluent use of the
Scriptures by Jehovah's Witnesses should not be allowed to
obscure the utter remoteness of many of their teachings from
Christianity in any generally-accepted sense. A Lutheran
scholar, Dr Einar Molland, has aptly called these faiths
'religious systems containing elements derived from
Christianity'. They are ignored in this discussion.

Secondly, candour compels a Catholic to recognize that
there are many members of the smaller Protestant denominations whose attitude towards Rome is characterized by an
almost obsessional fear and distrust. For them, she is
'Babylon the great, the mother of the fornications and the
abominations of the earth' (*Apoc*. 17:5). Religious sociologists, in exploring the history and social and intellectual
atmosphere of these sects, can help us to understand the
human reasons for this attitude. If it is to be modified,
however, a powerful solvent will be the Christ-like conduct
of Catholics, in the social and political, as well as personal,
spheres. Many of us have had an opportunity to note the
impression, on acquaintances accustomed to view Rome
with no friendly eye, plainly made by the life and death
of John XXIII. In such ways it will become easier for them
to recognize in the Church that other figure of the
Apocalypse, 'a woman clothed with the sun' (*Apoc*. 12:1).

A common feature of many of these denominations is the
marked sense of fellowship within the congregation. This

[1] H. Davies, *Christian Deviations*, p. 118

characteristic tends no doubt to be most marked where a strictly Calvinist view of predestination, rather than an 'Arminian' one (with its clearer recognition of the universality of Redemption), is held and where the theory of the Church is congregational, rejecting larger units and jurisdictions: where, in short, there is the conviction of a 'gathered church' of the 'elect'. But neither of these conditions are essential to it. It owes something to the fact that, at least in their beginnings, these are typically churches of the poor. They have grown up in defiance of Churches closely allied to the State and to the dominant social classes; their membership has therefore largely been composed of the 'converted' and faithful, without a vast fringe of nominal adherents held in association by little more than the inertia of custom and social convention. Members are more conscious of their separation from the world and their union with each other. But the characteristic owes much also to ardent reading of the Epistles. Passages such as those dealing with the collection for the Christians at Jerusalem (1 *Cor.* 16:1-4; 2 *Cor.* 8-9) and the 'greetings' chapter (16) of *Romans*, could not fail to drive home the idea of the Church as the household of God, in which the fellow-servants might be in intimate contact. (We Catholics of course are constrained to point out that this conception ignores that the kingdom of heaven is like to a mustard-seed that will become a great tree, and that obedience to Our Lord's final charge of the universal mission could not but modify the familial atmosphere of the early Church.)

The characteristic is well put in words from the First Baptist Confession of Faith, 1646: 'The Church is a company of visible saints, called and separated from the world by the Word and Spirit of God, to the visible profession of the faith of the Gospel: and all His servants . . . are to lead their lives in this walled sheepfold and watered garden . . . to supply each other's wants, inward and outward . . .'.[2] It has often been expressed in practice by other groups, such as—to take an example with a special Irish interest— the 'Plymouth' Brethren. The roots of the Brethren lay in

[2] H. Bettenson, *Documents of the Christian Church* (1st ed., Oxford, 1943), pp. 349-50

private religious meetings held in Dublin (and later, con-
spicuously, in Plymouth) in the early nineteenth century.
John Nelson Darby (1800-82), who had already become a
barrister and taken orders in the Established Church, joined
the emerging movement in 1828 and became its most
notable figure. Indeed, the Brethren were sometimes simply
called 'Darbyites'. The Brethren came to reject all existing
denominations, all permanent ecclesiastical office and the
sacramental conception. Adult Baptism and a weekly
Breaking of the Bread are the only ceremonies. Although
rent by a schism between the 'Open' and 'Exclusive' Brethren
—the 'Open' accept a measure of fellowship with some
other Christians which the 'Exclusive' reject—the Brethren
have survived. Congregations of both groups still meet in
Dublin. They form strikingly close-knit communities.

It would be wrong to suggest that the charity which exists
between members of a given denomination always remains
pent-up within it. The Quakers have earned for themselves
a glorious reputation for generous concern with suffering
and, not content with palliatives, they have often been to
the fore in deeper consideration of social problems. This
has not been least the case in Ireland, where they have borne
their quiet witness for three centuries and with Catholics
and other dissenters endured the Penal Laws. It is fitting
that the Religious Society of Friends in Ireland is the only
one of the denominations with which we are here concerned
to be expressly recognized in Article 44 of the Irish Constitution.

Even more relevant, perhaps, is the welcome to their
warm community life which the Pentecostal Churches offer
all comers. It is saddening to read the comment of a Puerto
Rican who joined a Pentecostal Church in New York: 'I
used to go to the Catholic Church, but there nobody knew
me . . . now, in my church, they call me sister'.[3] Is it not a
reproach to us that a stranger can come to an urban Catholic
parish and live there for months without contact with
fellow-worshippers? Admittedly, social conditions prevent
this particular problem from being acute in our own

[3] Quoted by D. J. O'Hanlon, S.J., 'The Pentecostals and Pope
John's "New Pentecost" ', in *America*, 4 May 1963, p. 634.

country. Nevertheless, it is difficult not to feel that we have something to learn from the fellowship displayed by many congregations of our separated brethren, even when, on the one hand, we discount the influence on them of a mistaken theology of redemption and ecclesiology and, on the other, we remember our growing-together by participation in the Eucharistic Sacrifice.

A description which many Christians of these denominations are prepared to accept is 'conservative evangelical'. Not only do they hold firm to the dogma of the inspiration of the Bible, but they are strongly inclined to suspicion of modern biblical scholarship. Hence in part arises the attitude of reserve which they display towards the ecumenical movement. (It must be said that among the more extreme a further ground of objection is the evident desire of the leading Protestant ecumenists to maintain a dialogue with Roman Catholics.) In ecclesiology 'there seems scarcely any doubt that many Baptists, Congregationalists and Disciples of Christ hold that the continuity of the Church is essentially that of the preaching of the true doctrine and the sole test of this is Scripture'.[4] Two of the three bodies just mentioned, the Baptists and the Congregationalists, represent very ancient strains in Protestantism. The Baptists take their name from their distinctive doctrine of Adult Baptism. The English movement, from which the small Irish one derives, began in the early seventeenth century. Its history was chequered by dissensions about predestination. However, in the late eighteenth century there was a more constructive development—the foundation in 1792 of the Baptist Missionary Society, under the influence of William Carey (1761-1834). Through it the Baptists were in the forefront of the Protestant missionary endeavours of the nineteenth century. Baptist strength today is chiefly in the United States, among the Negro Baptists and in the 'Bible belt'. 'The only necessary furniture of a Baptist church is a Bible'.[5] Baptists use two 'ordinances', externally similar to sacra-

---

[4] B. Leeming, S.J., *The Churches and the Church*, p. 138

[5] Quoted by E. A. Payne in R. J. W. Beavan, *The Churches and Christian Unity*, p. 137.

ments, but not founded upon a sacramental theory: Baptism
and Holy Communion.

The Congregationalists insist on the total independenc'
of congregations. Their importance in this country has been
very slight. On the other hand, the founders of the Disciples
of Christ ('Churches of Christ' or 'Campbellites') were two
Irish Presbyterians, Thomas Campbell (1763-1854) and his
son Alexander (1788-1866). Their original aim was to help
Christians towards unity, but circumstances forced them to
settle down to the life of a separate denomination, combining
the theory of Adult Baptism with Congregational Church
government. The Disciples have retained their concern with
unity and were officially represented at the opening sessions
of the Second Council of the Vatican, which were similarly
attended by Congregationalist and Quaker observers,
although not by any of the other denominations considered
in this chapter.

Christians of these denominations are not all of them, to
use an unsatisfactory and disliked word, 'fundamentalists'.
Many belong to 'liberal' schools of thought. An extremely
'conservative' viewpoint does, however, appear to be typical
of powerful elements in the Baptist Churches of the United
States. In any event many, of whatever 'school', it can be
argued, show in practice the truth of what Pius XII wrote in
Divino Afflante Spiritu (1943): 'Christ . . . will be better
known by men, more ardently loved, more faithfully
imitated by them, according as they are moved with an
eager desire to know and meditate upon Holy Writ, and
especially the New Testament'.[6]

Conservative evangelicals often show an ascetic and even
puritanical strain. This must not be considered to be merely
an undervaluing of the natural order and its legitimate
pleasures (a judgment into which what might be called
'Chestertonian' Catholics are tempted) or a rationalization
of social and economic deprivation (as some sociologists
might have us believe), though these elements may well
often be present. The existence of a strong ascetic tradition
in Irish Catholicism should help towards a more understanding evaluation. The Christian ought to put from him

[6] Paragraph 58 of C.T.S. translation by Canon G. D. Smith

whatever may distract from the search for the Kingdom. In their practice of this hard Christian counsel, Protestants of some of these denominations at times remind one of the religious orders in the Catholic Church; Macauley's famous dictum about Wesley (that if a Catholic he would have been an Ignatius Loyola) is peculiarly apposite here. (Among the more Adventist bodies the impulse to be ready for the coming of the Lord is also a stimulus to detachment from the things of this passing world.)

No denomination suggests the religious order more forcibly than does the Salvation Army. The founder, 'General' William Booth (1829-1912) and his wife, Catherine (1829-90), shared an eager zeal for souls, which led him to repudiate Calvinist predestination and once inspired her to write to him: 'It is impossible to live a holy life without winning souls'. They had no wish to form a sect or to withdraw their adherents from existing denominations. But inevitably the claims of the Army crowded other religious activities out of the lives of most recruits. The Army's outlook is characteristically biblical and ascetic. 'More than any other sect . . . their acceptance of the Bible is unquestioning'.[7] By the Articles of War, which recruits must sign after a probationary period, Salvationists accept the principal doctrines held by most Christians and renounce worldly amusements, alcohol and tobacco. An intense devotional life turns on consideration of God's universal love, the enormity of sin and the sufferings and death of Christ in making atonement for it. The thought of the Precious Blood of Our Lord, freely shed for men, is dear to Salvationists. The uniform of the Army (again suggestive of the religious habit) is a familiar sight in the great cities, including Dublin and Belfast, where in the spirit of the early Franciscans, it pursues its apostolate. Few can be unaware of the wide range of its charitable work or of the manner in which it tried to approach the urban masses of Victorian times in terms of their own culture. Since the early days when Cardinal Manning gave fraternal encouragement to General Booth many Catholics have felt deep respect for Salvationists and kinship with their spiritual outlook,

[7] D. Woodard, *Our Separated Brethren*, p. 104

though the Army's lack of interest in the sacramental
system is a distressing barrier.

Since the beginning of this century a remarkable movement has spread among our separated brethren and, what
is more, has made a substantial impact upon what we have
traditionally looked upon as Catholic countries. This is the
Pentecostal movement. In the United States, the combined
membership of two leading Pentecostal bodies increased
tenfold between 1925 and 1958—from 50,000 to nearly
500,000. It has been claimed that in Chile membership rose
from 182,000 in 1955 to 700,000 in 1962. So striking has
been this progress and so conspicuous the peculiar features
of the movement that some writers have urged the replace-
ment, in our ways of thinking, of the twofold division of
Catholic and Protestant with a threefold one, Catholic,
Protestant and Pentecostal. Even treating the movement as
'Protestant', we cannot but see in it a development demand-
ing close attention.

Of course there is nothing new in Christians becoming
dangerously fascinated by the mysterious role of the Holy
Spirit in the beginning of the Church and the bestowal of
charismatic gifts which accompanied it. In the middle ages
this played its part in the strange teachings associated with
Joachim of Fiore and the Spiritual Franciscans. Seventeenth-
century England had many sects who believed these gifts
could again be enjoyed. In their origins, the Quakers showed
some of the features of modern Pentecostalism: waiting for
the guidance of the Holy Spirit, ardent missionary zeal
and simplicity of life. But calm and decorum soon asserted
themselves as Quaker characteristics, while the other, wilder
sects of the time vanished from sight.

A Norwegian Pentecostalist has described the views of
his brethren: 'On the question of Justification they are
Lutherans, on Baptism, Baptists, on Sanctification, early
Methodists, in their work of winning souls, Salvationists,
but with regard to baptism by the Holy Spirit they are
Pentecostalists, as they believe and preach that it is possible
to be baptized in, or filled by, the Holy Spirit as on the day

of Pentecost'.[8] The beginnings of modern Pentecostalism were multiple, though it is primarily a fruit of revivalist movements on both sides of the Atlantic about the turn of the century. In January 1900 there was an alleged case of speaking with tongues at Topeka, Kansas, while the Welsh revival of 1904-5 was marked by ecstatic phenomena. Particular importance seems to have been attached to an incident on 9 April 1906 at a prayer meeting in Los Angeles, when an eight-year-old boy supposedly began to speak with tongues. Soon similar events were reported from Canada, England and Norway. Thus was the Baptism of the Holy Spirit experienced. Its effects have been described as follows: 'Its function is to confer power for service; to assist in unfolding the word and witness for Christ; to help in the overcoming of sin. It is held to lead to deeper communion with God, prayer of greater force, and more searching understanding of Scripture'.[9] The speech in tongues which is claimed to accompany it is distinguished by Pentecostalists from the charismatic gift of tongues (1 *Cor.* 12:28) which may later be bestowed upon those 'baptized in the Holy Spirit'. As Pentecostal thought has developed, the manifestations of the charismatic gift have been regulated by the requirements of order and profitable interpretation. There was evidently need for this: a Pentecostal writer has declared that in the early days there were 'scenes of indisputable fanaticism'.[10] The other gifts mentioned by St Paul are of course claimed, but the gift of tongues is evidently the most spectacular and exciting.

Apart from these special features, Pentecostalists have beliefs very much those of conservative evangelicals in general. Contrary to what one might expect, there is no particular development of doctrine concerning the Third Person of the Most Holy Trinity. Pentecostalists are zealous missionaries and their propaganda is often intemperate and violent. They are decidedly puritanical. A Catholic writer, Father Legrand, has written of their 'deep feeling of their Redemption by Christ, real detachment from

---

[8] Quoted in E. Molland, *Christendom*, p. 303
[9] B. R. Wilson, *Sects and Society*, p. 22
[10] Donald Gee, quoted ibid., p. 25

material goods, great zeal, great generosity', but has also drawn attention to their 'excessive emotional element, the trances and hysterical phenomena to which it leads, and the poverty of doctrinal teachings'.[11] Church government was originally typically Congregationalist, but various denominational alliances and groupings have arisen: the Assemblies of God, the Apostolic Faith Church and the Church of God in Christ.

One Pentecostal body had strong Irish connections. A Welsh revivalist, George Jeffreys, who had adopted Pentecostalism, was invited to campaign in Ireland some fifty years ago. From his evangelism emerged what is now the Elim Foursquare Gospel Church.[12] According to Jeffreys himself, Monaghan was the birthplace of the movement. The success of Pentecostalism in the economic and political uncertainties of the Ulster of those days has been thought significant of the appeal which it makes to the deprived and threatened. To these origins may also be attributed something of Elim's very marked anti-Catholicism: 'papacy is for Elim . . . the great evil in the world'.[13] Elim is still well represented in Northern Ireland. Belfast has eight Elim churches, while there are twenty-two meeting places elsewhere in the province. Elim's origins in a revival movement has helped it to abstain from exclusivist claims. It has no true sacramental conception, but Breaking of the Bread, Baptism by immersion and an anointing of the sick are practised. Elimites meet for two Sunday services and others during the week. In these, sermons, hymns and spontaneous prayer involving the use of 'gifts' occur in varying proportions. Elimites are discouraged from mingling with the 'worldly'; they are expected to abstain from alcohol and tobacco, as well as from gambling and most organized amusements.

[11] Quoted by Leeming, op. cit., p. 235
[12] The elements of the name are derived from *Exod.* 15:27, 'And the children of Israel came into Elim, where there were twelve fountains of water, and seventy palm trees: and they encamped by the waters', and from the Foursquare Gospel of the evangelist Aimee Semple McPherson, 'Christ is the Saviour, the Healer, the Baptizer in the Holy Spirit and the Coming King'.
[13] Wilson, op. cit., p. 94

In the 'Four-Square Gospel' the fourth description of Christ is 'the Coming King'. As in the case of Pentecostalism, Adventism can be traced in Christian history long before the emergence of the modern movement. It has been an ingredient in many 'left-wing Protestant' positions. Emphasis on the Second Coming is a feature, for example, of the teaching of the Brethren. The modern movement stems from a curious episode in mid-nineteenth-century America, when thousands fell under the prophetic influence of William Miller (1782-1849), a self-educated New England farmer. The Second Coming failed to occur on 22 October 1844, as calculated, but many of Miller's followers formed religious congregations to prepare for it when it should. 'In Church polity they were Congregationalist, in their Baptismal practice Baptist, in their doctrine extremely Protestant, with a strong predilection for apocalyptic speculation'.[14]

Some of the Adventists were in touch with a small Baptist body which had existed since the seventeenth century, the Seventh Day Baptists. The result of the meeting of these influences was the sect of Seventh Day Adventists, organized in 1863. To Adventist ideas these Christians added, as their name suggests, the peculiar doctrine that Saturday should still be kept as the day of rest. The difficulty presented by the non-occurrence of the Second Coming in 1844 was met by an explanation advanced by Mrs Ellen White (1827-1915) that in that year Christ entered into the 'sanctuary of heaven' to complete the work of salvation. The sect has adopted many of the precepts of the Old Law. Members abstain from pork and the flesh of strangled animals. They are persuaded that only those who share their faith will be eligible to be among the 144,000 elect who will live for ever with Christ on a renewed earth. The Seventh Day Adventists are the only Adventist group of importance outside the United States. They have eager evangelists, well equipped with scriptural quotations.

Seventh Day Adventism may perhaps be regarded as the extreme position which can at all meaningfully be called Christian. It is significant that the Witnesses of Jehovah owe

14 Molland, op. cit., p. 317

many ideas to it. Yet the Adventists may at least serve to
remind Christians of the Last Things. It is said that some
of the Orthodox, with their eschatological outlook, tend to
suspect Western Christians of ignoring this element in their
faith. In the midst of Adventist extravagances there may be
a preoccupation we ought all in a measure to share.

These are of course merely a selection of the characteristics found in 'Protestants of other denominations'. Others
could have been singled out instead. It would seem a pity,
however, to concentrate on such negative aspects as the
substantial rejection of the sacramental system and the
frequent dislike of worship according to any set form; these
are things we must, sadly, recognize, but in this context
need not dwell upon. One might also point to the contrasts
between different denominations. Thus the Exclusive
Brethren rigidly segregate themselves; the Disciples of Christ
are eager to co-operate with other Christians. Most of these
Protestants constantly appeal to the Bible; but for the
Quakers the Inner Light (the guidance experienced by those
who are obedient to the Spirit) is the ultimate guide.
Another line of approach would arise from consideration
of the fact that a good many denominations are clearly heirs
to the Puritan ethos of seventeenth-century England.

More than once in this essay reference has been made to
the extent to which the newer denominations (which are
also, in general, those most active in propagating their
views) draw their membership from the poor and despised
of the world. In addition, they often display a distinct anti-
intellectualism, a contempt for the wisdom of men, as they
view it. For the most part this has meant that they have
lacked educated leaders capable of carrying on a worthwhile
theological dialogue. Surely in their case, more than in
any other, progress towards understanding must depend on
a contact of hearts rather than of minds? It is easy to smile
a trifle pityingly at the simplicities, indeed the absurdities,
of an unlearned and unsophisticated enthusiasm and at the
sometimes all-too-obvious function of religious exhibition-
ism in compensating for unimportance in the world of men.
It is also easy to feel natural irritation at the aggressive and

persistent proselytizing of some deviant sect. In Ireland we are happily not faced with the sobering reproach that many seem to be reached by no message of hope but that brought by, say, a Pentecostal mission. Yet we cannot ignore that a deeply-felt love of the Redeemer may burn within an exterior of very odd doctrines and disciplinary practices, and that the union of Christians must include them all.

Suggestions For Further Reading

Among general surveys of denominations, Rev. D. Woodard's little book *Our Separated Brethren* (C.T.S., London) is useful. It is written from a firmly Catholic and apologetic standpoint, but unfortunately neglects Pentecostalism. A longer Catholic account is *Christian Denominations* by Mgr Konrad Algermissen (English edition, London, 1953). Particularly valuable is Dr Einar Molland's *Christendom* (English edition, London, 1961). A Norwegian Lutheran, Dr Molland writes without a controversial intention. In R. J. W. Beavan, *The Churches and Christian Unity* (London 1963), there are helpful Baptist and Congregationalist contributions by Dr. E. A. Payne and John Huxtable, respectively. H. Davies, *Christian Deviations: the Challenge of the Sects* (S.C.M. paperback, revised edition, 1961) has good chapters on the Seventh Day Adventists and Pentecostalists. The author's approach is decidedly critical and controversial, from a broadly ecumenical Anglican viewpoint. Mgr Algermissen's *The Christian Sects* (Faith and Fact Books no. 139) is a rather similar Catholic work, but has for us the disadvantage of being markedly concerned with German conditions. Bishop Lesslie Newbigin, *The Household of God* (London 1957), contains (chapter 4) general reflections on the Pentecostal strain; the author wrote as a prelate of the Church of South India. B. R. Wilson, *Sects and Society* (London 1961) is a remarkable sociological study. One-third of it is devoted to the Elim Church; it is not directly concerned with purely religious issues, but gives a fascinatingly detailed account of the way of life of these Christians.

THE HOLY SPIRIT

Desmond Wilson

*The grace of the Lord came upon me in a full tide of faith
and love, the love that is in Christ Jesus* (1 *Tim.* 1:14).

THE surpassing generosity of God's giving is beyond our
grasp because we cannot think in terms of infinite goodness.
That God should give generously to those within the law,
that he should give lavishly, pressed down, flowing over,
to those who keep it, is understandable; but that he should
show mercy to those outside it passed the understanding
even of the Apostle John: 'Lord, wouldst thou have us
bid fire come down from heaven and consume them?'
(*Luke* 9:24). As for us, we are tempted simply to set aside
this mystery of God's free giving and seek salvation by
obeying the law to its last letter, for this at least we think
we can understand. St Paul never ceased to wonder at how
lavish were the gifts of God, even to the outsider: 'So rich
is God's grace, that has overflowed upon us in a full stream
of wisdom and discernment, to make known to us the hidden
purpose of his will' (*Eph.* 1:8-9).

The Spirit of God is not constrained in the number of his
gifts or by the condition of those to whom he is willing to
give them. Mary in Nazareth and the unbaptized in Caesarea
(*Acts* 10:44 *seq.*); the apostles in Jerusalem (*Acts* 2) and
the man who without authority worked miracles in the
name of Jesus (*Mark* 9:37-39), for these the outpouring of
the Holy Ghost was governed by no law except that God
can act only with infinite love. In our time the Holy Ghost
does not withhold his inspiration from his people because

of their bettered condition within the solid framework of an ancient and experienced Church, nor does he cease to touch souls as though they were now guided well enough by the law.

When we pray, 'Come, Holy Ghost', we admit the ever-present necessity of being inspired by him day by day. Wisdom, understanding, counsel, fortitude, knowledge, piety, fear of the Lord are not given once for all. They need to be renewed like the other daily gifts of God, like the sunrise, like the wind bringing rain, for man can only live in the hope of grace from one day to the next.

And if, for whatever mysterious reason, one gift is given, another is not, if like the wind blowing into odd corners the Spirit breathes upon some to move them to speak the name of God but not to accept all Revelation, upon some to cry out the name of God in the streets but not to seek authority, we should be glad when such as these are touched by the Spirit. The Spirit who in his infinite wisdom has not led them yet into the fullness of truth sweetens their exile with his gifts.

It is for them we pray today, that having been blessed already by the Spirit they may be inspired to pray and wait for the best gifts of all, Catholic faith and complete submission to his will; and for ourselves, that we may for our part recognize the marvel of God's giving to all of us, and turn again to the Comforter whom we have so often forgotten.

'It is the same God who manifests his power everywhere in all of us. The revelation of the Spirit is imparted to each, to make the best advantage of it. One learns to speak with wisdom, by the power of the Spirit, another to speak with knowledge, with the same Spirit for his rule; one, through the same Spirit, is given faith; another through the same Spirit powers of healing; one can perform miracles, one can prophesy, another can test the spirit of the prophets; one can speak in different tongues, another can interpret the tongues; but all this is the work of one and the same Spirit, who distributes his gifts as he will to each severally'. (1 *Cor.* 12:6-11).

A PRAYER

May the Comforter who proceeds from thee bring light into our minds, we pray thee, Lord, and guide us to all truth, as thy Son promised.

Collect for Wednesday in Whit Week in the Roman Missal.

Suggestions for Spiritual Reading

Psalms 8, 18, 33, 145; *Ecclesiasticus* 1-2; 17-18; *Acts* 1-15; 1 *Corinthians* 12-14; *Romans* 9-12

A. M. Henry, O.P., *The Holy Spirit*, Faith and Fact Book 18, London: Burns and Oates, 1960

E. Leen, C.S.Sp., *The Holy Ghost*, London: Sheed and Ward, 1937

A. Lyons, *Come Holy Ghost*, Dublin: Clonmore and Reynolds, 1957

C. Marmion, O.S.B., 'The Mission of the Holy Spirit', *Christ in His Mysteries*, 2nd ed., London: Sands, 1931, pp. 323-41

Suggestions for Hymm-singing

Psalm 26 (27) 'The Lord is my Light and my Help', *Thirty Psalms*, pp. 18-20

Psalm 32 (33) 'Ring out your Joy to the Lord', ibid., pp. 24-5

Psalm 138 (139) 'O Lord, You search me and You know me', ibid., p. 64-5

'Holy Paraclete Life Giver', *Westminster Hymnal*, no. 66

'Veni Sancte Spiritus', *Holy Ghost Hymnal*, no. 19

'Veni Creator Spiritus', ibid., no. 20

'Come, O Creator Spirit Blest', *Laudemus*, Dublin: CTSI, 1955, p. 39

THE UNITY IN CHRIST OF ALL MANKIND

Seán O'Riordan

ON the last day of the Church Unity Week we pray for the Unity in Christ of All Mankind. This theme carries our thoughts beyond the frontiers of Christianity to all those who have not received baptism of water, who are not members of any Christian Church or denomination, but who have been redeemed, as Christians have been redeemed, by the saving blood of Christ and are called, as Christians have been called, to spiritual unity in him.

It is necessary for us to realize that the unbaptized constitute the great bulk of the human race. Outside the areas of western civilization they practically constitute the human race. Africa and above all Asia are substantially non-Christian continents. Even within traditionally Christian countries the number of the unbaptized is increasing. This is due on the one hand to the growing falling-away of the masses from the traditional Christianity of their forebears and on the other to growing immigration into traditionally Christian areas of people from traditionally non-Christian areas of the world. In all kinds of ways—ways of partnership, co-operation, opposition or conflict—the world of our time is becoming increasingly one world. The traditionally Christian world is gradually being merged in this larger unity of the entire world. This condition of things raises many problems for the Church, but it also creates new and vast possibilities of working for the unity in Christ of all mankind.

If we are to pray intelligently for this final intention of the

Church Unity Week we must understand aright what exactly we are praying for. Let us note the two terms of our intention: *unity in Christ* and *all mankind*. We pray that all mankind may be brought to unity in the Saviour of the entire human race. Buddhists, Hindus, followers of the great and small nature-religions of mankind, the many millions who live by the Koran, the relatively small but immensely important race that lives by the Old Testament but not by the New, the many millions again who profess no religion, who positively deny the truth of any religion or at least reduce its significance to that of a purely subjective experience—for all these we pray today, praying that they may be brought to unity in Christ. In a word, we pray today for Jew and Gentile that the will of God may be manifested in them—his will 'to demonstrate his justice now in the present, showing that he is both himself just and justifies any man who puts his faith in Jesus. . . . Do you suppose God is the God of the Jews alone? Is he not the God of Gentiles also? Certainly, of Gentiles also, if it be true that God is one. And he will therefore justify both the circumcised in virtue of their faith, and the uncircumcised through their faith' (*Rom.* 3:26, 29-30).[1]

Redemption is for all mankind. The mercy of God is for all mankind. All mankind are summoned, invited and drawn by God to spiritual unity in his Son. It is God's will 'that all men should find salvation and come to know the truth. For there is one God and also one mediator between God and men, Christ Jesus, himself man, who sacrificed himself to win freedom for all mankind' (1 *Tim.* 2:4-5).

Yet in all mankind we are not to see an undifferentiated mass of men, all of them equally remote from him who is the light of the world. His grace and light extend to them all and touch them all in varying degrees of clarity and obscurity. The redemption of all mankind would be only an empty formula if somehow it were not possible for all to enter by faith into union with Christ. St Paul welcomed the inscription which he noticed on an altar in Athens: 'To an

---

[1] Scriptural quotations are from the New English Bible, which is used here because of its simplicity and clearness in the passages I wish to quote.

Unknown God'. He took the starting-point of his discourse
on the Areopagus from that phrase. 'What you worship
but do not know', he said, 'this is what I now proclaim'.
He went on to remind his hearers that God 'created every
race of men of one stock, to inhabit the whole earth's surface. He fixed the epochs of their history and the limits of
their territory. They were to seek God and, it might be,
touch and find him; though indeed he is not far from each
one of us, for in him we live and move, in him we exist;
as some of your own poets have said: "We are also his
offspring" ' (*Acts* 17:23-28).

Among the unbaptized, however, an absolutely special
place is held today as it has been held since the time of
Christ himself by his own people, the Jews. They are not
just one people among the unbaptized peoples in general:
they are a unique people in that vast assemblage of humanity. Jew and Gentile: that differentiation of all mankind
made by both the Old and the New Testament is valid still.
In our prayer for the unity in Christ of all mankind we pray
firstly for the Jew and secondly for the Gentile. It is the
right and necessary order of our prayer for the unbaptized.
'The Jew first, but the Greek also' (*Rom.* 1:16): that is the
divinely-established hierarchy of humanity. 'There will be
grinding misery for every human being who is an evil-doer,
for the Jew first and for the Greek also; and for every
well-doer there will be glory, honour and peace, for the
Jew first and also for the Greek' (*Rom.* 2:9-10).

Even apart from the consideration of the missionary
function of the Church we have an excellent reason for
keeping clearly in mind this differentiation of mankind into
Jew and Gentile. These two distinct strands of humanity
enter into our own very being. We are by natural origin
Gentiles, bearing within us the spiritual heritage of peoples
'outside the pale of the Law of Moses' (*Rom.* 2:12). It is a
mixed spiritual heritage, a heritage of evil and good. Our
distant ancestors 'bartered away the true God for a false
one' and 'offered reverence and worship to created things
instead of to the Creator, who is blessed for ever; amen'.
This led them 'to break all rules of conduct'. But it never
cancelled 'the light of nature' within them—a light that

like the Law of Moses came from God himself. There were
good Gentiles too, Gentiles who displayed 'the effect of the
law inscribed on their hearts'. Of them St Paul writes:
'Their conscience is called as witness and their own thoughts
argue the case on either side, against them or even for them,
on the day when God judges the secrets of human hearts
through Christ Jesus' (*Rom.* 1:25, 28; 2:14-16). And then
there is the Jewish strand in our Christian being—the
strand of salvation, deriving from the Jews. 'It is from
the Jews that salvation comes', said Christ to the woman
of Samaria (*John* 4:22). 'Spiritually we are all semites',
said Pius XI in words which we can never afford to
forget. To understand the Jews, to see their rightful place
in relation to Christ, himself 'the king of the Jews' (*Matt.*
27:37), 'the Lion from the tribe of Judah, the Root of David'
(*Apoc.* 5:5), is to understand ourselves better as Christians
and to have the true key to the understanding of the unity
in Christ of all mankind.

Today more than at any previous time of history we need
to gain this deeper understanding of ourselves, of Judaism,
of humanity, of the Church, of Christ.[2] We can well apply
in this context the words spoken by Paul VI in reference to
the Oriental Churches in his discourse of 17 August 1963:
'We are all a little deaf and dumb. . . . May the Lord make
us capable of hearing the voices of history. . . . May he
enable us always to hearken fully to his voice—to the
resounding Gospel which should always be our law and
our strength, since it is the word of God'.[3]

Who and what are the Jews? What *do* they mean for us
and what *should* they mean for us as Christians and Catholics?[4] Most Irish Catholics have no direct contact at all
with Jews. This is due to the fact that there are in the whole
of our country only about 7,000 Jews, 5,000 approximately
in the Republic of Ireland and 2,000 in Northern Ireland.

---

[2] On the ecumenical movement in relation to the Jews see *The
Ecumenist* (New York: Paulist Press), vol. I, no. 3, February-March
1963.

[3] Translated from the *Osservatore Romano*, 19-20 August 1963.

[4] See A. Gelin, *The Religion of Israel* in the Faith and Fact series,
n. 65.

Practically all of them live in or near our two principal cities, Dublin and Belfast.

Jews in Ireland belong almost entirely to Orthodox Judaism: that is, they observe the full requirements of Jewish religious law and custom. In other countries Liberal or Progressive Jews, as they are called, are strongly represented. They distinguish between the essentials of Judaism, to which they hold fast, and secondary or accidental elements which they regard themselves as free to discard in modern conditions of living, for example the dietary laws, which it is certainly quite inconvenient for a Jew to observe strictly when he lives in a non-Jewish community. There has been a Progressive synagogue in Dublin since 1953 but its congregation is small, numbering only a few hundred.

In its more advanced forms Liberal Judaism approximates to that kind of Liberal Christianity which prevailed in Protestant theological circles, especially in Germany, in the last decades of the nineteenth and the first decades of the twentieth century. Or rather it would be more accurate to say that this form of Christianity represents a reduction of Christianity to the two great tenets of Liberal Judaism, namely the fatherhood of God and the brotherhood of men. Liberal Judaism to a greater or less extent abjures the Law, and Liberal Christianity similarly abjures the Trinity, the Incarnation and other specifically Christian doctrines. The result on both sides is in practice a substitution of religious philosophy for faith. Superficially the liberal Jew fits in with a broadly Christian tradition of life and social custom, and to that extent he assimilates Christianity and is assimilated to it. In reality, however, the very liberalism of his Judaism moves him farther away from the authentic common ground of Israel and the Church. This common ground is 'the hope of Israel' which the Church sees as fulfilled in the incarnate Son of God and Orthodox Judaism does not. The essential point at once of union and of cleavage between the Church and the Synagogue lies here. Did Jesus of Nazareth fulfil the hope of Israel or not? The Church says yes, the Synagogue says resolutely no. St Paul explained the matter in the clearest terms to King Agrippa: 'It is for a hope kindled by God's promise to our forefathers that I stand in the dock today. Our twelve tribes hope to see the fulfilment of that promise, worshipping with intense devotion day and night; and for this very hope I am impeached and impeached by Jews, Your Majesty. Why is it considered incredible among you that God should raise dead men to life?' (*Acts* 26:6-8). He returned to the point later in addressing the local Jewish leaders in Rome. 'My brothers', he said, 'I, who never did anything against our people or the customs of our forefathers, am here as a prisoner; I was handed over to the Romans at Jerusalem. They examined me and would have liked to release me because there was no capital charge against me; but the Jews objected, and I had no option but to appeal to the Emperor; not that I had any accusation to bring against my own people. That is why I have asked to see you and talk to you, because it is for the sake of the hope of Israel that I am in chains, as you see'. On another day, talking again with the Jews of Rome, St Paul 'dealt at length with the whole matter; he spoke urgently of the kingdom of God and sought to convince them about Jesus by appealing to the Law of Moses and the prophets'. St Luke tells us that the discussion 'went on from dawn to dusk' and that some of the Jews 'were won over by his arguments; others remained sceptical' (*Acts* 28:17-24).

From the Church's point of view that is still the problem of Israel. They, the bearers of the divine promises and of the hope of salvation, need to be 'convinced about Jesus by appealing to the Law of Moses and the prophets'. Some are convinced from time to time and enter the Church as first-born members of the Mystical Body of Christ, for they more than any other people have their full and rightful place there; but Israel as a whole 'remains sceptical', cherishing its hope but rejecting the fulfilment of that hope in Christ.

There are of course very many Jews who reject the hope of Israel altogether, irreligious or anti-religious Jews. In a religious context they are properly described as ex-Jews in all save blood and nationality. In no sense of the word do they constitute Judaism, any more than ex-Catholics constitute Christianity.

The Orthodox Synagogue is still the core of Israel. The true glory and the true sadness of Israel meet there. Both together, the glory and the sadness, the seeing and the not-seeing of the hope of Israel, constitute the noble and tragic fidelity of the Synagogue. It is a moving experience for a Catholic to encounter the fidelity of the Synagogue in an intimate, personal way. I remember one evening in Rome when the sun was already setting meeting an elderly Jewish couple from New York; they were on their way to Jerusalem for the Passover and had broken their air journey for a day in Rome. They had had no main meal all day, for, being Orthodox Jews, they would have to eat in a *kosher* restaurant and did not know where to find one. They were hungry and tired, but they had borne it rather than break the Law. It gave me great pleasure to be able to conduct them to a *kosher* restaurant in the Via Cavour. Their gratitude for this little service was touching: nobody in the world is more grateful for kindness and help than the grateful Jew. They invited me to share their meal, unconsciously reproducing the invitation of the disciples on the way to Emmaus to Christ: 'Stay with us, for evening draws on and the day is almost over' (*Luke* 24:29). Unfortunately I had no time to accept the invitation; so we parted, exchanging the greeting *shalom*, peace, familiar to Jews from the Old Testament and to Christians from the Old and the New.

Anti-semitism is an ugly word and an ugly thing. I do not propose to go deeply into the matter here. It has been adequately dealt with from a Catholic point of view by Mrs Barbara Ward Jackson in her brief but thorough article, 'Christians and Jews: Rooting out the Fatal Myths'.[5] Unquestionably Jews themselves often enough give ground for anti-semitic feeling and action—just as Irishmen often enough give ground for anti-Irish feeling and action or negroes similar ground for feeling and action directed against them. Dr Theodore Herzl, the founder of Zionism, himself wrote about Jews: 'In the ghetto we have taken on a

[5] *The Observer*, 18 August 1963. This article and a preceding one, 'Catholics and Jews: Removing the Stain of Guilt', by Dr. Zachariah Shuster, European Director of the American Jewish Committee, have been reprinted as an *Observer* pamphlet.

number of anti-social characteristics'. Anti-social characteristics that may be found in Jews do not, however, bring us
to the heart of the matter in the question of anti-semitism,
as far as Catholic feeling about Jews is concerned. Nor
does the medieval institution of the ghetto as such explain
things fundamentally. The deepest harm among Catholics
has been done by what Mrs Ward Jackson calls 'the fatal
myths'—the myth that all Jews somehow bear a personal
responsibility for the crucifixion of Christ, a notion that is
without any biblical or theological foundation whatever,
and a host of minor myths about Jewish murders of Christian
children for ritual purposes and the like. All this fatal
mythology has badly and sadly tainted Catholic thinking
about Jews for many centuries and has frequently been
given a pseudo-theological status in Catholic writing about
Jews. This problem is now being taken firmly in hand by
the Secretariat for Christian Unity established by John
XXIII with Cardinal Bea as its head and Mgr John M.
Oesterreicher and Fr Gregory Baum, O.S.A., both distinguished priest-converts from Judaism, among its con-
sultors.[6]

But the eradication of pseudo-theological anti-semitism
from Catholic thought is only one of the objectives of the
contemporary movement in the Church for a better understanding of Judaism. The other, the positive and more
important, objective of this movement is to make Catholics
more aware of what they themselves owe to Israel. To
Israel we owe the word and the revelation of God: to it we
owe Jesus of Nazareth and his mother Mary: to it we owe
the apostles, the foundation-stones of the Church, and the
first Christian communities: to it we owe the command-
ments of God, the foundation of our moral life: to it again
we owe the basis of our liturgy. True, 'we must not . . .
minimize . . . the importance of the influence of the Greek
and Latin culture upon the Christian liturgy. Nevertheless,
when we come to list those elements which are purely
Jewish, we may think it no exaggeration to say that not

[6] Father Baum's *The Jews and the Gospel* (London 1961) is dedicated
'to my mother, who died in the Berlin of 1943, where extermination
had been decreed for all Jews'.

only the idiom and mode of thought of the scriptural readings, psalms and antiphons but also the whole background of the Mass is Jewish'.[7]

The Israel that refuses Christ is, says St Paul quoting the Old Testament, 'an unruly and recalcitrant people' (*Rom.* 10:21). But he immediately continues: 'I ask then has God rejected his people? I cannot believe it! I am an Israelite myself, of the stock of Abraham, of the tribe of Benjamin. No! God has not rejected the people which he acknowledged of old as his own' (*Rom.* 11:1-2). He continues: 'What follows? What Israel sought Israel has not achieved, but the selected few have achieved it. . . . I now ask, did their failure mean complete downfall? Far from it! Because they offended, salvation has come to the Gentiles, to stir Israel to emulation. But if their offence means the enrichment of the world, and if their falling-off means the enrichment of the Gentiles, how much more their coming to full strength!' (*Rom.* 11:7, 11-12). St Paul reminds the Gentiles that Israel always remains the root of the tree of life. 'Remember', he says to them, 'that it is not you who sustain the root: the root sustains you' (*Rom.* 11:18). He concludes: 'For there is a deep truth here, my brothers, of which I want you to take account, so that you may not be complacent about your own discernment: this partial blindness has come upon Israel only until the Gentiles have been admitted in full strength; when that has happened the whole of Israel will be saved. . . . Just as formerly you were disobedient to God, but now have received mercy in the time of their disobedience, so now, when you receive mercy, they have proved disobedient, but only in order that they too may receive mercy' (*Rom.* 11:25-26, 30-31).

The 'deep truth' that St Paul preaches to us Gentiles is, in a word, humility before the destiny of Israel which includes our destiny also. Such humility excludes anti-semitism from the roots upwards. Anti-semitism, especially as a theological attitude, is suicidal for Christians, for it strikes at the very root of their own faith and their own life—that root which is Israel.

[7] Edward K. Taylor, 'Jewish Forms in the Liturgy', *The Furrow* 14 (1963), p. 516.

In the early seventeenth century an extraordinarily
interesting clash between pseudo-Catholic anti-semitism and
genuinely Catholic respect for Israel occurred within the
Society of Jesus in connection with its second General,
Laynez, who had died in 1565. Laynez was of Jewish blood
and the official historian of the Society, Sacchini, mentioned
this fact in the second volume of the *History* published in
1622. Thereupon the Province of Toledo demanded that
this 'slur on the sweet memory of so great a Father' should
be expunged from the *History*. Sacchini's defence of what
he had said about Laynez's Jewish ancestry is magnifi-
cently Christian:

> The Fathers of Toledo contend that by revealing the
> Jewish origin of Laynez I have inflicted a wound on
> the whole Society. How so, pray, when none but
> themselves felt any wound? My book has been cir-
> culated in all our provinces and read at table in many
> refectories, but only from Spain has come so much as
> a syllable of complaint. And where, anyhow, is this
> infamy of which they speak? St Epiphanius, that great
> light of the Church and opponent of heresy, was a Jew
> on both sides. So was St Julian, archbishop of no less
> a place than Toledo itself, and still its patron. And
> how many saints and doctors besides were of that same
> blood of the Saint of Saints! The Church glories in
> such men and so should we glory in our Laynez, whose
> so-called stain is an ignominy only to vulgar and
> prejudiced minds. It is our duty to make war on such
> prejudices and destroy them. Why this fear where there
> is no cause for fear? Is it an ignominy to find Christ
> our Lord, however late in the day? What stain remains
> in the new man who has put on Christ and become a
> temple of God, a son of God, an heir of God and co-
> heir of Christ? Must we blush to have the same mind
> as the Apostle of the Gentiles? It is he who forbids
> the wild olive to boast against the broken branches of
> the true olive, into which through no merit of their
> own the alien shoots have been grafted. Armed with
> this thought, how can any man who loves Christ be

offended by the return to him of his own racial kith and kin? But I am not pleading the cause of the New Christians. I merely wish to indicate that I in no way repent of what I wrote about Laynez. As a Christian, his Jewish blood was not an ignominy but an ennoblement, for he was not a wild shoot, as each of us is, but a fallen branch of the good olive grafted again sweetly and fitly into the parent stock'.[8]

I said above that understanding of and respect for the mystery of Israel provide the key for a right understanding of the unity in Christ not only of the Jews but of all mankind. We respect Israel because it is, as St Paul says, a 'consecrated root': we respect the Gentiles because, though they are by nature 'a wild olive', they are nevertheless destined to 'share the same root and sap as the olive' of Israel (*Rom.* 11:17). The divine destiny of all mankind is to unity in Christ, and it is this understanding and conviction that has inspired the Church's whole missionary prayer and labour from the beginning. Her ecumenical prayer is the continuation of Christ's own prayer for unity: 'But it is not for these alone that I pray, but for those also who through their words put their faith in me; may they all be one: as thou, Father, art in me, and I in thee, so also may they be in us, that the world may believe that thou didst send me' (*John* 17:20-21). 'I am a free man and own no master', said St Paul proudly; 'but I have made myself every man's servant, to win over as many as possible. To Jews I became like a Jew, to win Jews; as they are subject to the Law of Moses, I put myself under that law to win them although I am not myself subject to it. To win Gentiles, who are outside the Law, I made myself like one of them, although I am not in truth outside God's law, being under the law of Christ. To the weak I became weak, to win the weak. Indeed, I have become everything in turn to men of every sort, so that in one way or another I may save some. All this I do for the sake of the Gospel, to bear my part in proclaiming it' (1 *Cor.* 9:19-23).

[8] The story of this controversy is given in J. Brodrick, S.J., *The Progress of the Jesuits* (London 1946), pp. 310-6.

That is the fundamental spirit of the Church's missionary and ecumenical activity. In his own conversion and in all his subsequent labours St Paul spelled out for her a headline that she has never ceased to follow. Human weakness ('we are all a little deaf and dumb', said Paul VI) has at different times and in different ways prevented this spirit from finding its full and rightful expression in practice in relation both to Jews and Gentiles. For this we must humbly beat our breasts, consoled by the fact that even St Peter on one occasion had to be straightened out by St Paul when his missionary conduct 'did not square with the truth of the Gospel'. 'If you, a Jew, born and bred, live like a Gentile, and not like a Jew, how can you insist that Gentiles must live like Jews?' (*Gal.* 2:14).

In this connection we must also note the missionary work of the Protestant Churches and denominations, for they have played a very considerable part in bringing the knowledge of Christ to the non-Christian world. Actually Protestant foreign missionary activity is a late development in the history of the Churches of the Reformation: it was no part of the programme of the Reformers themselves. Once this activity did get under way, however, it was carried forward vigorously and in many fields of activity, for example the lay apostolate and medical and social work, it has remarkable achievements to its credit, often outstripping our own endeavours in those fields.

Many Irish Protestant organisations sponsor and further foreign missionary work. Since 1954 they have all been united in the Dublin United Missionary Council which established Koinonia House in Dublin as an international hostel for overseas students. Incidentally we may observe that apart from scattered individuals the only representatives of non-Christian cultures and religions whom we have in this country are students who come here for university or some other form of higher education.

Among the foreign missionary organizations sponsored by the Church of Ireland[9] the oldest is the Irish branch of

[9] See O. A. C. Irwin, 'The Missionary Work of the Church of Ireland in Modern Times', *Pan-Anglican* 7 (1956), pp. 59-61; *Church Handbook* (Dublin 1962).

the Society for the Propagation of the Gospel, established in 1714. Next in date comes the Hibernian Church Missionary Society, founded in 1814 and carrying on missionary work today in various parts of Africa and Asia. Two overseas missions sponsored by Trinity College, Dublin, are the Dublin University Far Eastern Mission (formerly the Dublin University Fukien Mission), founded in 1885 and at present supporting missionaries among Chinese in Singapore, Malaya and Sarawak, and the Dublin University Chota Nagpur Mission, founded in 1890. The centre of the activities of this mission is Hazaribah in the diocese of Chota Nagpur, where there are also Women Missionary Associates from the Church of Ireland.

The Presbyterian Church in Ireland has sponsored foreign missionary work since 1840. The first public act of the General Assembly of that year was to appoint two missionaries to India. The first missionaries were clerical, but subsequently lay missionaries were added—doctors, printers, agricultural and other specialists. In 1874 this missionary effort was supplemented by a women's auxiliary movement which sent out women for evangelical work in the fields of teaching and medicine. In 1860 the Presbyterian Church in Ireland began work in Manchuria in conjunction with the Church of Scotland and in federal relations with the Danish Lutheran Mission. Another mission was opened in Nyasaland in 1956, taking over part of a mission-field which had hitherto been administered by the Church of Scotland.[10]

Irish Methodists are also active in missionary work. They take part in all the missionary activities of the Methodist Missionary Society in the West Indies, Africa and Asia.[11] Dr Charles W. Ranson, a former President of the Methodist Church in Ireland, was from 1947-58 General Secretary of the International Missionary Council, which forms an integral part of the World Council of Churches.

Finally, in connection with the foreign missionary activity

[10] From information kindly supplied by Foreign Mission, the Presbyterian Church in Ireland, Church House, Belfast.

[11] From information kindly supplied by the Irish Auxiliary to the Methodist Missionary Society, Aldersgate House, Belfast.

of the Irish Protestant Churches, we must mention the
Church of Ireland Jews' Society, an auxiliary to the London
Church Mission to Jews; this staffs mission centres in
Israel, Iran, Ethiopia, Tunis, Algiers, Morocco, Great
Britain and Ireland.

The foreign missionary work of the Protestant Churches
has assumed special importance in modern times as a
contributory factor to the growth of the ecumenical movement among Protestants.[12] As Protestant missionary
activity developed, it was realized more and more clearly
that this activity was hampered by the doctrinal and
institutional disunion of the Churches of the Reformation.
If all mankind was to be brought to unity in Christ, there
must first be some kind of true unity among Christians into
which the nations might be gathered. From this it was a
logical step to go on to the consideration of the vital
importance of Christian unity for its own sake. And so the
modern ecumenical movement in the Protestant Churches
gradually grew out of their missionary preoccupations,
which led to the foundation of the International Missionary
Council in 1921. Accordingly the Catholic Church today,
which through the Secretariat for Christian Unity is devoting
special attention to the Protestant ecumenical movement,
must at the same time give similar attention to the aims and
aspirations of Protestant missionary movements in the
non-Christian world. The good they have done and are
doing not only in the temporal but in the spiritual sphere
must be frankly recognized. They seek to bring and in no
small measure succeed in bringing the knowledge of the
Gospel of Jesus Christ as Lord and Saviour to millions who
would otherwise never hear it.

Let us recall again the words of St Paul on the Areopagus:
'All men were created to seek God and, it might be, touch
and find him; though indeed he is not far from each one
of us, for in him we live and move, in him we exist' (*Acts*
17:27). Israel possesses the word, though not the final word,
of God. Islam possesses some of his word too, derived from

[12] See M. Hurley, S.J., 'The New Delhi Programme', *The Irish
Theological Quarterly* 29 (1962), pp. 61-7. The subject is extensively
treated in B. Leeming, S.J., *The Churches and the Church.*

Jewish and Christian sources. The other great religions of mankind present man's groping after God—their seeking of 'an Unknown God'. Mingled with their errors there is the measure of truth, greater or less, which each of them contains. This grain of truth must always be respected in our missionary efforts, as St Paul respected the elements of truth and goodness which he discerned in the life of the Gentile world. The Gentile world outside the frontiers of Christianity, even as it stands, is not wholly in darkness. Every human heart is open really even if unconsciously to the life and grace of Christ. 'Without faith it is impossible to please God; for anyone who comes to God must believe that he exists and that he rewards those who search for him' (*Heb*. 11:6). But this much faith—not the fullness of faith but sufficient faith for a man to belong to Christ in heart and spirit—is possible for every man of good will, even though he has never heard explicitly the name of Christ. This follows from the teaching of St Thomas Aquinas that wherever you have real human goodness—not just the goodness of this or that particular act but the fundamental goodness of the human person—there you have faith and grace. 'Straightway, when a man comes to the maturity of the use of his free will, if he prepares himself for grace he will have grace'.[13] As Garrigou-Lagrange says, this is 'a beautiful form of the baptism of desire'.[14] Through it a man is already established in the depths of his being in union with Christ. He belongs to Christ, he belongs, though invisibly, to the Church.

Taking the good will of men where she finds it, the Church enlarges their faith until it becomes the fullness of the grace and truth of Christ. Where she does not find good will, she first labours to create it, becoming like St Paul 'weak to the weak, to win the weak'.

> 'Awake, sleeper,
> Rise from the dead,
> And Christ will shine upon you' (*Eph*. 5:14).

That is the first and last message of the Church to Jew and Gentile—her summoning of all mankind to unity in Christ.

[13] *De Veritate*, q. 24, a. 12 ad 2: cf. I-II, q. 89, a. 6
[14] R. Garrigou-Lagrange, O.P., *De Gratia* (Turin 1947), p. 410

Suggestions for Further Reading

G. Baum, O.S.A., *The Jews and the Gospel*, London: Bloomsbury
     Publishing Co., 1961
     'Christians and Jews', *The Quest for Unity*,
     London: Sheed and Ward, 1963, pp. 242-62

T. Candlish, 'Edith Stein (1892-1942)', *The Furrow* 4 (Sept. 1953),
     pp. 500-509

C. Couturier, S.J., *The Mission of the Church*, London: Darton,
     Longman and Todd, 1960

P. Démann, *The Jewish Faith*, Faith and Fact Book 134, London:
     Burns and Oates, 1961

*I. Epstein, *Judaism, an Historical Presentation*, Harmonds-
     worth, Penguin Books, 1957

A. Gelin, P.S.S., *The Religion of Israel*, Faith and Fact Book 65,
     London: Burns and Oates, 1959

H. Graef, *The Scholar and the Cross*, The life and work of Edith
     Stein, London: Longmans, Green, 1955

O. Karrer, *Religions of Mankind*, London: Sheed and Ward,
     1936

R. Lombardi, S.J., *The Salvation of the Unbeliever*, London:
     Burns and Oates, 1956

J. M. Oesterreicher, *Walls are Crumbling*, London: Hollis and
     Carter, 1953

J. M. Oesterreicher (ed.), *The Bridge*, A Yearbook of Judaeo-
     Christian Studies, New York: Pantheon Books

K. Stern, *The Pillar of Fire*, London: Michael Joseph Ltd., 1951

*Jewish author

UNIVERSAL REDEMPTION

Seamus Grace

*I tell you God has the power to raise up children to
Abraham out of these very stones (Matt. 3:9).*

THE Pharisees of old came down to the River Jordan to
listen to the preaching of John the Baptist. But they came
with curiosity and with the intention of judging him rather
than of being converted by him. Since they were the descendants of Abraham and the most punctilious observers of the
Law, they were convinced that nothing could be wanting
to them.

It was to these Pharisees that John addressed the rebuke:
'Do not presume to say in your hearts: We have Abraham
for our father; I tell you, God has power to raise up children
to Abraham out of these very stones. Already the axe has
been put to the root of the trees so that every tree which
does not show good fruit will be cut down and cast into the
fire!'

In the world of today the same rebuke might perhaps be
directed to us.

We can be like the Pharisees, too sure of our own virtue.
Perhaps we feel too sure of heaven because we are 'good
Catholics', strict observing members of the Catholic Church.
As was the case with the Pharisees, no fault can be found
with our external observances; but this was not enough
in their case nor is it enough in ours. Evidently neither pious
practice nor religious orthodoxy nor penance nor alms-
giving is the 'good fruit' that is required of us. The Pharisees

had all of these, but they were far from being enough. Do we in our turn rely too complacently on the same things? Do we search our lives anxiously to see what good fruit are we producing? Are there others outside the Church less favoured by God whose lives are in fact more fruitful than ours? To whom much is given from them much will be required.

The existence of Faith outside the chosen people and outside the Catholic Church is a fact we cannot doubt. It was a Roman Centurion who said: 'Lord, I am not worthy that thou shouldst enter under my roof' and his words are enshrined in the solemn moments of the Mass. Presumably this man was a pagan, but our Lord could say of him: 'Truly I have not found such great faith in Israel'. It was a Chanaanite woman who said: 'The dogs feed on the crumbs that fall from their masters' table'. That table was God's special providence for the Israelites, but those same Israelites did not always appreciate what God had done for them. In comparison with the superabundant provision made for the chosen people, the rest of the world received only the crumbs that fell from their table.

Nevertheless amongst the least favoured there were souls —very many souls—who eagerly responded.

In the world of today we are the ones most favoured by God, we have his revelation, his sacraments, his Church. So generously endowed are we not extraordinarily indifferent? On the last day will it not be our shame to see how little we have done with all that we have received, while beside us we will, no doubt, see Mahommedans, Hindus, pagans fed only from the crumbs of our table who will surpass us in faith and in generosity.

God wills the salvation of every man. Through and in Christ he has given us all one common destiny: the beatific vision hereafter and its anticipation by faith and charity here and now. No soul therefore enters this world and comes to the use of reason without receiving from God graces sufficient to lead him to faith—at least to that minimum of faith that will be necessary for his salvation. We know that the hand of God is held out to all men of goodwill, we know that the voice of God speaks to them in their hearts, we know that the revelation which we receive in its entirety reaches them in the apparently fortuitous ways of Divine Providence. We believe that among all the religions of the world and even among apparent unbelievers there must be many—we hope very many—who have given their assent to the crumbs of revelation which have reached them. We are moved with gratitude to God and with hopeful reverence towards all our fellow-men. However remote they may seem from us, it is our hope that God by faith and his divine grace may be dwelling in their souls.

If we cannot be complacent about our own salvation neither can we be complacent about the salvation of others. Every adult person in the world will come eventually either to heaven or to hell. Without the abundant aids which we enjoy we must feel that salvation is precarious. This is enough to move us to the most earnest prayer and to the greatest labour for the myriads of unbaptized. If we are in practice indifferent to their fate we are hardly better than the Pharisees. If at the end of our lives we are to be judged by the charity we have shown to our fellow men, no charity will be equal to this—concern for their eternal salvation. No want of charity will be greater than our unconcern.

A PRAYER

God, who desirest that all men should be saved and that all should come to know the truth, we pray thee send forth labourers to thy harvest, and give them strength to proclaim thy word with all confidence, so that thy teaching may be received with honour throughout the world and all nations may acknowledge thee, the true and only God, and him whom thou hast sent, Jesus Christ, thy Son, our Lord.

Collect from the Votive Mass for the Propagation of the Faith in the Roman Missal.

Suggestions for Further Reading

Jonah 1-4; *Acts* 10-11:18; *Romans* 2; 1 *Timothy* 2:1-7

Y. Congar, O.P., *The Wide World, My Parish*, London: Darton,
    Longman and Todd, 1961

H. de Lubac, S.J., 'Salvation through the Church', *Catholicism*,
    London: Burns and Oates, 1950, pp. 107-25

C. Davis, 'Can Unbelievers be Saved?', *The Study of Theology*,
    London: Sheed and Ward, 1962, pp. 127-33

H. Küng, 'Outside the Church No Salvation?', *That the World
    May Believe*, London: Sheed and Ward, 1962,
    pp. 61-70

R. Lombardi, S.J., *The Salvation of the Unbeliever*, London:
    Burns and Oates, 1956

Suggestions for Hymn-singing

Psalm 23 (24) 'The Lord's is the Earth', *Twenty-Four Psalms*,
    pp. 12-13
Psalm 116 (117) 'O Praise the Lord!', ibid., p. 19
Psalm 144 (145) 'I will Give you Glory', *Thirty Psalms*, pp. 66-7
Canticle of Simeon, ibid., p. 53
'Hail Redeemer King Divine', *Holy Ghost Hymnal*, n. 83
'Holy God! We Praise Thy Name', ibid., n. 71
'Holy Church', ibid., n. 102

PRAYERS FOR UNITY

Assembled by Michael Hurley

Thou, O Lord, wilt open my lips
And my tongue shall announce Thy praise
Glory be to the Father and to the Son and to the Holy Ghost
As it was in the beginning, is now and ever shall be, world without end. Amen.
Let us pray to the Lord for the Unity of His Church.
Remember, O Lord, all Thy children who carry the sign of Christ upon their foreheads.

> Lord, have mercy on us.

Draw them, who were purchased by Thy blood, closer to Thee in the union of love.

> Lord, have mercy on us.

Remove from their hearts all stubborness and pride and whatever impedes respect and love for fellow Christians everywhere.

> Lord, have mercy on us.

Make Thy Church, O Lord, to shine more gloriously before men through that Unity which is Thy gift alone.

> Lord, have mercy on us.

Hasten the day, O Lord, when Thy scattered children will be drawn together in that Unity for which Thou didst pray.

> Lord, have mercy on us.

Glory be to the Father, and to the Son and to the Holy Ghost. As it was in the beginning, is now and ever shall be, world without end. Amen.

From The Furrow *Unity Leaflet, 1963.*

Preface of Unity

It is truly meet and right,
our joy and our salvation,
that we should at all times and in all places
give thanks unto Thee, O Lord, Holy Father,
Almighty, Everlasting God, through Christ our Lord.

Who on the eve of His passion,
prayed for the unity of all faithful people,
in Him and in Thee,
by the Holy Spirit in the Church;
we believe that Thou wilt hear His prayer.

We give thanks unto Thee
for the unity of the body of Christ,
and we await with joy
the day when we shall perfectly be one,
that the world may know that Thou has sent
Thy Son
and that He loved us as Thou didst love Him.

Wherefore,
with angels and archangels,
with thrones and dominions,
and with all the army of the hosts of Heaven,
we sing the hymn of Thy glory,
and, without ceasing, cry:
Holy, Holy, Holy,
Lord God of hosts,
Heaven and earth are full of Thy glory.
Hosanna in the highest.
Blessed be He that cometh in the name of the Lord.
Hosanna in the highest.

'*Preface of Unity*', The Eucharistic Liturgy of Taizé, *London:
The Faith Press, 1962, p. 81. This preface is used at Taizé on
Sundays from Michaelmas Day until the feast of Christ the
King and every day during the January Unity Week. Taizé (in
France) is an international inter-denominational ecumenical
monastic community, neo-Calvinist in origin and inspiration.*

O God of infinite goodness, who dost eternally rejoice in the unity of peace, Thou who art the author of peace and by the choirs of angels hast proclaimed peace, grant in Thy merciful goodness that by this bond of love with which, at Thy Ascension into heaven, Thou didst unite all Thy disciples, we may be drawn into an ever deeper love for Thee and for our brethren. Amen.

From the Mozarabic Missal, as printed in Prayers for Christian Unity, *ed. Donna Myers, New York: The Paulist Press, 1962, pp. 10-11.*

O God, our Father, good beyond all that is good, fair beyond all that is fair, in whom is calmness, peace and concord; reconcile we pray Thee Thy servants separated one from another by dissension, and lead us back into a unity of love which may bear some likeness to Thy sublime nature. And as Thou art above all things, grant that we may be united in generosity of spirit; that by the bonds of love and ties of affection we may become spiritually one, as well within ourselves as with each other, through that peace of Thine which maketh all things peaceful in the grace, mercy and pity of Thy beloved Son. Amen.

A shortened and slightly modified version (taken from the 1959 Unity Week leaflet prepared by the Faith and Order Commission of the World Council of Churches) of the prayer before the Pax in the Syriac Liturgy of St Dionysius of Athens. Cf. E. Renaudot, Liturgiarum Orientalium Collectio, *Paris 1716, II, p. 202.*

Almighty and everliving God, who by thy holy Apostle
hast taught us to make prayers and supplications, and to
give thanks for all men; We humbly beseech thee most
mercifully to receive these our prayers, which we offer unto
thy Divine Majesty; beseeching thee to inspire continually
the universal Church with the spirit of truth, unity and
concord: And grant, that all they that do confess thy holy
Name may agree in the truth of thy holy Word, and live in
unity and godly love.

*From the Communion Service in the Church of Ireland Book of
Common Prayer. Also regularly used by Irish Methodists in
their monthly celebration of the Sacrament of the Lord's Supper.*

O God, the Father of our Lord Jesus Christ, our only
Saviour, the Prince of Peace; Give us grace seriously to lay
to heart the great dangers we are in by our unhappy divisions.
Take away all hatred and prejudice, and whatsoever else
may hinder us from godly union and concord: that, as
there is but one Body, and one Spirit, and one hope of our
calling, one Lord, one Faith, one Baptism, one God and
Father of us all, so we may henceforth be all of one heart,
and of one soul, united in one holy bond of truth and peace,
of faith and charity, and may with one mind and one mouth
glorify thee; through Jesus Christ our Lord. Amen.

A prayer familiar to Anglicans and Presbyterians at least. Cf.
Book of Common Prayer *and* Book of Common Order of the
Church of Scotland *(in use also in Presbyterian Church in
Ireland). A modified version of this prayer is printed in* Prayers
for Christian Unity *(ed. Donna Myers, New York: Paulist
Press, 1962), p. 11, and is said there to be 'from the Liturgy of
St James' but the experts in Eastern liturgies whom I consulted
could not recognize it.*

O God of Peace, who through Thy Son Jesus Christ didst set forth one faith for the salvation of mankind; send Thy grace and heavenly blessing upon all Christian people who are striving to draw nearer to Thee and to each other, in the unity of the Spirit and in the bond of peace. Give us boldness to seek only Thy glory and the advancement of Thy Kingdom. Unite us all in Thee as Thou, O Father, with Thy Son and the Holy Spirit, art One God, world without end. Amen.

From Book of Common Order of the Church of Scotland (*used also by Presbyterian Church in Ireland*).

O God, the physician of men and nations, the restorer of the years that have been destroyed; look upon the distractions of the world, and be pleased to complete the work of Thy healing hand; draw all men unto Thee and one to another by the bands of Thy love; make Thy Church one, and fill it with Thy Spirit, that by Thy power it may unite the world in a sacred brotherhood of nations, wherein justice, mercy and faith, truth and freedom may flourish, and Thou mayest be ever glorified; through Jesus Christ our Lord. Amen.

From Book of Common Order of the Church of Scotland.

Let us Pray

that we may be delivered from all in us that hinders the coming of unity: from selfish unwillingness to leave old ways; from a sectarian spirit; from pride masking principles as prejudices; from willingness to sacrifice conviction to expediency; from pessimism and defeatism, impatience and sloth; from setting either the hopes or fears of men before the will of God;

that we may serve the cause of unity according to the gifts that are in us;

that we may not set back the good cause by lack of charity, but that honouring the convictions of others we may seek the truth in love; that the Church may be ever more outward turning and forward looking; that invigorated and renewed the Church may go forward in its missionary apostolate towards mankind.

From The Prayer Manual of the Helpers' Union *of the Methodist Missionary Society, which 'is widely used in private devotions and also regularly in most public services each Sunday'.*

The Communion of Saints

Christ, from whom all Blessings flow,
Perfecting the Saints Below,
Hear us, who Thy Nature share,
Who Thy Mystic Body are:
Join us, in One Spirit join,
Let us still receive of Thine,
Still for more on Thee we call,
Thee, who fillest All in All.

Closer knit to Thee our Head,
Nourish us, O Christ, and feed,
Let us daily Growth receive,
More and more in Jesus live:
Jesu! we Thy Members are,
Cherish us with kindest Care,
Of Thy Flesh, and of Thy Bone:
Love, forever love Thine own.

Move, and actuate, and guide,
Diverse Gifts to each divide;
Plac'd according to thy Will,
Let us all our Work fulfil,
Never from our Office move,
Needful to the Others prove,
Use the Grace on each bestow'd,
Temper'd by the Art of God.

Sweetly now we all agree,
Touch'd with softest Simpathy,
Kindly for each other care:
Every Member feels its Share:
Wounded by the Grief of One,
All the suffering Members groan;
Honour'd if one Member is
All partake the common Bliss.

Many are we now, and One,
We who Jesus have put on:
There is neither Bond nor Free,
Male nor Female, Lord, in Thee.
Love, like Death, hath all destroy'd,
Render'd all Distinctions void:
Names, and Sects, and Parties fall;
Thou, O Christ, art All in All!

Representative Verse of Charles Wesley, *ed. F. Baker, London: The Epworth Press, 1962, pp. 28-9;* Methodist Hymnbook, *n. 720, which prints a slightly different version. Composed for the Methodist Love-Feast and familiar to all Methodists.*

Ubi Caritas et amor

Refrain: Where there's charity and love of one another, God
is there with us.

Vv. 1. Hither, love of Christ has summoned us, His
People, to assemble.
2. Let us glory and rejoice in Him who made us and
redeemed us.
3. The living God let us revere and worship; let us
love Him.
4. And from our hearts sincerely love each other—as
he told us.

Repeat *Refrain.*

5. Wherefore when we, God's own chosen holy people,
here are gathered,
6. Let us meet with minds and spirits undivided, being
brothers,
7. Let quarrels cease, and every sharp dissension now
be ended,
8. And let us welcome thus to be amongst us, Jesus
Christ our Lord.

Repeat *Refrain.*

9. Soon, together with the Blessed Ones of Heaven,
may our vision
10. Rest upon Thy Sacred countenance in glory,
Christ most holy!
11. Joy greater than the mind of man can measure,
there awaits us;
12. Through all eternity our souls possessing bliss
unending. Amen.

*This translation suitable for singing to the plainsong melody is
by Dom Bede Lynch, O.S.B. of Glenstal and embodies suggestions made by Mother J. Sweetman and Father K. Kane, S.J.
The original Latin is sung during the Maundy or Washing of
the Feet on Holy Thursday and can be found in the missal.*

Prayer for the Council

O Holy Spirit, sent by the Father in the name of Jesus, to assist the Church and keep her from error, pour forth Thy gifts in their fullness on the Ecumenical Council.

Gentle Teacher and Comforter, enlighten the minds of our bishops, who will come together for this Council in ready obedience to the Supreme Pontiff.

Grant that this Council may bear abundant fruit, that the light and strength of the Gospel may fill the lives of men, that the Catholic religion and its missionary activity take on a new vigour, and that men may come to know more fully the teaching of the Church and realise it more profoundly in their lives.

Strengthen our minds in truth, dear Guest of the soul, and dispose our hearts to obedience, so that we may accept humbly and sincerely what the Council decrees and willingly carry it out.

We pray also for the sheep who still remain outside the One Fold of Jesus Christ, that they too who are proud to be called Christians, may finally unite under the guidance of the One Shepherd.

Let this age of ours, like another Pentecost, see once more the evidence of Thy power, and grant that Thy Holy Church, guided by Peter and united to Mary, the Mother of Jesus, in constant and unceasing prayer, may spread the kingdom of our Divine Saviour, the kingdom of truth and justice, of love and peace. Amen.

This prayer was composed by Pope John XXIII for the Second Vatican Council.

O Lord Jesus Christ, who hast promised to be with thy Universal Church to the end of the world; hear our prayer for our brethren, members of the Roman Catholic Church, who are about to assemble in Council to consult for the good governing and unity of thy Church; and vouchsafe to pour out a new measure of the Holy Spirit on them, and also on us; so that thy whole Church may be renewed in the unity of the Spirit, in the bond of peace, and in right-eousness of life; and that the world may see and believe that thou alone art the Way, the Truth and the Life; who livest and reignest with the Father and the Holy Ghost, world without end. Amen.

Prayer for the Vatican Council approved by the Anglican Archbishops of Armagh and Dublin and commended for use in churches. Church of Ireland Gazette, *24 August 1962.*

Appendix

THE GREYSTONES CONFERENCE MESSAGE

THIS Conference was held in late September 1963 under the auspices of the United Council of Churches and Religious Communions in Ireland. According to the *Church of Ireland Gazette* (18 October, p. 6) the delegates recommended that the Conference Message be read in churches throughout the country during the January Unity Week. For this reason among others it seems particularly appropriate to print here the text of the message as given in the *Irish Times* (1 October):

We ask the Churches which appointed us, to consider seriously the matters which have occupied us here. We believe that the Churches in Ireland, in common with Churches everywhere, are being called by the Holy Spirit to give clearer outward expression to the unity which is 'both God's will and his gift'. We believe that we must seek to be reconciled, not merely for reasons of convenience or efficiency or neighbourliness, but in obedience to the truth of the Gospel and the Lord of the Church. We believe that concern for unity among our people will be deepened only as we accept more faithfully that the Church exists not to maintain itself, but to reach out in service to men and as a witness to the Gospel, in Ireland and in all the world.

We cannot yet see clearly the nature of the unity to which we are being led, and we believe it will include a rich diversity of worship and structure. Yet, because we are the servants of him who to reconcile mankind laid down his life, we call our Churches to acknowledge that the search for unity may involve the death of our separate denominations and of much that we have cherished in order that the whole Church may be renewed according to his purpose.

We therefore commend to our Churches the following measures:

(1) To commit themselves to apply seriously the now familiar formula, 'to do together all things except those which deep differences of conviction compel us to do separately'.

(2) In particular at the national level to co-operate in such matters as evangelism, church extension, youth and adult education, broadcasting and television, and social action: to make the United Council of Churches in Ireland a more effective instrument of common action, and to provide the necessary staff to this end.

(3) And at the local level, to encourage congregations to observe the Week of Prayer for Christian Unity, and to join in prayer, study and action, whether through local councils of Churches or in other appropriate ways.

(4) To take steps to provide for members of our Churches to worship regularly together, while retaining their allegiance to their particular traditions, and to provide where appropriate for the use of one building for worship by members of different denominations.

(5) To consider in what ways we ought to respond in truth and love to our Roman Catholic brethren who express their sense of fellowship with us.

We believe that in ways such as these our Churches may grow together towards the unity which we see to be God's will. But co-operation is not enough. We welcome the inauguration of Union Conversations between several of our Churches, and we ask that such Conversations shall be continued and enlarged as a matter of urgency.

We believe that in seeking to be reconciled as one people we are being led by the Holy Spirit.

Today we see openings which only faith could discern yesterday. But there is far to go. Our faith is in him who is calling us, for he is faithful and he will do it (1 *Thess*. 5:24).